CW00954222

Malcolm Rifkind

'This book should be read of central and southern A and white. They are a fine honest, articulate and worthy champion, as rigorous, objective and professional in this book as in his journalism as Africa Editor for the *Financial Times*. He has an energy and an eloquence in recording not just what he knows or has analysed but also what he feels to be the reality of his homeland's tragic experience, under white, colonial domination and the black-led governments that followed.'

Ed Balls

'With a professional lifetime spent chronicling the opportunities and calamities of the continent, Africa has no fiercer critic and no greater advocate than Michael Holman. Passionate, sometimes angry but also caring and often hilarious, he once again delivers his trademark combination of beautiful prose and compelling storytelling. This book is a delight and a tragic tale of hopes still unfulfilled.'

John Githongo

'Throughout his career as a journalist and author, Michael has been a rebel with a clear cause. He has a seamless capacity to get under the African skin, and a ruthless insight for sniffing out what's working, even though it may not look it, and what's an utter waste of time, even though no one else will admit it. He has brought this insight and unapologetic attitude in his quest for the truth to everything he has ever done, on and for Africa. All of it is informed by a deep sense of empathy for the land of his upbringing, warts and all, and a biting sense of humour. This is therefore an important book by a special man with a special understanding of Africa who continues to live it wherever he is in the world.'

Alexander McCall Smith

'If you want to see what a good man in Africa has done, read this book. It contains profound observations of real and lasting significance on virtually every page. In Holman's company we are there—right there —seeing what he saw, listening in on conversations with politicians, businessmen, ordinary people. We are admitted to the company of those who wield considerable power; we hear what it is like to be caught up in an era of hope, of dashed dreams, of privation. And all the time, in a style which is as courteous as it is elucidating, we are led to the heart of the problem. A tyrant may be a tyrant, but who made him what he became? Whose responsibility is the suffering that is the lot of so many talented and hard-working people in Africa who have had such bad luck in their venal governments? What happened to the dreams that people dreamed? Holman is not censorious. His judgements are necessarily stern, but what shines through is a wonderful humanity that is humbling in its power. This is wise writing, the testimony of a witness who, in difficult times, has consistently testified truth. That there are such journalists, and that they do their job in the way in which Michael Holman has done his, makes this book a beacon in dark times, a wonderful, exhilarating affirmation of all that is good and worth believing in.'

Michael Holman was brought up in small-town white Rhodesia, establishing his political credentials in Salisbury (now Harare) as a University of Rhodesia student leader opposing UDI in 1965. In August 1967 he was served with a government order confining him to his hometown (Gwelo, now Gweru). Allowed to leave after a year, he completed an MSc at the University of Edinburgh, before returning to Zimbabwe to work as a journalist. He narrowly escaped arrest after refusing to accept military call-up and after three weeks in hiding, left the country illegally. He soon returned to Africa, basing himself in Lusaka, Zambia and writing as the *Financial Times*'s Africa correspondent. After moving to London he became the paper's Africa Editor, taking early retirement in 2002 following surgery for Parkinson's disease, but continues to visit his old beat regularly. In addition to an earlier collection of reports, he has written three satirical novels set in the imaginary East African nation of Kuwisha.

Also by Michael Holman
African Deadlines
Last Orders at Harrods
Fatboy and the Dancing Ladies
Dizzy Worms
Stripey and the Post Box

Postmark Africa

DEDICATION

To Gabrielle—with my love
London 2020

ACKNOWLEDGEMENTS

The book was researched and edited by Stephen Games of *Booklaunch*, whose intellectual drive and enthusiasm made it possible in this form. Alexander Peel and Hans Georgeson provided valuable editorial assistance at an earlier stage. I am grateful to the *Financial Times* for, while not formally endorsing this book, letting me include some of my FT articles in it.

MICHAEL HOLMAN

POSTMARK AFRICA

HALF A CENTURY AS A FOREIGN CORRESPONDENT

EDITED BY STEPHEN GAMES

First published 2020 in Great Britain by
EnvelopeBooks
with *Booklaunch*
A New Premises venture

EnvelopeBooks
12 Wellfield Avenue
London N10 2EA
England

editor@envelopebooks.co.uk

Republished January 2021

A CIP catalogue record for this title is available from the
British Library

ISBN 9781838172060

Typset in Quadraat and Arial Black
Designed by *Booklaunch*

An EnvelopeBook
www.envelopebooks.co.uk

CONTENTS

The 2000s

The 2010s

Appendices

PREFACE

Unpublished, 1990s

It gets bitterly cold in Gwelo, my hometown in the heart of Zimbabwe—so cold that in midwinter there would often be an early-morning layer of ice on the cement dog bowl at the foot of the garden tap. When I rode to school, shivering in my school uniform of khaki short trousers and green blazer, the route took me from the family home at 8 Kopje Road, which ran along the foot of the small hill or *kopje* that gave it its name, and emerged from the surrounding savannah, peppered with acacia and flat-topped msasa trees. Had I cycled further, I would have come to the mining town of Selukwe, where Ian Smith, the prime minister to be, had his farm, with its herd of prize-winning cattle.

But one year we spent three months on the other side of town, and the journey was longer and even colder. The road dipped down into a *vlei*, shrouded in mist in the winter months. As I approached its low bridge, my legs pumped away at the pedals of my bike, as much to generate warmth as speed.

This journey to school took me past Gwelo's jail, which from March 1959 to April 1960 was home to Hastings Banda, a black politician feared and loathed by white Rhodesians, and which in 1964 briefly housed Robert Mugabe. It was a whitewashed building with walls topped by barbed wire, and surrounded by a fence and sentries.

Twenty years later I got to interview Banda, who by then had become the first president of a newly independent Malawi (formerly Nyasaland). I began by telling him that he and I had three things in common: we both had degrees from Edinburgh University; we both had spent time against our will in Gwelo (now known as Gweru); and we both had received an early-morning knock on the door from the Special Branch.

Banda, then in his eighties, looked at me impassively from behind dark glasses, and said not a word. With his pinstripe suit, red rose in his lapel and ever-present ivory-handled flywhisk, he radiated a combination of Victorian values and African voodoo. He demonstrated that in Africa age need not be a handicap, but an asset—and when combined with the status of his country's founding president, his personality alone was a powerful and disturbing force.

My opening line had not captured his interest however. So much for what I hoped would be an ice-breaking opening question for someone who rarely gave interviews. Then the old man, sitting behind his desk in a room in Blantyre's Sanjika Palace, broke his intimidating silence: 'Tell me more about Gwelo.'

AFRICA HAS ALWAYS been kind to me. I was six when I ran away from kindergarten and began the long, hot tramp that left home behind me. I was spotted by a delivery 'boy', one of the men who carried the orders from stores such as Meikles, pedalling their bicycles fitted with huge wicker baskets and filled with grocery orders, to the homes in the white suburbs. He scooped me up, deposited me in the basket, and delivered a six-year-old parcel to my grateful mother.

I remember night hikes as a boy scout, navigating by the stars, fearful only of snakes, falling asleep to the rhythmic thump of the ore crushers on the small gold mines that dotted the Midlands province, and waking up within a circle of cows looking down on the stranger in their midst.

To be brought up in small-town Southern Rhodesia in the 1950s was to enjoy a combination of Arthur Ransome and *Scouting for Boys* with the innocence of the Famous Five.

Roof-rattling expeditions after nightfall, when we threw stones on neighbours' roofs and ran giggling when the householders emerged and gave chase, was the limit of anti-social behaviour. So-called 'duckies'— youths who defied convention by growing their hair an inch or so longer than white society deemed appropriate, and with the help of Brylcreem carefully combed it so it met at the back of their heads—were leaders of adolescent rebellion. The nearest we came to a drug culture was a beer —Castle lager—and a Sportsman cigarette. Most of my peers were members of either the Boys Brigade or Boy Scouts. School 'socials', dance evenings policed by members of staff, were a model of rectitude and the highlight of our year was the annual school athletics day, with the houses—Sparta, Athens, Corinth and Troy—vying for the trophy.

Television didn't come to Rhodesia until the early 1960s, along with commercial radio. Until then we listened to a station broadcasting from Lourenço Marques (now Maputo), with the highlight being the LM Hit Parade, introduced by David Davies.

White Rhodesia—all 270,000 of us at our peak—was a tight-knit society. You would not know everyone but most of us meeting a fellow Rhodesian for the first time would find we had a friend in common. The European population of Gwelo when I was young was 8,439. Africans numbered 43,578 according to official figures. In reality there were twice that, living in the townships or white suburbs, breaking the law of the time, which saw Blacks as temporary residents in areas classified as European. Their official home was in the Tribal Trust Land, out of sight.

Opposite the house at 8 Kopje Road lived a lawyer, Desmond Lardner-Burke, in whose pool I and friends would enjoy midnight swims. A few years later the same man, by then Minister of Law and Order, signed a notice restricting me to the European area.

'On the basis of information placed before me,' his order declared, 'I am satisfied that you have associated yourself with activities prejudicial to the maintenance of law and order in Rhodesia. I am unable to disclose any details of the information ... for the reason that it would be contrary to the public interest. I consider it desirable for the purpose of maintaining law and order in Rhodesia, to make an Order against you ... that you should remain in the area of land in the district of Gwelo.'

'The boy has gone off the rails,' Lardner-Burke explained to a mutual friend. That I did not mind. I did think less of him when he discovered that the area to which I was restricted included the town's 18-hole golf course, of which he was president, and banned me from playing on it.

By my early teens, Africa was changing rapidly. African nationalism was surging across the continent, and the march to independence from colonial rule, beginning in Ghana in 1957, headed south. It was at its most brutal and chaotic in the Belgian Congo, and the reverberations reached even into my cloistered world as a white schoolboy.

By then the rumbles from what Ian Smith called 'those countries to the north' had reached Gwelo and its black townships. It often took the form of an internecine rivalry between the supporters of the divided nationalist movement, a split that has never been resolved.

One Sunday evening, when my parents were at church, the household cook came knocking at the door, panting with fear and exhaustion. He had run the several miles from the troubled townships to the sanctuary of our house. 'I ran and ran, and I thought my engine would burst,' he said breathlessly. At that stage I had reached my mid-teens, and started looking more closely at my curious white tribe, whose values I was beginning to reject and whose objectives I opposed, but which nevertheless helped shape me.

Although the myth of a frontier society was encouraged, of a pioneer nation born and bred on the African veld, the fact is that a majority of Rhodesians were immigrants—like me. My mother had been born in South Africa, and brought up in King William's Town, but my father was a Cornishman, and had met her while serving in the Royal Air Force, in Queenstown, during the Second World War. He took her back to Cornwall, where they married, and I was born in Penzance. But in 1947 we emigrated to Durban, South Africa, and four years later to Gwelo, then still a small town. Rhodesia, at the time, was a self-governing colony; in 1953 it became part of the Central African Federation, also known as the Federation of Rhodesia and Nyasaland.

Some years later I was called up to serve in the Rhodesian army, but managed to avoid the military police and cross the border into Botswana. For a long time afterwards I used to think that I had escaped from Gwelo. I now look back grateful for the good fortune that brought me to a town I remember with affection as well as frustration, even though some of the memories are painful. Thirty or so years later, it seems incongruous that Africans were excluded from Saturday matinees in the Royal cinema, and that Indians and Coloureds were permitted discreetly to occupy the back rows.

So petty, so futile, so inconsequential a manifestation of prejudice, keeping Africans out of the bioscope, as we called it, that it now seems incomprehensible that it could be a way of life that 30,000 men and women would one day die over, in the war for majority rule.

Other memories are as vivid as if they happened yesterday rather than in my childhood. To this day the words 'Tokwe' and 'Lundi' have a magical, thrilling ring to them, for they are the names of the two rivers that often blocked our way south on our five-day journey to spend Christmas at Kei Mouth, on the Natal coast.

These safaris followed the onset of the summer rains in mid-December, when the two rivers were invariably in flood and the low-level bridges—more causeways than bridges, with frail handrails—became impassable. Each bridge had a hotel on the bank, and trade flourished when traffic came to a standstill, sometimes for two or three days at a time. And then the water level would drop and the men would gather in groups to assess when it would be safe to brave the torrent, stained reddish-brown by run-off. Slowly the handrails re-emerged, battered by tree trunks that had been swept downstream, but sufficient to guide us to the other side. I would know we were ready to move off when I heard the word 'convoy', and, bumper-to-bumper, the cars would inch across to the other side, fearful that a flash flood could yet sweep us downstream.

It was on these journeys that the demeaning nature of racism began to dawn on me. It came not from the relationship between White and Black but between White and White. I was struck by the almost contemptuous way English-speaking Rhodesians treated Afrikaans speakers, who shared the lower rungs of the white Rhodesian class structure, together with Greeks and Portuguese. One side of my mother's family is Afrikaner, and during those Christmas journeys to the coast we passed through the northern Transvaal. The Afrikaner men and women who sold the fruit from the farms—*leechies* (lychees) and *naartjies* (like mandarin oranges) and delicious home-made melon *konfyt* (preserve)—seemed dour and unfriendly: until, that is, my mother spoke Afrikaans. The effect was dramatic. Seemingly sour faces broke into smiles, and an extra handful of leechies would be added to what was already piled in the car.

TODAY MANY OF the 'Europeans' who flocked to Rhodesia in the mid-1950s, followed by a second wave of immigrants in the early 1970s, are scattered around the world. Born perhaps in Birmingham, they lost their heart to Bulawayo, and then emigrated to Brisbane as Rhodesia's guerrilla war intensified, eventually forcing Ian Smith to capitulate to independence at the Lancaster House talks in London in 1979.

They are now part of a curious diaspora, a forgotten footnote to colonialism, cherishing their memories and perpetuating their myths, in tribute to their passion for an ersatz culture, racist at heart, not even true to the philosophy of the man after whom the country was named. Cecil John Rhodes had at least nominally advocated equal rights for all civilised men, by which he meant 'a man whether white or black who has sufficient intelligence to write his name, has some property or work, in fact is not a loafer', but even such a restrictive doctrine was unacceptable to Ian Smith, the Rhodesian prime minister who made a unilateral declaration of independent (UDI) on 11 November 1965, a gesture doomed to failure.

'Rhodesian-born, Rhodesian-bred, strong in arm, thick in head,' went one disparaging ditty about the tribe Smith led and to which I belong, albeit as a renegade member.

Strong of arm, certainly. At one stage Rhodesia had enough cricketers in English county sides to have made up a decent Test XI. Not so thick in head, however. Those who have made their intellectual mark abroad include a former editor of *The Economist*, a senior member of the British government and a host of businesspeople, writers and academics.

Not bad for what was sometimes called 'Surbiton in Africa', after the uninspiring London suburb with as many residents as Rhodesia had Whites. Much of the tribe is now scattered around the globe. A contact magazine called *Rhodesians Worldwide* offers nostalgia, advertisements of army memorabilia, and the news that 'Jock and Hazel, ex-Fort Victoria, offer a bed and beer to "Rhodies" passing through Vancouver'.

Yet for nearly 15 years Jock and Hazel and their like defied the world. Never more than 275,000 of them, and outnumbered 15 to 1 by Africans, they were eventually ground down by sanctions and a guerrilla war. Thousands of people died—468 white and 1,790 black civilians, 1,361 members of the security forces (just under half of them white) and 10,450 guerrillas.

By comparison South Africa got off lightly. Apartheid's death toll over the past decade was under 10,000. On a deaths-to-population ratio, South Africa would have had to endure 120,000 fatalities before reaching a settlement. UDI brought out the best and the worst of white Rhodesia, caught up in the myth of a frontier society. They kept Morris Minors on the road, and Viscounts in the air, longer than anyone thought possible. They broke sanctions with ingenuity, and either manufactured what they formerly imported, or managed without.

The dark side is that white Rhodesia tortured its enemies, executed jailed guerrillas in secret (and lacked the decency to tell next-of-kin) and compulsorily regrouped thousands of peasant families in 'protected villages' which became urban slums. All this was known at the time, but Ian Smith retained the loyalty of most Whites to the very end. Other truly terrible deeds have since been revealed.

Ken Flower, Smith's intelligence chief, recruited a black church minister to supply poisoned clothing to youngsters who thought they were joining the guerrillas. Hundreds died a horrible death. Flower had the minister assassinated to avoid exposure but recounts the tale in his autobiography, *Serving Secretly*. As the deported Catholic bishop Donal

Lamont observed, in their battle to defend what they considered Western, Christian values, white Rhodesians abandoned any morality.

Omens of what was to come were apparent well before UDI. The African nationalist movement within and beyond the Central African Federation began flexing its muscles and the mood in southern Africa started changing as the 1950s drew to a close. Although hardly into my teens, I felt the rise in political tension as tangibly as the build-up of those awesome African storms, when purple-black clouds gather, and the atmosphere becomes electrically charged, to be relieved only when the first heavy raindrops raise little explosions of dust as they fall on the powder-dry earth.

For me and my family, secure in our segregated white suburb, the black townships were a world away, but clashes between rival African nationalist parties brought home a very different reality. Night after night, the 'boys'—which is what we then called the men who worked for us as cook and gardener—returned from their outings in the townships with tales of factional fighting.

'My head, he ache; my nose, he bleed,' complained our cook as he took refuge in the kia, the servants' quarters, at the back of our garden.

For this white Rhodesian Gwelo boy, it marked the end of an era.

THE IMPACT OF the bloody upheaval in the Belgian Congo (now Zaire) in the early 1960s created ripples extending to Gwelo as white refugees made their way south. Newspapers carried advertisements for mercenaries and the psyche of white southern Africa was being prepared for the Rhodesian Front's victory in the 1962 election, which brought Ian Smith to the premiership a year later.

The turning point for white southern Africa came when I was in what was then Salisbury (now Harare), not very long after I had returned from Edinburgh in 1973 to work as a freelance journalist. I remember sitting with a Roman Catholic priest in the open-air section of a restaurant on the first floor of a building overlooking the city, as we digested the news of the 1974 coup in Portugal. It was a time when black students in southern Africa were beginning to rebel. In Rhodesia, that same year, I went with the priest to Regina Coeli mission on the eastern border with Mozambique, and learnt that students were crossing the border in their hundreds to join the guerrilla forces of ZANU. Not long afterwards school students in Soweto took to the streets, and the war against white rule took on a new dimension.

It was about that time that I saw my first dead body. The sickly-sweet stench of death wafting over the whitewashed walls of the police compound in north-east Rhodesia gave advance warning of what I and other journalists had been flown in on an ageing Dakota to see: three bodies, curled up in foetal position, so charred by fire that they were reduced to skeletal figures, captured weapons neatly laid out beside them, and a captured terr (terrorist) standing to one side, available for questioning.

IN THE YEARS that followed, much of my reporting was on the sensitive subject of torture by the Rhodesian security forces and the round-up of as many as 200,000 peasant farmers into so-called 'protected villages'. It was inevitable that my time would run out. Call-up papers were served on me and military police came to my office to arrest me and I unsuccessfully took my case to an exemption board. (A transcript of the hearing can be found in Appendix 2, page 254.) I failed in my bid and ultimately found it necessary to flee the country. The following account of my escape was published by The Observer in July 1977:

> The warning call from a friendly source came in mid-afternoon on 10 June. The Military Police were on their way to my office. Emergency powers regulations published that day arbitrarily ended the protection the courts had afforded during my six-month battle against military service for a regime which 10 years ago restricted me to Gwelo, and 12 months ago, unsuccessfully tried to deport me.
>
> The court case based on the contradiction of expecting a 'security risk' to serve in the Army, was due to be heard in the Appellate Division of the High Court in July. However, one of the new regulations stated that irrespective of court proceedings, call-up papers would take effect. Should a conscript win his case, he would then be released. It was a version of guilty until proven innocent and it was undoubtedly aimed at me. Apart from a case brought by a Quaker conscientious objector, there had been no other challenges.
>
> I missed the MPs by a few minutes. Later in the day a contact in the Special Branch warned me that I would not be allowed to leave the country. I decided to stay in hiding. Four weeks later, having shaved my beard and dyed my hair, I crossed the border and made my way to London. To protect those who helped me and so that the route might be used by others, the less I write about the journey the better.
>
> I left behind a country which has inextricably slipped into

tragedy. A divided black-nationalist movement with two armies and a ruling white elite which clings to power is a formula for disaster. Despite a depressed economy and a rapidly worsening guerrilla war, I doubt if Mr. Ian Smith is ready to throw in the towel.

While he may grudgingly accept a black majority in Parliament and Cabinet, he is likely to insist that the 270,000 Whites have a guaranteed social, economic and political role which includes the power to veto unacceptable constitutional changes. Knowing as well as any black leader that constitutional guarantees are worthless, Mr. Smith will insist that Whites control the Rhodesian armed forces.

It is this outline which I believe will form the basis of Mr. Smith's international settlement offer to tribal chiefs and any nationalist leader, such as Bishop Abel Muzorewa, and the Rev. Ndabaningi Sithole, he thinks might accept these terms. It will not work, because the overwhelming majority of Blacks will not concede a white veto, and would desert those leaders who did. Nevertheless, it is a strategy worth taking seriously. Although the white right-wing has accused Mr. Smith of being politically bankrupt, they have failed to take into account his shrewd appreciation of his South African audience.

As the black nationalist Patriotic Front increases its demands, Mr. Smith must hope that his internal settlement proposals will become more attractive to Mr. John Vorster, and win South Africa's powerful protection. In the meantime, one of the most disquieting develop-ments is the dominance of the Rhodesian armed forces whose leaders have never been more outspoken.

Recently, for example, Army Commander Lt-Gen John Hickmann firmly rejected either the dismantling of the Rhodesian Army or the integration of the guerrilla forces during a transition period. While this stance is entirely compatible with Mr. Smith's ambition, it nevertheless is ominous that, for the first time in Rhodesia's history, serving soldiers are making political speeches.

It is also worrying that the recently formed right-wing Rhodesia Action Party draws from angry young servicemen and conscripts, convinced that a more ruthless conduct of the war, including the 'eradication' of the guerrillas' political wings (the Zimbabwe Africa Peoples Union led by Mr. Joshua Nkomo and the Zimbabwe African National Union, led by Mr. Robert Mugabe) would pave the way for their version of an international settlement consisting of black and white territorial assemblies.

It is now clear that Whites are being prepared for the breakdown of the Anglo-American initiative. From Government ministers comes a steady stream of hard-line comment. One senior minister recently bitterly attacked Britain, suggesting that Sir Roy Welensky's passionate condemnation of Britain's handling of the break-up of Federation in 1963—a story of 'treachery and deceit seldom equalled … (even) in negotiations between nations which have hated each other …'—had relevance today. Two days later, the Foreign Minister Mr. P. K. Van der Byl made his notorious scorched earth threat, promising to 'contest every hill and every river … indescribable chaos and irreparable destruction that will follow … .'

An outsider might think that this appalling prospect would double the emigration figures overnight. However, Mr. Van de Byl's brand of patriotism should be set against years of political conditioning of the white community. The Rhodesian Front came to power in 1962 and has controlled broadcasting ever since. It has replaced the overt newspaper censorship introduced at UDI with an equally effective D Notice system and a press liaison officer (Colonel 'Mac' Knox) who ensures that contentious copy has to receive Government clearance. For 15 years, then, Whites have had their news doctored. Many of those bearing the brunt of the fighting—the 17–30 year olds—are the 'UDI generation', cushioned from criticism of their Government and its values, and the repeated warnings of the outside world.

I doubt whether the grim nature of their predicament has really sunk home among most Whites. The war confirms their prejudices rather than shakes their convictions. The Government line is readily accepted: a small 'Communist terrorist' minority rapes, loots, mutilates and murders, and wins the grudging support of tribespeople by intimidation.

Perhaps the greatest irony is that Whites do not realise how fortunate they are that most of the black leaders they revile are part of the old guard of black nationalism—teachers, clerics, trade unionists, professional men, who began their political careers in the fifties. The same men are now struggling to keep at the forefront of a movement increasingly influenced by young guerrillas.

I fear the epitaph for my fellow Whites will be that their dilemma was of their own creating, their prophecy of chaos under black rule self-fulfilling.

Looking back, I am starting to conclude that Africa's crisis has as much to do with its state of mind as the size of its external debt or the frailties of its governments. I fear the continent has been traumatised, by the slave trade, by colonial rule, by the Cold War, and latterly by the imposition of structural adjustment, the medicine of economic reform proving too harsh for a frail patient. Its peoples have lost confidence in themselves and in their capacity to bring about a recovery, and to remedy the consequences of the poor leadership they have allowed and endured during the post-independence era.

Meanwhile, Africa's relationship with Europe has become that of a bad marriage. The two parties have known each other intimately, but no longer can surprise, inspire, delight or engage the other. Indeed, the relationship is dominated by expectations of failure or disappointment, which in turn helps shape response. Europe now despairs of Africa's recovery. Africa for its part despairs of Europe's capacity to recover the enthusiasm for the continent to which it was once so closely bound.

Once enslaved, later colonised, and then marginalised in the 1980s, the continent faces a continuing crisis in the 1990s—but with a new dimension. Africa is not only in danger of losing the battle for economic recovery and political stability, the world is losing interest. The countries that led the scramble for Africa's resources some 130 years ago are now disengaging.

No longer are the great trading houses of West Africa seen as offering long-term careers in Ghana or Nigeria, and nor do ambitious young diplomats dream of following in the footsteps of an earlier generation. Fewer voices are raised in Africa's defence, fewer supporters are in Africa's corner.

As for the bad marriage, I have perhaps unwittingly been part of it, and maybe still am, for many of my reports have been bleak, as you will read in this book. Some will put that down to my temperament, or to a Western media predisposed to gloom and doom. I believe they reflect reality.

Whatever the weaknesses of my profession, especially its susceptibility to bad news rather than good, no colleague I know takes pleasure in Africa's pain. The reporting of South Africa's joyous, miraculous transition lifted our spirits, and made us realise the toll bad news takes.

I have been called an Afro-pessimist. My response is that I am an Afro-realist, refusing to patronise, or condone failure, or conceal short-comings. Hopes that the emergence of multi-party politics would prove a simple stepping-stone to good governance have proved premature. Opposition parties have turned out to be weak, fractious and susceptible to patronage, owing more to ethnicity than policy for their support.

Meanwhile the policy at the heart of relations between Africa and the West is failing. 'Good governance', the concept which links aid to Africa with economic reform, human rights and democracy, has not reached the heart of the continent's predicament.

Admirable in principle, complex in practice, the policy today appears confused. Increasingly the West is leaving responsibility for Africa to the World Bank but providing neither adequate mandate nor clear guidance. For the industrialised world, the will to help may emerge only when an ailing Africa is seen as a threat to self-interest, whether in the form of immigration to southern Europe, a rise in Muslim extremism, growth in drug-trafficking, increasing health risks posed by a continent that cannot be ring-fenced, the depletion of flora and fauna with medicinal value or other environmental concerns.

Western involvement must ultimately be motivated by self-interest as much as compassion in its response to the African crisis. Possible solutions will only be implemented when an ailing Africa is seen as a threat and as a loss. One day, I hope, the world will realise what is at stake: something more complex than lives, precious though they are, but an interdependent relationship between Africa and the world which we ignore at our peril.

I WROTE THE above three decades later, on a Johannesburg veranda with a panoramic view of the city before me and a glorious jacaranda tree in full purple bloom in the foreground. Perhaps I was too impatient. I should have put my near-thirty years of adult experience against a perspective of 300 years and more of white domination going back to the days when Dutch settlers planted the seeds of white rule in the Cape in 1652.

In those three decades I saw undone the work of three centuries and concluded that redressing that legacy would take at least a further three decades. I reminded myself that I had followed three revolutions: the ending of white rule in southern Africa, the impact of the Cold War and the consequences of its ending, and the impact of structural adjustment.

At the same time I celebrated the fact that for the first time in those 30 years, southern Africa was within reach of lasting peace. The battle over apartheid was fought on neighbouring territory, as much as in South Africa itself. Millions died, whether directly or through disease that could have been prevented, or through famine that need not have been or that could at least have been ameliorated but for war.

Now a region whose resources encompassed the oil of Angola, the diamonds of Botswana, the vast stretches of arable land and copper mines in Zambia, the natural gas fields of Mozambique, the commercial farms of Zimbabwe, the industrial muscle of South Africa, and an unspoilt coastline, could at last realise its potential. And as I looked out over a city once synonymous with apartheid, what came to my mind was a joyous evening in June 1995, an evening that left an abiding image and served to mark the end of a chapter of my life:

> I am in Johannesburg with friends and South Africa has just won the Rugby World Cup after Nelson Mandela has called on black South Africans to rally behind their team. As we drive from the ground to a city-centre hotel, a small black boy on the street corner joins in the celebrations. With his hands cupped aside his head, forefingers jutting above his ears like budding horns, back curved, rump high, the street urchin metamorphoses into a youthful black springbok, prancing with delight at his country's success. A white motorist hoots in response, and both exchange grins as wide as Nelson Mandela's, as he celebrates a victory in which he had played no small part.

The event symbolised South Africa's miraculous transformation, and its recollection still revives my spirits and sustains my faith.

The 1960s

Prime Minister not practising what he is preaching

Letters, *The Chronicle*, Bulawayo, 10 September 1964

Sir—In the Rhodesian Front advertisement in the *Sunday Mail* (Sept. 6) Mr. Smith is quoted from his eve-of-departure speech as saying that 'people are entitled to their freedom of expression, their freedom of thought, their freedom of worship and their freedom of action—always provided that in the exercise of this freedom they do not interfere with the freedom of other people, or that this freedom is not used as a subversive means of undermining the constitution.'

This statement certainly supports democratic principles, but it can be seen from recent events—the banning of the *Daily News*, PCC, ZANU[1] and ZAPU[2]—that it contradicts Government practice.

For while the rights of the white minority should be protected, this same minority has not the right to impose its wishes on 4,000,000 Africans and still claim to represent what Mr. Smith calls a 'democratic system'.

---

[1] ZANU, the Zimbabwe African National Union, was a militant organisation that in 1963 split from ZAPU, the Zimbabwe African People's Union, to fight against white minority rule in Rhodesia. In 1975 ZANU split again into wings loyal to Robert Mugabe or to Ndabaningi Sithole, later called ZANU–PF and ZANU–Ndonga respectively. It won the independence elections of 1980.

[2] ZAPU, the Zimbabwe African People's Union, is a socialist political party, founded by Joshua Nkomo and others in December 1961 to campaign for majority rule in Rhodesia. Robert Mugabe was originally its information and publicity secretary, and ZIPRA, the Zimbabwe People's Revolutionary Army, was its military wing. Standing as the Patriotic Front party in the 1980 independence elections, ZAPU lost to ZANU but the two bodies merged in 1987 to form the Zimbabwe African National Union–Patriotic Front (ZANU–PF). It was relaunched in 2008.

In the same speech the Prime Minister said that the 'era of civilised control in Southern Rhodesia isn't estimated in a period of two years, 10 years, or even 100 years. It has got to be for all time.'

I assume that this 'civilised control' will be maintained by denying majority rule. My assumption becomes conviction when at the end of his speech I read that he will fight for independence 'whether there is Unity or not'.

Together with the events mentioned above, this speech and its implications lead me to the conclusion that the Southern Rhodesian Government has adopted an authoritarian view as a desperate substitute for democratic rule.

Michael Holman
Gwelo

Apartheid, Rhodesian-style
Myths of Separate Development
The Scotsman, Friday 27 August 1971

There exist several schools of thought about Rhodesia Front (RF) doctrine. A few years ago Whites espoused 'partnership' like Samuel Butler Christians: with an equal horror of those who practised the concept and those who doubted it. Today apartheid is disavowed by the very people who put it into practice.

There is not a single RF MP who will publicly admit that Rhodesian separate development is not substantially different from apartheid, partly because they wish to avoid a word which has become synonymous with brutality, partly because they wish to avoid any suggestion that Rhodesia is a mere client state of South Africa, and partly because they are confused about the precise implications of Rhodesia's apartheid plans.

Mr. Smith's own description of the Rhodesian Front doctrine as 'trying to create a little bit more of what already exists' is misleading and perhaps this accounts for the confusion of some of his MPs.

Similarities with present RF doctrine can be found in the policies of the 30s, and leading RF politicians quote with approval certain speeches by the prime minister of the time, Sir Godfrey Huggins (later Lord Malvern) in order to back their claim that current policy is 'traditional'.

They do not point out that the speeches they quote were made during the first few years of the Huggins administration, and Huggins began to change his policy in the forties. The RF have, since UDI, taken up a policy which was tried and found wanting 30 years ago.

Prejudice
Where there is no misunderstanding is in the determination to reduce

social contact between the races, hence the decisions to ban multi-racial school sport, reduce the number of multiracial bars, to introduce separate parks and toilets, to enforce segregation of the few residential areas which have non-white residents, and to move the families of servants who work in white areas to townships situated a safe distance from white suburbs.

'Problems of race are intractable,' the Deputy Prime Minister has said, 'especially when there is the problem of differing races coming into social or cultural contact. Where there is such contact, you get innumerable cases of tension and strain occurring between people, arising from such things as dissimilarity of religion, morality, courtesy, property ownership, differing ideas and conceptions as to work and time and money.' Here is the glib and specious rationale for racial prejudice which for those white Rhodesians who need convincing, gilds their bigotry and racial obsessions.

But when separate development is taken beyond segregating toilets and children's sports meetings there is not the same unanimity. Before the 1970 general election the party chairman sent a memo to all divisional and constituency branches, asking them to ensure that the MP they returned was dedicated to the concept of separate development.

There was an angry response from one MP: 'His reference to the National Party in South Africa makes it obvious that he would enlarge and extend separate development in the same direction. If that is Mr. Nilson's idea of separate development it is not mine, and I am certainly not dedicated to its implications.' In his belief in the distinction between Rhodesian separate development and South African apartheid the MP was presumably relying on the definition of his leader.

'Apartheid means the division of the country into areas and ultimately the Africans having the autonomy to control their own areas, doesn't it,' said Mr. Smith. 'Like the Bantustans, the Transkeis and so on. I mean the two things (apartheid and separate development) are as different as chalk is to cheese, aren't they?'

Are they? An RF advertisement in 1968 proclaimed: 'We support the principle of separate facilities for different races. We believe the different races should live in their own areas.' The 1969 Constitution has provision for provincial governments in African areas, based on a further division of the races in Rhodesia, a tribal division between the Mashonas and the Matabele.

'The solution,' said Desmond Lardner-Burke, 'is to remove the inevitability of conflict between the races at its sources by eliminating, as far as is constitutionally possible, the likelihood of political competition between the races.'

A start has been made, for African local councils in rural areas provide the foundations of provincial governments for African areas. 'I look forward to the time,' one RF MP told the House of Assembly, 'when it is found possible in Rhodesia to implement the Rhodesian Front policy of provincialisation which will allow the Africans to run their own minor parliaments in their own parts of the land,' and several of his fellows expressed similar sentiments. A far cry from 'a little more of what already exists.'

The executive of the party have long been determined to introduce an apartheid system based on the structure which exists. A few months after UDI the Secretary for Internal Affairs, one of the most influential men in Rhodesian politics, outlined RF doctrine concisely and unambiguously.

'If we accept at the outset that there is no solution to be found in racial integration ... then from the start we must recognise and plan on the basis of ultimate territorial segregation of the two major races— European and African.'

Since then the regime has set up its own version of the South African border industries, under the auspices of the Tribal Trust Development Corporation.

'Minor parliaments' with limited responsibilities are all the Africans can expect, for power and skills remain with the white man. The present African rural councils are presided over by a white district commissioner—there is not a single African DC, or even cadet officer. Nor is there a senior African official in any of the spheres which deal with African affairs, such as the Ministry of Internal Affairs, the Ministry of Education, the Ministry of Local Government and Housing; not a single African township superintendent; no Africans have become patrol officers in the police force; there is no African commissioned officer in any of the services: and in no sphere, administrative, health, education, or in the services, does a white man take orders from a black man.

In the period 1960 to 1969 only six Africans were apprenticed in government service, and in the private sector from 1962 to 1969 only 78 Africans were registered as apprentices, against 3,299 Whites and 114 Asians and Coloureds. When set against these figures, the concern expressed for one section of his pupils by a headmaster of a white school unwittingly reveals the waste, inefficiency and brutality of 'separate development'.

Wretched

'I am talking,' he told parents at speech day, 'of the boy who, as often as not, is a good member of the school community, seems to have common sense, makes friends, is quite good with his hands, but somehow cannot get his COP certificate (the basic school leaving qualification) and is thoroughly frustrated when he tries to find worthwhile employment such as trade involving apprenticeship ... It is tragic when they are debarred from apprenticeship because of being as little as 5 per cent short of the pass in such an academic exercise as the writing of an essay or doing a comprehension task in a normal two-hour examination.'

In 1969 nearly 4,000 Africans had to leave school after Form II, which is the level required for apprenticeships. Talent is wasted because white Rhodesians believe that colour is more important than ability, and those wretched white students of below average ability struggle to acquire basic skills before taking their reserved place in the Rhodesian elite.

Of the 118,453 African children who entered school in 1961, over 110,000 were on the labour market by the age of 14 or younger. There is 'plenty of work available for them in both the European and African agricultural sections of the economy,' says the Minister of Labour, meaning that they can weed farms. Would the white headmaster have been satisfied with that reply to his problem?

There are jobs to be filled—both the railways and the mining industry are badly in need of skilled personnel—but the jobs will go to white men, often to immigrants who become 'Rhodesians' overnight. There are over a thousand African graduates working outside Rhodesia, and 400 to 500 currently in training, who will not get jobs in Rhodesia, as unemployed African graduates of the University of Rhodesia have proved.

Credibility

At some stage Mr. Smith will have to give a clearer lead on what timetable he has in mind for provincialisation. No doubt the Rhodesian Front party managers and executive feel that it is unwise to press for the full development of provincial parliaments while there is any prospect of a settlement; and when the South African government is increasingly bothered by black and coloured leaders in South Africa making adroit use of the platforms provided by Bantustans and coloured Assemblies, the Rhodesians can hardly be blamed for refusing to rush where the neighbours are now treading warily.

Yet this caution may be costly for the Rhodesian Front. The effect of the 1969 Constitution is to ensure that there can be no constitutional progress towards majority rule; to the right of the RF new ground has opened up for those who wish to apply a rigid interpretation of separate development, and those who chafe at delay. Concepts which would have been dismissed before the RF came to power now have credibility in Rhodesian eyes at least.

The foundations of an apartheid state in Rhodesia have been laid. If the RF does not build on them, it will be threatened by a party which will.

Letter to friends in London
Salisbury, Rhodesia, 11 March 1974

An obituary in the British South Africa police magazine *Outpost* begins:

> The term 'complete Rhodesian' can be applied to several local personalities but never with as much justification as when we refer to the late Police Reservist Delville Vincent who was killed in action (against guerrillas) in Northern Mashonaland on April 3, 1973.
>
> Del was born in South Africa in 1929 ...

And that is, and will be, Rhodesia in the 70s. White immigrants dying, defending with the gun the country Whites took by the gun.

> Because we're all Rhodesians and we'll fight through thick and thin,
> We'll keep our land a free land, stop the enemy coming in,
> We'll keep them north of the Zambezi till that river's running dry,
> And this mighty land will prosper 'cos Rhodesians never die.
>
> We'll preserve this little nation for our children's children too,
> Once you've known Rhodesia no other land will do.
> We will stand in the sunshine with truth upon our side,
> If we have to go alone we'll go alone with pride.

This charming ditty, 'Rhodesians never die,' is sung by an immigrant (he happens to be Prime Minister Ian Smith's son-in-law). He is one of 60 per cent of the 'white Rhodesians' who were born outside Rhodesia.

I met another immigrant not very long ago. Hitching from Gwelo, in the heart of the Rhodesian Midlands, my friend and I were given a lift. The driver was a young, lean, deeply-tanned South African farmer, with a broad Afrikaans accent. He managed a pyrethrum estate on the eastern border. No, he didn't miss his home.

'You can talk to the munts[3] here; you can't in South Africa. Here I can say, "Bugger off, you shithouse." I say that in South Africa and I get into trouble. You just can't talk to the munts there anymore.'

One reason for his satisfactory labour relations no doubt lies in the fact that black agricultural workers and domestic servants—no less than 55 per cent of all Blacks in employment—work under the Masters and Servants Act. This harsh and archaic piece of legislation ('it is illegal in terms of the Act for any of his family, by desire of his master on any journey within southern Rhodesia ... on which his master orders him to go ...') was enacted in 1901 and is based on legislation introduced into the Cape Province of South Africa in 1856. There is no provision in the act for trade unionism, collective bargaining or other wage-setting machinery. No wage minimum is established under the Act.

You can, however, get guidance on wages—as far as domestic servants are concerned—from the Information Booklet issued to new members of staff by the University of Rhodesia Women's Club. It recommends $10–$12 a month plus rations (one dollar is about 75 pence) and 'Hours of indoor servants are usually about twelve hours in duration'—two more than the minimum permitted by the Master and Servants Act.

The wages of black farm workers average about $10–$15 a month plus rations. In real terms there has been a decline in their income over the past decade. There is a farm workers union, but there is also a catch: it does not receive recognition and is thus prevented from acting as a negotiating body. There is not the slightest chance that it will be recognised.

Addressing one farmers' meeting, an official of the Rhodesia National Farmers Union warned: 'Trade unions are ready and willing to exploit any grievance the worker may have. A recent example was the intervention of Mr. Mpofu (the general secretary of the Plantation and Agriculture Workers Union) at a chicken farm near Salisbury. A pay dispute was built up by this individual to include grievances over housing and latrines and many other aspects the employees had not originally complained of.' Both Mr. Mpofu and the president of the

---

3 Munt (plural munts). (Rhodesia, slang, originally military, derogatory, offensive, ethnic slur). A black person, usually a man.

union were restricted last year, joining about 60 of their colleagues from other unions.

'We have a very sympathetic Minister of Labour,' the official continued, 'and you can rest assured that an agricultural trade union will not get recognition.' (The speech from which I take these extracts was not published.) Seventeen of the 49 Rhodesia Front MPs are farmers; 10 of the 18 cabinet ministers are farmers.

One must assume that Mr. Macmillan[4] was not aware of the Masters and Servants Act—and several other acts for that matter—when he wrote (in the last volume of his memoirs) that before the Rhodesia Front came to power in 1962 Rhodesia enjoyed 'a tradition of moderation and even of liberalism'. But he is not the only one who believes in this tradition. Sir Alec[5] does, and so does the main white opposition in the country, the Rhodesia Party, who see themselves as the inheritors of that tradition. 'Rhodesia's long and proud history of racial tolerance, harmony and understanding,' proclaims the RF manifesto, 'is today yielding to petty and unnecessary racialism.'

After persistent questioning Allan Savory (leader of the RP) admitted to me that the RP does not see its way clear to pledging repeal of the Act should it ever get into power.

The truth of the belief in this tradition of 'moderation' is possibly not as important as the role it plays in British policy. Around the belief is built the theory that as pressure on white rule increases, so white Rhodesians, becoming aware of their folly and their predicament, will get together and sort things out.

Every one of the dozen or so by-elections since UDI puts the theory to the test, and always it takes a battering when RF candidates are returned by substantial majorities, occasionally being threatened by extreme right-wing candidates. The two by-elections on February 28 this year were no exception. The votes in the two constituencies were:

- Sinoia-Umvukwes: RF 553, RP 249, Rhodesia National Party (extreme right wing) 199, Centre Party (moderate white) 27,
- Raylton, Bulawayo: RF 783, RP 371, CP 31.

Yet the pressures on white rule were apparent in February not simply to those with inside information, but to all those who read the leading

---

4 Harold Macmillan (1894–1986), British Conservative prime minister 1957–63.
5 Sir Alec Douglas-Home (1903–95), British Conservative prime minister 1963–64.

daily, the Rhodesia Herald. Three Whites were killed in guerrilla attacks in the Centenary area, which is part of the Sinoia constituency (in the north-east of Rhodesia) just ten days or so before voting took place.

Men over 25 with no military commitments at present are now liable to call-up periods of one month. Rhodesians look with concern at Mozambique as rail links with the coast come under attack by Frelimo.[6] Hardly a day goes by without anxious reference to a black birth rate of 3.6 per cent which annually exceeds the white population of 280,000 in Salisbury. Stringent petrol rationing began in February, due more to a shortage of vital foreign exchange than any supply problem.

All this and much else is public knowledge. Yet in the ninth year of UDI there is little evidence that the Rhodesia Front is losing any substantial support. I visited Centenary the day after the shootings, but I heard no reappraisal of white rule, no questions about the cost of white rule. Instead there were demands from local farmers for harsher punish-ment of tribesmen and farm workers who aided 'terrorists'. (Although just two weeks previously 110 tribesmen had been taken into custody at Bindura, for allegedly collaborating with guerrillas in the murder of several Africans in the Madziwa TTL. Their crops and huts were destroyed and their cattle impounded. The Rhodesia Herald, falling over itself in an effort to plug the government line, headlined the news: 'Terror Murderers Aided by Tribesmen', although they had no evidence other than the allegations in the government communique.) The farmers also wanted a dusk-to-dawn curfew in the area, and the right to shoot 'anything that moved' during the curfew period.

The cattle that are impounded are generally sold. There have been cases where the cattle have been shot. One needs to know something of the importance of cattle to the people to appreciate the immensity of this. Cattle are not measured in terms of so many pence per pound of flesh. One African writer says: 'A family without cattle in Shona society is like a house built on sand … . Cattle are the enduring foundation of traditional Shona society.' Their slaughter is part of the ritual at marriage and death. 'They plough the fields and carry crops … pull carts.' 'In Shona society, one's social status and wealth are determined by numbers of cattle. Thus to have many cattle is the summit of a Shona's desire. Except in cases of extreme necessity, a Shona does not

---

[6] The Mozambique Liberation Front (FRELIMO), founded in 1962, is the ruling party in Mozambique. It began as a nationalist movement fighting for independence from Portugal, which it achieved in June 1975, a year after this article was published.

sell his cattle ... . Keeping cattle provides a link between neighbours. The people of a whole village take turns in herding the cattle ... . They remain the life blood of Shona society ... .'

I was talking to a wise old friend of mine, a middle-aged African who has a farm near Inyanga. He was not personally affected by confiscations, but he was telling me of his anguish when he heard what was happening in the north-east. He tried to explain the pain, the sadness, the shock of what was happening. 'You know, Holman, they are treating our *mombies* (cattle) like animals.'

Not one farm is vacant in the Centenary area although there have been a number of guerrilla attacks there. There seem to be three main reasons. It is one of the wealthiest farming areas in Rhodesia. Many of the farmers have private planes and landing strips. One farm manager, I was told, was getting a salary of $14,000 a year. Secondly it is a very close-knit community, and I imagine that it would not be an easy thing for one farmer to tell his neighbour that he was selling up, knowing full well that empty farms are security risks. Finally the Whites in the region devoutly believe that they are holding the front line for Rhodesia; should their morale crack, white Rhodesia will fall.

It is harder to judge morale in the rest of the country. Looking at the latest migration statistics I noticed an interesting trend, though. These are the figures for net migration in the age group 19–24, July 1972 to January 1973:

July-December	+ 73	October	− 1
January	+ 74	November	− 12
July	− 4	December	− 35
August	− 3	January	− 60
September	− 60	TOTAL LOSS	− 174

Over the same period there was a net gain of 169 for all other age groups. I meet very few young people who don't plan to go to Britain. One hears snatches of exchanges in shops and cafes and during cinema intervals. Like this one

'I'm off next week.'
'Ah, bull.'
'Swear t'God. M'ma's lent me the fare.'
'Jesus. Well, good luck in England, hey, and don't come back
    married to a wog.'

Still on the theme of immigrants: I went to a report-back meeting given by the Rhodesia Front MP for Mabelreign, Salisbury, one John Cleig. Addressing an audience of predominately middle-aged Whites, he warned them of 'the Communist-trained scum whose sole object is to smash this government and take over the country.'

What were the answers to this? Apart from military retaliation Whites must use every means at their disposal to increase the white population. There must be a halt to Africanisation, a halt to the influx of Africans into the cities, and control must stay in white hands.

'We Rhodesians must never be ashamed to be white. We must be proud to be white. We must be proud to be Rhodesians.'

This was delivered in a nasal Manchester accent. He has lived in Mabelreign for 17 years.

From his audience at question time came a barely concealed loathing and contempt for Africans. Two or three times questioners choked over the word 'Africans' and referred to '*kaffirs*'. There were three MPs on the platform, including the Minister of Power, Roger Hawkins.[7] But despite Smith's oft-repeated call for respect and racial harmony, no correction or rebuke was forthcoming.

Father David Bird ended six years' ministry to the army last year. 'I was sitting in a pub in a hot little town in the lowveld last week when two smartly dressed men came in and were refused service. You know the reason: wrong race. By not doing or saying anything I was just as much part of the hate-making process as the barman ... . Maybe I have a violent streak in my nature, but I later thought that if I were in their shoes there would have been another recruit for the terrorists.'

Father Bird's tale and its moral can be repeated a hundredfold. The common point is the individual responsibility for the 'hate-making process'. No single white Rhodesian can say 'I didn't know it was happening.'

African reaction to a British Labour government has been muted. I think it is appreciated that Rhodesia is very low on the scale of concerns.

Further, although Blacks I talk to see Labour as a party which is more concerned about its own problems than the Tories, the leadership is sceptical as to whether Labour has the political will required to initiate real change.

But there is the feeling that Smith will find the Labour Government

---

7 Roger Tancred Robert Hawkins (1915–1980) was one of the founding members of the Rhodesian Front and a member of Ian Smith's cabinet in the years after UDI.

harder to convince than the Tories, should he claim that he has achieved an internal settlement based on the support of chiefs and the black pro-settlement (i.e. in favour of the Smith-Home proposals) groups. These groups—there are about five at the moment—have been joined by the African Progressive Party, formed on 2 February. It is led by Chad Chipunza, once a junior minister in Sir Roy Welensky's cabinet. The African Progressive Party took half a page in the Sunday Mail to announce its policies. Rhodesian television and radio gave the announcement extensive coverage, which immediately made it suspect. Both the Centre Party and the Rhodesia Party called it a party of white business.

Chipunza ('CC') himself has had a chequered career. In April 1964 the Railway African Workers' Union demanded the withdrawal of a concessionary store CC was operating on its property, alleging that he was 'anti-African'. He was declared a Prohibited Immigrant (P.I.) in Zambia in 1966, after being called a 'sell out' by President Kaunda.

CC denies that the APP receives white backing from businessmen who would dearly love to convince Britain that Blacks in Rhodesia have changed their minds about the No recorded by Pearce.[8] He claims that the money has been raised over two years, the time during which the party was being prepared and planned. There is no evidence of such a period of preparation.

Back to the ad in the Sunday Mail. It had no telephone number for the APP. The party address was given as a box number. After several enquiries I got the phone number, and it was answered by a white man, one Moss. He arranged for me to interview CC and the party secretary Samson Chibi at his office at African Safari Products. This is a souvenir shop, selling copperware, skin and hide products, and soap-stone carvings. When I got there I was met by one Maurice Leapman (who has a record of association with African pro-settlement groups) and was taken in to his office to meet CC and Chibi.

I went through my questions prior to recording the interview. Leapman had something to say on every point, occasionally reminding me that 'It's their party, the whole thing is their idea.'

---

[8] The Pearce Commission, chaired by Lord Pearce, was sent from the UK to Rhodesia at the start of 1972 to test the acceptability to black Rhodesians of an agreement that would legalise the Smith government's rebellion but which black parties had not been allowed to take part in. The efforts of the Commission gave rise to increased guerrilla unrest and after two years were rejected.

Messages of support had been 'flooding in'. This was strange. How did these spontaneous supporters get hold of an unpublished number? Ah, the 30 or so organisers in the African Progressive Party had been receiving messages of support and *they* had phoned in with these messages. Could I meet one of these organisers? Unfortunately not, only CC and Chibi were authorised to speak to the press.

As I was about to leave the office after the interview I noticed that Leapman had a framed photograph of Ian Smith (shaking hands with Eddie Calvert,[9] of all people) on his desk. And as you enter the shop a large oil painting of Smith greets you. Leapman was once, and possibly still is, a member of the Hatfield branch of the Rhodesia Front.

CC now claims that over 3,000 APP groups have been formed. There is not a tittle of evidence to back this.

The African National Council inaugural congress held in the Stodart Hall, in the black township of Harare, Salisbury, was another matter altogether. It was an historic occasion, the biggest nationalist gathering in Rhodesia for over ten years. Eight hundred delegates attended from all over Rhodesia.

The Bishop (Bishop Muzorewa) entered the hall to the accompaniment, strange to white ears in that situation, of a sort of slow hand clap; and once on the stage, he was saluted by the audience, arms thrust forward, palms facing him; women ululated. His concluding address ended with the singing of the black national anthem, *Nkosi Sikelel' iAfrika* —God Bless Africa. As the last line was sung, the Bishop held up his hand for silence. 'I see some people shedding tears. I want you to know that I believe God recognises your tears.'

The purpose of the ANC, the Bishop had declared on the Saturday morning, was to 'seek and try to achieve majority rule and end the Rhodesian Front totalitarianism and fascism which have haunted us for the last painful and wasted 11 years'. He attacked the 'segregatory and repressive laws' passed since the Pearce Commission was in the country two years ago:

> The RF government are writing the blackest chapter in the history of this country.
>
> When we stop to think that there are people who are languishing in prisons, detention and restriction camps, and of the innocent persons dying in the North Eastern border area, we are

---

9 Albert Edward 'Eddie' Calvert (1922–78) was an English trumpeter who had seven instrumental hits in the UK Singles Chart between 1953 and 1958.

motivated incessantly to demanding our immediate emancipation.

Day-to-day humiliation and insults through racial discrimination we face everywhere, all the time … .

And the Bishop added a warning to Whites: 'The way they are treating Africans now will determine how free they will be in the future.'

Time and time again the points he made were greeted by applause, by cries of 'Shame! Shame!' and by deep reverberating murmurs of assent. These gut rumbles of approval sent shivers down my spine, and the singing of *Nkosi Sikelel' iAfrika* brought tears to my eyes too.

His audience were for the most part workers and peasants, dressed for the occasion almost without exception in ties and threadbare jackets. The Bishop himself had discarded his clerical garb for the congress. He wore a loose sleeved, open necked Afro-patterned shirt. On the table before him were not the usual speakers' aids of glass and water jug but traditional long-handled carved wooden scoops and clay pitchers. It was all part of the background when he said 'I am so sick and tired of seeing so many who are ashamed to be Africans. They want to be someone else. We are looking forward to a time when people will cotton on to the idea that black is beautiful.

'Respect your colour, respect your culture. You are a child of God: respect yourself.'

The Bishop ended his opening address: 'Let not the struggle for freedom in Zimbabwe be given up, but let the struggle be vigorously pursued until the freedom chimes ring from the tower of Zimbabwe.' He then led the singing: 'Free, free, free, Zimbabwe shall be free.'

The three Special Branch policemen in the balcony of the hall watched impassively.

THE POLITICS OF Britain is without a stark cause—or so it seems to me. Maybe multinational companies and international capitalist conspiracies wrack the bowels of a Labour party worker, but I could never find a response on that level. But in the Stodart Hall there were people suffering the cruellest indignities and affronts. They were for the most part poor, and yet they were inspired by a message which promised nothing but dignity. The politics of Rhodesia are so fundamental. They are seen as power and abuse on the part of the Whites, and servitude and humiliation on the part of the Blacks.

It would be fruitless (at this stage) to warn that audience about black elitism, neo-colonialism and inequitable international trade relations.

All that may come to pass, and then their grinding poverty will become inexplicable to them, because manipulators will mystify the business of politics and deliberately place the issues beyond the grasp of the ordinary people.

But at the moment that audience acutely understands the politics of Rhodesia. Their needs are seen in stark terms and they have an immediate objective which to achieve requires an immense struggle, but never can the objective be lost sight of in that struggle. Never will it appear remote and irrelevant to their daily lives. And perhaps for a nation there are only few occasions in its history when an issue is so clearly defined. And when it happens there is magic in the air, a sense of inspiration and a mood of sacrifice. That was why the congress was a thrilling and precious occasion. It was a fine reassertion of nationalistic dignity and went to the hearts of all those there, and that is why people were crying.

So it was heady stuff. But I cannot help feeling that the Bishop has had to adopt the adage of many white politicians here: 'Talk tougher than you act.'

He described the mandate to continue talks with Smith which the executive (re-elected *en bloc*, unopposed) had received from the congress as a breakthrough in African politics in Rhodesia. It marked, he said, the adoption of a strategy of negotiation (accompanied by a reaffirmed congress pledge of non-violence) and not confrontation.

In fact there is little choice. Talks have to continue whether the Rhodesia Front makes concessions or not. As Edson Sithole, the ANC publicity secretary, said to me in an interview: 'If we broke the talks, then what? We are in talks for two important reasons. To reach an agreement if we can get it and also for our own existence. If we broke up the talks, how will the government treat us? You can't say you don't want to talk and at the same time say you're not going to do anything. You must have an alternative.'

The ANC has no adequate alternative at this stage. Not one of the 50 resolutions before the congress suggested tactics which might replace negotiation. Although the 800 delegates were convincing evidence that the ANC has national support, that in itself is not enough. In the eyes of Whites (and the ANC has chosen to work within the white political frame-work) it is the talks themselves which form a vital part of the ANC claim to legitimacy, and it is the talks which reinforce the ANC claim to be the main black opposition which should be recognised by the RF and Britain.

(One could see the ANC as a political arm of the guerrillas, exploiting white weaknesses in constitutional terms, but I see no evidence of this yet.)

It is for these reasons that during two years of harassment by the white authorities, the ANC continued to meet Smith and his representatives.

It is worth recalling some of the background to these years so that one can appreciate what a remarkable event the congress was. The RF has been picking off its opponents one by one. Business sectors anxious for a settlement have been tamed through personal meetings with Smith; through the planting of false hopes about the progress of the Smith government's management of negotiations with Britain (business gullibility seems unending—but there is also the weapon, often used, that unless they play ball they won't get foreign exchange for their imports); and by judicious announcements on the state of the economy. The government investment programme, for example, for 1973–76 amounts to a 29 per cent increase in spending over the 1972–75 programme. Flue-cured tobacco this season will fetch a guaranteed price of 60 cents a kilogram, five cents up on 1972–3.

By mid-73 the guerrilla offensive which had begun in December 1972, taking security forces by surprise, had been contained. Up to this point the regime could not take the risk that moves against the ANC might have had repercussions in urban unrest.

But at the end of 1973 they took action. Over a three-week period at least 33 ANC executives had been detained and four had fled the country. At least five and possibly more of the eight provincial executives had lost key members.

Bearing in mind the organisational problems I describe earlier in this letter, the ANC has had a rough time. Given this background, then, the congress was a triumph. It was an occasion on which the troops were rallied, confidence re-instilled and trust confirmed. The wretched failure of the attempts to demoralise and split the ANC must leave the regime tempted to take even more drastic action.

But there cannot be another congress like the inaugural one. At some stage talks will, unless the leopard changes its spots, lose their tactical value—and as Edson Sithole says, then what? As I wrote earlier the ANC claims that time is on its side. But it seems that Whites will only be forced to the negotiating table by guerrilla successes (and judging by the reaction at Centenary this is a long way off, for so far the mood is one of intransigence and not doubt) and not by ANC persuasiveness, moderation and non-violence.

Why should black Rhodesians, when this stage is reached, choose the half loaf which Whites may concede, instead of the whole loaf the encroaching guerrillas will promise?

WHEN I LOOK over this letter it seems very impersonal. I think that is because it is duplicated, and ideally I would like to write a slightly different letter to each of my friends.

I miss Britain a great deal: London and Edinburgh. Perhaps that is not only because I became assimilated in my time there. I feel under some strain here, and there are few occasions for relief. While I can mingle with them when need be, white society is alien to me.

There is a vigorous, perhaps radical, perhaps intellectual, group of young white Rhodesians who try to work for change. But the group is very small. The size is not so important though. What is important is their especial problem, the sapping, destructive, depressing agonising search for an identity. People like John Cleig (that MP) and those in Centenary may have solved it; maybe others see Britain as a permanent escape hatch. But God knows how a member of a tiny group, a white Rhodesian radical (it even sounds ludicrous), defines his position to his satisfaction. He or she is acutely aware that the legitimacy of the very term 'white Rhodesian' is an historical accident, like some sort of grumbling colonial appendix, having at some distant stage had a potential function, but now just an irritant in the body politics. For several reasons I fail to see how these young Whites can play a useful role in this polarised country, but one reason is that black rejection seems inevitable. I don't think they can, or can afford to, tolerate the self-doubt which haunts white radicals.

I've been writing all evening; it's very late, and I'm tired.

Dr. Sithole's success story

The Scotsman, 26 June 1974

Edson Sithole,[10] publicity secretary of the African National Council, joins 350 political prisoners held in jail and detention camps in Rhodesia. He is no stranger to imprisonment without trial. Now in his late 30s, he has spent a total of 12 years in detention since he was first arrested at the age of 23.

This is by no means the first time that an ANC official has been detained, presumably in an attempt to split the so-called 'moderate' and 'hard-line' wings of the ANC. In July and August last year at least 33 senior ANC executives were arrested.

Dr Sithole is known to have thought that settlement negotiations with Ian Smith have a tactical value for the organisation. But at the same time, he has long been suspected by the Rhodesian Front as being the leading 'hard-line' member of the ANC executive, responsible for the failure of the latest round settlement talks.

Earlier this year I spoke to him in his office in Salisbury. He is a small, dapper man, regarded by Whites with a mixture of fear, suspicion, and reluctant admiration. His career is a success story, in the best tradition of African politics. And according to that tradition, in which African leaders invariably serve an apprenticeship in jail, the latest move by the Rhodesian authorities will simply add to his stature.

From tea-room waiter, factory hand and newspaper vendor, he became a journalist and trade unionist. In 1963 he was the second African advocate to be admitted to the Rhodesian Bar. A man whose

---

[10] Edson Sithole (1935–75) was a cousin of Ndabaningi Sithole (see page 58), then head of ZANU.

education was mainly through night school and correspondence course, he is now acknowledged to be one of the most highly qualified lawyers in the country. That the detention order should have been served on him during one of his cases at the High Court has an ironic touch that even the Rhodesian Special Branch will appreciate.

He was born in the Eastern Districts, the beautiful rugged mountain region on Rhodesia's border. His formal education ended at Standard IV. From then on he helped himself. Standard V and VI were passed at night school, and his GCE taken by correspondence.

'Are you married?' I asked.

'No, I've never been given the opportunity,' he said, and recounted his history of periodic arrest, detention and release.

He was first detained in 1959, and like so many detainees, turned his cell into a classroom. When he was released four years later in 1963 he had an LLB.

Then came two years of freedom, working in the Nationalist movement and as a trade union official. A 12-month restriction order cut short the activity, but it gave him time to complete his master's degree in law. Released in 1965, two months later he was back in detention, this time staying in jail until 1971. Again the time was not wasted. Last year he was awarded a doctorate in law.

Over the past two years there has been increasingly bitter criticism of members of the ANC, including Dr. Sithole, from nationalists in exile. In Lusaka, London and Dar es Salaam the very fact that the ANC were engaged in talks with Ian Smith was ominous. From being the heroes of the day, responsible for the mobilisation of African rejection of the Douglas-Home–Smith settlement proposals, Bishop Muzorewa, Dr Sithole and other members of the executive had become 'sell-outs'— perhaps the harshest term of abuse in the vocabulary of African colonial politics.

It does not concern Dr Sithole unduly. In nationalist politics one's credentials are in part measured in terms of detention orders and years spent at places whose names are exchanged like a list of battle honours: Gonakudzingwa, Wha Wha, Khami, Marandellas,[11] Goromonzi, Gwelo and Salisbury Central.

Some of the names are on Sithole's escutcheon with an impressive length of service for a man not yet forty.

'The criticism doesn't bother me at all,' he said to me. He suspects

---

[11] Now known as Marondera.

that in some cases the attacks on the ANC are made because an uncompromising line is expected of nationalist exiles.

'But if they genuinely say the policies we are following are wrong, then I would consider them to have lost touch with real events here. How on earth could you proclaim violence as your policy and then continue to exist?'

He is above all a pragmatic politician. 'What really matters is not the vote, but who is governing you. If Africans were to be told today that despite a limited franchise the Parliament would be dominated by Africans, they would accept that. The question of one man, one vote, would come later. 'When we were formulating our franchise proposals we immediately accepted a qualified franchise, and not one man, one vote. Not one of the 50-member national committee of the ANC opposed this, yet most of them had been involved in earlier nationalist parties.'

It is this sort of admission—he is on record as saying that 'one man, one vote' is just a slogan—which disturbs some nationalists outside Rhodesia. It is quite possible, however, that he is in fact subtly teasing white Rhodesia and its claim to 'civilised standards'.

He points out that if the ANC concede the right to vote to every white adult irrespective of education, in return for giving the vote to every African adult with eight years' education, there will be more than 300,000 Africans with the vote compared to 120,000 Whites.

He relishes this statistic. It forces those who claim that white rule in Rhodesia (where the 50 white MPs in the 66-seat Parliament are elected by 85,000 white voters) is based on merit to admit that franchise qualifications have more to do with race than education.

In his inimitable fashion, Mr. Smith has blown hot and cold, announcing a round-table constitutional conference two days before Dr Sithole's arrest. It may well be his way of paying off 'moderate' and right-wing sections in the Rhodesian Front. But the angry reaction from Bishop Muzorewa, calling off settlement talks and scorning the constitutional conference, suggests that Mr. Smith's behaviour has been the last straw for the ANC.

On 3 December 1974, Edson Sithole was taken from prison and flown, with others, to Lusaka for talks on the future of the ANC. He was flown back to Salisbury (Harare) on 12 December and released. On the evening of 15 October 1975 he and his secretary disappeared while in Salisbury, and were never seen again. It was rumoured at the time that he had been re-arrested by the Rhodesian Special Branch and had died or been killed while in their custody.

Mr. Smith in the black books
South Africa issues a warning
The Scotsman, 23 July 1974

Michael Holman considers the growing irritation in South Africa at Rhodesia's inability to reach any kind of accommodation with its black community. The Portugese coup, he finds, and consequent Mozambique hopes of independence, have added to Mr. Smith's worries.

Nothing illustrated the turn of events in Southern Africa as graphically as the television interview recently with the Rhodesian leader, Ian Smith, and Marcelino dos Santos, vice-president of the Mozambique liberation movement, Frelimo. Dos Santos's face positively glowed with the assuredness of a man who knew that events were going his way. Ian Smith looked grey and exhausted, his face etched by strain and tension. The implications of the Portuguese coup were taking their toll.

It was the face of a man who had suffered his second traumatic political shock in two years. In May 1972, the commission of inquiry under Lord Pearce had reported that Rhodesian Africans over-whelmingly rejected the Home–Smith settlement proposals. For the first time the white Rhodesian political consciousness registered the fact that black Rhodesians hold the power of veto over any settlement with Britain—the cherished 'first prize', as Smith calls it.

Today he finds himself in a position of enormous responsibility in southern Africa without the power to influence events. Intransigent in his determination to maintain white rule on Rhodesian Front terms, he awaits the consequences of decisions taken in Lisbon, Pretoria, London and Lusaka.

His first comment on the May coup illustrated his helplessness. Rhodesia, he said, did not interfere in the internal affairs of other countries and therefore the political changes in Portugal were 'essentially matters for the Portuguese'. This was hardly assuring for his followers—'two sentences, two platitudes', commented the *Rhodesia Herald*.

At the same time, it was clear that the African National Council's hand had been immensely strengthened. A new confidence was reflected in its first reaction to the coup. It warned that Whites might find themselves negotiating for their very survival if they continued to reject the power-sharing offered by the ANC.

There were good grounds for ANC confidence. Mozambique, together with South Africa, is Rhodesia's lifeline to the outside world. The bulk of Rhodesia's fuel requirements come through that country and Lourenço Marques and Beira are landlocked Rhodesia's principal ports.

A hostile government applying sanctions would be a devastating blow. The country has been an invaluable staging post for sanctions busting. For example, Austrian trade statistics have 29,000 tonnes of chrome—one of Rhodesia's most valuable exports—as imported from Mozambique. Yet Mozambique lists no exports to Austria.

The 700-mile border with Mozambique has been policed with Portuguese co-operation. As Sir Roy Welensky, the former Federal Prime Minister, pointed out: 'It is no secret that some of the terrorist incursions have been mounted in Mozambique even though the Portuguese authorities are doing their best to destroy them. It is obvious that any change on their part could greatly embarrass Rhodesia.'

Given these circumstances. it came as no surprise when soon after the coup Mr. Smith visited John Vorster, the South African Prime Minister. Two of the topics on the agenda would undoubtedly have been alternative trade routes in case the Mozambique border is closed, and the continuance of South African military assistance to Rhodesia.

At the moment Rhodesia does not have a direct rail link with South Africa. From Bulawayo the line goes through the independent African state of Botswana. Preliminary work has been done, however, on closing an 80-mile gap between the rail points of Rutenga in southern Rhodesia and Messina, on the South African border. No firm date has been set for completion, but work on the link is now treated as urgent. Further work will have to be done on the section from Messina to Johannesburg, for there are reports that it cannot carry a heavy flow of traffic. But even with the line completed it will be an expensive and inadequate alternative to the Mozambique routes.

As far as South African military commitment to Rhodesia is concerned, it is doubtful whether Mr. Smith received substantial comfort from his neighbour, for the short-term paramilitary South African police in Rhodesia, variously estimated at between 2,000 and 5,000 men, will remain. Warnings are emerging from South Africa, however, that this cannot continue indefinitely.

The relationship between the two countries has always had an undercurrent of strain. At a General Election in the 1940s the *Rhodesia Herald* appealed in an editorial for racial issues to be kept out of the election. It was referring not to Black and White, but to Afrikaaner and English-speaking Rhodesians. This antipathy between 'British' Rhodesia and Afrikaaner-ruled South Africa almost disappeared in the emotional aftermath of the former's unilateral declaration of independence in 1965.

Nevertheless, regular sniping by the Afrikaans press at Rhodesia's efforts to reach a suitable post-UDI constitutional settlement continued. It tended to suggest that Rhodesians were wet behind their political ears. It criticised them for dithering along somewhere between the crude maintenance of white power known as *baaskap* and separate development or apartheid, unable to formulate a workable political programme for peaceful progress in Rhodesia.

The sniping has become a broadside following South Africa's consternation at Mr. Smith's inability to come to terms with the ANC. The latest round of settlement talks ended with the announcement by the ANC earlier this month that they had been offered no substantial concessions. It seemed unbelievable to South African observers that the coup had not shaken the Rhodesian Front out of its intransigence.

Their irritation was expressed last week. A well-known Afrikaans columnist wrote: 'When a neighbour's problems upset your own matters, you have a right to show him and even pressure him into bringing things into rein. Rhodesia should realise what a brakeshoe it is for our good relations in Africa ... . It is time we put this clearly to the Rhodesians.'

The influential South African magazine *To the Point* warned earlier this year: 'As far as its attitude towards the Rhodesian conflict is concerned it cannot be taken for granted that South Africa will at all times and under every circumstance underwrite the status quo in that country. While it actively participates in resistance to terror by policing Rhodesia's borders with Zambia, South Africa realises that controlled political development is desirable.'

Those who see a long-term South African commitment to white-ruled Rhodesia do so out of a belief in a southern African domino theory. They have yet to make out a convincing case. On the other hand, a recent study of the military situation in Rhodesia and its implications for southern Africa points out: 'A variation of the "domino theory" as developed in the context of south-east Asia would, to be successful, require an organisational sophistication, logistic capacity and quality and depth of command and control well beyond the present scope of both the liberation movements and the Organisation of African Unity.

'It is conceivable,' the study continues, 'that in the event of uncontrolled conflict across the Zambesi—especially if the level of conflict threatened to draw in any of the major powers—rather than risk further escalation South Africa would be prepared to countenance and assist in a controlled implementation of majority rule in Rhodesia, in return for a controlled restoration of an acceptable measure of regional security.

The point at which South Africa will have to decide on her future role is drawing closer. The latest survey of military affairs issued by the Inter-national Institute for Strategic Studies warns: 'Unless the Rhodesian "Government" redresses underlying grievances, the white community faces the prospect of a protracted guerrilla campaign beyond its resources to contain.'[12]

Rhodesia's military resources are already strained. The move at the beginning of this year to call up those white males between 25 and 38 who had hitherto not been liable to military commitments was partly to ensure a fairer distribution of territorial army service. But it is also an indication that white Rhodesia has just about reached the limit of its manpower resources. The unpopularity of the demands of military service, largely borne by the younger men, is reflected in the migration figures for the male age group 19–24. During the period July to January 1972–73 there was a net gain of 169. In the same period 1973–74 there was a net loss of 174.

This comes at a time when Rhodesian forces are likely to be further extended. Reports suggest that Rhodesian guerrillas have accompanied Frelimo in the move south along the Mozambique border. As a result, what might be termed a 'second front' may open on Rhodesia's eastern border, not far from Umtali. White farmers are now receiving regular security briefings, and army and police activity in the area has markedly increased over the past three months.

---

[12] *Insurgency in Rhodesia, 1957–73: An Account and Assessment*, by Anthony R. Wilkinson (International Institute for Strategic Studies).

Given this background Mr. Smith's effort last month to reassure Whites about the impact of the coup was somewhat unrealistic: 'I believe that there is a chance,' he said, 'that it could lead to an improvement in Mozambique.' That is a candidate for the wishful thought of the year.

Daniel Madzimbamuto
The Scotsman, 25 January 1975

Daniel Madzimbamuto bears the unenviable distinction of having been Rhodesia's longest-serving political prisoner. From his dawn arrest in February 1959 to his release on 24 December, 1974, he has, with the exception of a 15-month period in 1963–64, been detained without trial in prisons and detention centres around the country.

His case became legal history, for when he challenged—unsuccessfully as it turned out—the validity of his detention order following the illegal declaration of independence in November 1963, he was in effect challenging the legitimacy of the Rhodesian regime.

I spoke to Mr. Madzimbamuto in his modest home at Highfield, one of Salisbury's African townships. He is a tall, impressive man, wearing glasses, as do many of the released nationalists. He explained this:

'People in detention were anxious to read and study, but the light was poor. And as a result of reading a lot of us strained our eyesight. We sought medical treatment but it depended on the type of doctor who came in. If you got a Rhodesia Front-supporting doctor, he was rough and unwilling to help in any way. That is the reason most of us wear glasses. Out of 48 detainees in our group, 46 now have bad eyesight.'

Like nearly every nationalist figure, Mr. Madzimbamuto comes from humble beginnings. His parents were peasant farmers, both illiterate. But they were determined that their son should get an education, and at intervals sold a few of their precious cattle to raise school fees.

His education began 40 years ago in what was called a 'kraal school'. 'There were no facilities whatsoever, except a small pole-and-clay building. The blackboard was painted on the wall, and most of the writing exercises we did were on the dusty ground.'

He completed primary school at a mission, and then went to Munali Secondary School, in what was then Northern Rhodesia. His mother died while he was there but his father, a brother and a sister died while he was in detention. Permission to visit them on their sick beds, or to attend the funerals, was refused. The memory hurts him. 'It's something that comes to me when alone, from time to time.

'I felt that as a person who was detained, without committing any crime, I should have been allowed, even under escort, to see them either before they died, or when they were dead, to fulfil obligations under our tribal customs. The requests were just brushed aside. To me it appeared immoral and cruel. I wouldn't do the same to anybody, even if I became a minister.' In some cases detainees were allowed to make such visits. 'But it was sporadic. One is allowed, the other refused.'

After completing his secondary education, he worked in South Africa as a travelling salesman. There he met his wife, who today is a senior nursing sister in the neuro-surgical unit of Salisbury's African hospital. He returned to Rhodesia in 1956.

Had he been influenced by politics in South Africa? 'I was more influenced by Northern Rhodesian politics, because it was a crucial time when the Central African Federation was being debated. By the time I went to South Africa, I knew more or less what the whole position was in southern Africa—the ill-treatment, the insults and the pass laws in South Africa simply brought home suppression as such.'

Back in Rhodesia, he took part in an organisation called the Youth League, together with men like James Chikerema,[13] George Nyandoro[14] and Edson Sithole, all figures in today's struggle.

'One of our major successes was a bus boycott in Salisbury, in protest against a rise in fares. We urged the people to walk to work, even if it meant being late. The company was forced to reduce its fare to the old price. From then people began to realise that there was an organisation which was the mouthpiece of the Africans.

'We realised that if somebody is there to speak out, something can be done. At that time, the old Southern Rhodesia African National Congress had only one branch in Bulawayo, with Joshua Nkomo (the

---

[13] James Chikerema (1925–2006) was president of the Front for the Liberation of Zimbabwe but went on to support 'internal settlements' in the late 1970s.

[14] George Nyandoro (1926–94) was one of the founders of the Southern Rhodesia African National Congress (SRANC) and was the general secretary of the Zimbabwe African People's Union.

present leader of the Zimbabwe African Peoples Union). We established branches throughout the country.'

'One of the most vigorously fought issues of the mid-1950s was the Land Husbandry Act, an attempt to limit African cattle stock and to introduce modern agricultural techniques, prompted by a concern at the rate of soil erosion in African areas. The nationalists opposed it.

'We were saying that there was erosion because of the Land Apportionment Act, which split the country into two. The land shared by the 3.5 million Africans couldn't carry the population, therefore there was soil erosion; while the 190,000 Europeans had a large area to operate and didn't get soil erosion because most of the land lay fallow.'

The opposition was succesful and the act was dropped. 'I believe that was the main reason we were banned in 1959.' Mr. Madzimbamuto and other nationalist leaders were rounded up.

'I was woken at 4 a.m. The police came in two jeeps, surrounded the house with guns pointed at the door. They searched everything in the house. When you are taken they don't even tell you where you are going. You are handcuffed, both hands and legs, and chucked into a truck.'

It was the beginning of a journey to Khami Prison in Bulawayo, where detainees were fingerprinted, photographed and classified as D Class prisoners—'which means you spend the whole day locked up in the cell, only allowed 15 minutes exercise in the morning and afternoon.

'The whole thing about detention is immoral. If you have no evidence against a person, you have failed. You have got the state machine, the police, informers, and yet they fail to get evidence to convict a person in a court of law. You don't just detain a person because he's an opponent.'

The then Minister of Law and Order was Julian Greenfield. Today he is Mr. Justice Greenfield, member of the Rhodesian High Court bench. Mr. Madzimbamuto may soon come face to face with the Judge, for he plans to become an advocate.

In January 1963, soon after the Rhodesian Front came to power, Mr. Madzimbamuto and other detainees were released. But in April 1964 there came once again the early morning hammering at the door. This time he was taken to Gonakudzingwa restriction camp in the remote south-east of Rhodesia, together with Joshua Nkomo and others.

Conditions at 'Gona' were more relaxed than in the prisons. Detainees' wives were allowed 33-hour visits, staying with their husbands in the camp, and overseas newspapers were permitted. But conditions were very different when he was moved to Gwelo: 'In prison there we were not allowed radios or overseas newspapers. Even the *Rhodesia Herald* had any reference to politics cut out.

'For the seven years we stayed in Gwelo the food was extremely poor. If you wanted bread and milk you had to make an application to the Minister of Law and Order because it was considered "European food".[15] On that application you had to have European witnesses who could testify that you had lived a "European" life and regularly ate bread. We refused to make this application.' But friends and relatives were allowed to send food parcels.

'Another thing in Gwelo was no bedding. We slept on mats thinner than a carpet; and only three blankets and no pillows. We were allowed to send one letter a week but because the superintendent there considered it immoral to withhold incoming letters, we received most of those.'

Most of the time in prison was spent reading: 'We were allowed to take correspondence courses, and once you qualified you became a teacher of the others. I first did a public relations diploma, then a marketing diploma, and finally an LL.B. through the University of London.'

All of these courses were made possible 'by our friends in Britain, especially from Amnesty and International Defence and Aid. I just don't know how to thank these people for the amount of work they did for our families and us detainees in particular.'

During his seven years at Gwelo, Mr. Madzimbamuto's wife managed to make the 350-mile return journey from Salisbury about twice a month. 'They put a glass partition between us, and you got hold of a telephone and spoke to each other through that for 30 minutes. It's not possible to touch at all, even to hold hands.'

It is remarkable that the marriages of all but a handful of the detainees have survived the strains of isolation: 'It shows that when we chose the road to freedom, although we knew it was a bitter road, you had to carry your partner with you. The wives understood what we were fighting for, and they had to keep the candle burning.

'Of course, there were problems which one has to solve even when in detention. And these problems sometimes made one go mad. Each time we got a case of mental breakdown in prison, it was because of family troubles—but there were very few.'

The eldest of Daniel Madzimbamuto's four children is at school in

---

[15] That is, food for Whites.

Britain. 'This son is bitter, extremely bitter. Some of his letters to me in detention got me into trouble because of what he was saying.

'He's staying with European friends in Britain and they treat him almost like a son. But when he comes here, he finds a different type of people.'

The anger and resentment is common among the children of detain-ees. 'It appears they reflect a new generation of feeling. We are now being accused of being too moderate. This is inevitable, being surrounded by independent African states, and only this country left ruled by Whites. (Leave South Africa out, that is a different question altogether.)

'There must be a reason, the children say. Either the present generat-ion are not capable of prosecuting the war to its conclusion, or we were just ineffective. Posterity will judge us, but I think we did our best. If I am locked up again, it is up to them to pick up the challenge.'

Did the prospect of renewed detention disturb him? 'No, certainly not. I am the stronger now than I was. I have met quite a number of people and I've heard what they want. Even if I die the next day, I know the battle will go on until it is won.

'My wife feels the same, though my detention would disappoint and depress her. Like any other woman, she'd like a husband with the child-ren, who have got to be taught good manners. But I suppose one has to make sacrifices.'

It was late afternoon when we finished talking. During our two-hour conversation, Daniel Madzimbamuto had spoken of the urgent need for racial reconciliation. 'The new leaders will be far more uncompro-mising than ourselves and the outcome will be tragic.'

As I drove away, a young well-dressed African, his face suffused with anger, shouted after me: 'What are you doing in Highfield, you white pig?' It starkly underlined the warning. But there is no evidence so far that Whites in Rhodesia appreciate the tolerance and compassion of men and women like the Madzimbamutos—and there are still, despite the Lusaka agreement, more than 200 political prisoners in Rhodesia's detention centres.

Eyeball to eyeball with Ndabaningi Sithole

Financial Mail (South Africa), 31 January 1975

The Rev. Ndabaningi Sithole is the leader of Rhodesia's militant Zimbabwe African National Union (ZANU), which broke away from Joshua Nkomo's Zimbabwe African Peoples' Union (ZAPU) in July 1963. In 1964 he was imprisoned on a charge of subversion. After completing his sentence in 1965, he was detained. While in detention he was convicted of plotting to assassinate members of the Rhodesian government. Sithole was re-detained on the expiry of his sentence last year, and released in November to take part in the Lusaka talks. At Lusaka, both Sithole and Nkomo signed a declaration of unity under the banner of the African National Council.

What are the prospects for a settlement?

I am not particularly hopeful, because the position of the white minority is fundamentally different from that of the African majority, and it would appear to me that the present regime would like to cling to power for as long as possible. On the other hand, the African people are not in the mood to give in.

How do you see ZANU's position in the African National Council?

I regard it, of course, as being the senior member and the most effective member of the partnership. It has fought very hard during the last two or three years, and I may point out that it is the fighting of ZANU that caused the present regime to rethink its position.

And the venue and chairman of a constitutional conference?

My feelings are that the venue should be outside Rhodesia, because if the conference were held in Salisbury and there was a breakdown, the chances are that government would have to re-detain some of the nationalist leaders. Whoever is chairman has to come from Britain. I am not particularly keen on the British Foreign Secretary. I think he has a set view against ZANU; that we are making the possibility of a successful conference very remote. He doesn't seem to understand that the African in this country wants majority rule immediately. He would rather we accepted something less.

When might the conference begin?
I have no idea. Mr. Smith would like it soon, but we are not very keen on that. We would like more time.

What if the conference fails?
There would have to be intensified guerrilla activity. Whatever the government may say against this view, it is only realistic to acknowledge that the African people have no stronger bargaining point than this threat. Expectations are so high that if the conference failed there is bound to be a risk of a racial explosion. I have met a good number of Africans who, while they rejoice that we are free after 10 years in detention, fear this may give the impression that the problem has been solved. This, they think, will undermine the actual liberation struggle. They feel talks will not solve much at this stage, and the only answer is fighting. My reply is: give the conference a chance, so that in future we can say that we tried all methods.

Is there pressure on you from the people?
Yes, they think I'm too moderate. Among the young, in particular, I detect anger, resentment, restiveness. They think we are moving too slowly. They think we must fight, right now, and not wait for conference talks.

Does the prospect of being re-detained worry you?
Not at all. Whatever happens to me personally is immaterial. The most important thing is that the struggle will go on until we establish majority rule.

Would a five-year transition to majority rule provide common ground?
What we want is an immediate solution to the problem facing us—the

solution is majority rule now. Immediate majority rule is not negotiable as far as I am concerned.

Exactly what is meant by 'immediate majority rule'?
That there shall be a government dominated by Africans in the shortest possible time—six months to a year, within that range. But not beyond that.

What about the franchise?
The question of the franchise is a very thorny one. If there is to be a qualified franchise at all during any transition, it must be very low. And it must give Africans a majority of the votes in the majority of the constituencies, thereby giving power in Parliament. And one man, one vote is our ultimate aim.

What would be the future of the Whites?
In some quarters it is believed that we are very anti-White. That is quite wrong. Whites will be welcome as citizens. ZANU policy is non-racialism. The white people needn't be afraid that when we take over we will throw them out of the country. The future Zimbabwe is the home of the Whites as well. They have as much right to their homes here as we have, provided they accept a non-racial society. The white man has no need to fear my leadership. What we hate is the system rather than the people themselves. They look at our leadership through the eyes of white supremacy. But once they put aside the spectacles of supremacy, they have no better friends than our present leaders.

What sort of future for Zimbabwe do you envisage?
Our basic policy would be socialist, but not based on ideology from other countries. It will be based on the communal customs of our people, in the tradition of African socialism.

How do you see South Africa's role today?
I think South Africa could play a very important part in finding a solution to the problem facing this country. During the last 10 years South Africa has interfered in the internal affairs of Rhodesia. If its troops had not been sent here I'm almost sure the Blacks and Whites would long ago have found a solution. But South African troops propped up the Smith regime so that it was impossible to see the reality of the situation. If troops were withdrawn, we would be forced to come to terms.

And future relations between South Africa and Zimbabwe?
I look forward to good relations. We would observe the principle of non-interference in the affairs of another state.

Last hide-out for the Tangwena

Observer Magazine, 6 July 1975

High in the Inyanga mountains on Rhodesia's eastern border with Mozambique, Chief Rekayi Tangwena, a fiercely independent old man, and nearly 600 of his followers are in hiding from the Smith Government. Some time ago I met Chief Tangwena in his forest hide-out: four grass huts built to merge with the trees, undetectable from the air.

The Tangwena tribe have been evicted from their narrow stretch of border land, which has been their home for centuries, because their land has been designated a European area. Rather than move to an 'African area', the Tangwena (their name comes from the boast of an ancestor: 'I am as strong as *ngwenya*, the crocodile') abandoned their cultivated valleys and hill slopes and took to the mountains.[16]

Look-outs on the hills keep 24-hour watch for police and army patrols, while the rest of the tribe shelter in small groups, never staying more than a few months in one place. They live off wild fruits, roots, bulbs and, when they can get supplies, *sadza* (maize meal). There are days when the 65-year-old chief goes without food. 'I used to feed my pigs and eat them,' he said. 'Now I feed on wild things as if I were a pig.'

Among black Rhodesians, to call someone a '*Tangwena*' is to pay them a compliment. The Tangwena's stubborn and determined resistance—what Rhodesian officials call 'self-inflicted misery'—has become a national issue. They have come to represent the hundreds of thousands of Africans who have lost their homelands.

---

[16] Ngwenya is also a town on the Ngwenya (Crocodile) river, bordering the Kruger National Park and South Africa.

On the earth floor of what was more a grass shelter than the usual African hut of pole, clay and thatch, Chief Tangwena squatted, tugging his beard as he spoke. As a guest, I sat on a carved wooden stool. Around us were arranged the chief's few possessions: blankets, sacks, tin mugs, an empty oil can and a kettle. In the middle of the hut were the embers of a fire. It was lit only before dawn and after nightfall, even during the bitterly cold winter months. Smoke during the day would draw attention to the camp.

Outside the hut there is a vantage point. It was a spot, said Chief Tangwena, where he could sit, smoke his pipe and watch police and army units move through the surrounding countryside. I asked him about the guerrilla war, which in north-east Rhodesia has cost several hundred lives since December 1962. In one incident, he said, Rhodesian troops had shot a Tangwena tribesman. 'This man, Mudagu, was moving along the border on the Mozambique side and he was shot dead. The soldiers dug a small hole where he was shot. We wanted to put him in a proper grave, but we thought they might have put some explosive under him. So we left him there where he was, and just put some more cover on him.'

Was he afraid of war? 'How can I be afraid when I am already dead, living in the mountain like a baboon. During the rainy season we get a lot of trouble. People have died because of the weather.' He listed some of his people's urgent basic needs: milk powder for the babies, stoves to provide hot food, especially for the children, warm clothes, blankets, raincoats and medicines.

Yet despite the strains, the traditional structure of the tribe is being maintained. The Chief is assisted, as in the past, by five village head men—'my mayors', he calls them—and five councillors. He makes no decisions without consulting them.

We looked out over the land, and Chief Rekayi Tangwena recited the names of the chiefs before him: Sakara, Chiwahwura, Nyamarihwodzo, Kubinha, Tsatse, Gwino … . He pointed to where he had played in the streams and hunted as a boy. From this grizzled and dignified chief, dressed in a shabby greatcoat, came a series of admonitions and rebukes addressed to both the Rhodesian and British Governments, and a vow that he would never voluntarily leave his land.

'I say I want my country,' he declared. 'This country is called Zimbabwe; it is our inheritance. The Europeans say they bought this land. Suppose I ask all the Africans who are living in England to buy the Queen's land—will the Europeans be happy?'

When the foundations of today's segregated State were laid in the early years, the Tangwena were among the victims. Their part of the country was officially listed as a white area in 1930, and a few years later the tribe, like other Blacks in their position, were officially classified as 'squatters'. In 1944 the land became part of the white-owned Gaeresi Ranch. Some of the Tangwena signed labour agreements with the farm owner in return for tenancy.

The Rhodesian Front came to power in 1962 on a platform of stricter segregation, and farmers were encouraged to evict those 'squatters' who didn't work for them. For the Tangwena this final indignity came in 1966, the year after UDI, when Ian Smith's regime broke away from Britain. They were offered new huts, and a beer hall, and later a school, in an African area, and the chief was promised recognition of his chieftainship with a government salary of £30 a month. Again the people refused.

The Minister of Lands promised that 'This blatant defiance of the law will of course be dealt with.' And so it was. Just before dawn on 18 September 1969 nine police Land Rovers and a bulldozer moved in to flatten Tangwena huts, crops and fruit trees. The people rebuilt their huts and planted new crops of maize and yams but in October and November they too were destroyed.

A year later their cattle were impounded. In Tangwena society cattle are regarded as a source of wealth, play a vital part in the dowry system and are slaughtered for important rites. Chief Tangwena found the confiscation not only unjust but demeaning. 'The Government has taken 473 cattle. Now they must be multiplying. They are drinking my milk; I cannot make money, my income is my cattle.'

In November 1970 a senior government official carrying an African ceremonial walking stick and a horsehair flyswitch was on hand to watch a Land Rover pull down 24 huts. The Tangwena who had taken temporary refuge in the mountains stayed there. They left behind over 100 children in the care of the small, local African co-operative farm, the Nyafaru Development Company, to which the area's primary school was attached.

But the school at Nyafaru was officially closed, in a final effort to get the Tangwena to move to an African area. The farm members continued to teach and care for the children until the day in 1972 when three army trucks drew up at Nyafaru. Crying and protesting, 115 children were forced into trucks and taken off to government welfare centres. The Rhodesians claim that it was a humanitarian exercise to 'shelter and succour innocent dependants who had been abandoned'. The chief calls it 'kidnapping'. The children are now scattered around the country, most of them at missions. Some haven't seen their parents for years.

Not all the Tangwena are in hiding. About 50 have become members of Nyafaru where in another way they are challenging the doctrine of land segregation. Nyafaru—on 2,000 acres of white land—became a co-operative soon after the land was bought from Gaeresi[17] in 1957. Throughout the people's troubles the farm has supported them. Already, Nyafaru has been prosecuted twice for infringing the Land Tenure Act. If the Government decides Nyafaru is a black-owned farm on white land, it can be closed.

In most African countries Nyafaru would be a model of a satisfying relationship between people and their land. But in Rhodesia a minist-erial *diktat* could put an end to life at Nyafaru. Chief Tangwena and his people have already suffered. 'If God is there, Smith shall get everlasting troubles,' said the chief. 'The dead shall ask him: "Smith, why have we died?" The dead shall judge him.' And he offered Mr. Smith some advice: 'There is nobody who dies carrying the country on his head. You leave it behind. I am a chief and this is the land I am looking after. But this soil shall consume me and I shall be manure. We must govern knowing this.'

---

[17] A white-owned farm.

Letter from Lusaka

Privately circulated, 8 July 1976

Got back on Thursday night from a fascinating and very enjoyable trip to Malawi. I left on Thursday 29 June planning to return that Sunday, but for three reasons decided to stay on. First, it was so interesting; secondly, the information department there had gone to so much trouble to arrange our trip that it seemed discourteous not to take advantage of their help; and finally, the highlight of the celebrations was a day of singing and daring and a speech by Kamuzu (Hastings Banda) on Thursday, 6 July.

I had to travel first class to Blantyre as there were no tourist-rate tickets when I went in to book. Very nice too, though the wrong time of the day to drink champagne. Sat in the first class waiting room at Lusaka airport until the last minute; wide comfortable seats in the first-class section; and drinks available from the moment one got into the cabin, including champagne and wine with the mid-morning snacks. This was followed by VIP treatment at Blantyre—no difficulties with Customs and Immigration, and met at the airport by an information official.

After checking in at the hotel, spent the afternoon visiting polling booths in the Thyolo area, a tea region about 30 miles from Blantyre. (I don't know how much you read of the whole business; it was the first general election since 1961: at intervening elections either all the candidates of the Malawi Congress Party were returned unopposed, or Banda appointed the MPs from a list submitted by the 87 constituencies. This time he again approved the final list, but did not appoint the MPs, leaving the electorate to choose between two, sometimes three, candidates in 40-odd of the contested seats. It was also the anniversary of Banda's return from Ghana on 6 July 1950, and the anniversary of independence.)

Letting in the press was almost unprecedented—two journalists were let in in November last year—and seems to be part of a general relaxation. A year ago 2,000 political prisoners were released and probably 20–30 now remain; no Asians have been deported recently though a year ago 40 Goan families were deported en masse, apparently because they turned off a radio broadcast of a Banda speech which was interrupting a wedding dinner; expatriates are more at ease.

Why the change, I'm not really sure. Diplomats suggest that it's an effort to remedy the poor press coverage, which in turn might have affected aid and investment, but that doesn't seem quite enough. Whatever, we journalists were treated as Royal Game, and it was often amusing; Malawi Young Pioneers—'a cross between the Boy Scouts and the Hitler Youth,' said one diplomat—seemed to twitch slightly when we pointed cameras at them (no doubt something they hadn't experienced in the past, or if they had, locked up the pointers) but put up with it.

There were about ten of us in all, from the Times, Reuters, Guardian, Financial Times, BBC and television and photographers from UPI and Time.

I packed my smart three-piece suit, and this is what I imagined: Banda would grudgingly give a press conference, and my colleagues would attend characteristically attired—jeans, no tie. Banda would be shocked (as you know, he always wears a three-piece). But ... he spots me, smartly turned out. 'Who's that?' he asks an aide; 'send the others away'—and I get an exclusive interview.

Alas, it didn't work out like that. We had a press conference on the Friday, but my colleagues were warned that best bib and tucker was obligatory. The interview took place at the luxurious Sanjika Palace, set high in the hills outside Blantyre.

We didn't see much of it, but it must have cost millions.

There was little that was especially newsy—he repeated his belief that white southern Africa shouldn't be isolated or boycotted—but the occasion was remarkable. From what I sent to the FT:

> The president, dressed in his characteristic three-piece suit, with flywhisk and ivory cane by his side, was answering questions during the first press conference in Malawi granted to foreign journalists for over ten years.

For over two hours the President lectured the press on the politics of the former Central African Federation, answered their questions good humouredly and sometimes with flashes of anger, and made it clear to the assembly that he greatly disliked the fourth estate.

'I have come here with great reluctance,' were Dr Banda's opening remarks. 'You newsmen have fixed ideas about everything and no matter what you hear, if it does not agree with your own fixed ideas, you stick to your ideas.'

Questions included Dr Banda's views on the Rhodesian internal agreement ('My opinion is not for the press'), relations with South Africa, the number of political detainees, treatment of Jehovah's Witnesses, and the role of expatriates and Asians in Malawi.

Dr Banda confirmed that several hundred detainees, held since 1964 following internal dissension, were released last July (informed sources say that nearly 2,000 were set free). Only a handful now remained in detention, said Dr Banda.

'Jehovah Witnesses in Malawi (many of whom have taken refuge in neighbouring Zambia) refused to pay taxes,' he said, and 'pestered others until they lost patience and the only thing they could do to chase them away was to beat them.'

Dealing with expatriates, who continue to hold senior posts in the civil service and the economy, Dr Banda said there would always be a role for them 'as long as I am here. After all, I lived in Britain and I like you people. I like to have British people about me,' he added, laughing.

The president denied there had been any harassment of the 3,000-strong Asian community, who may conduct business only in the three main centres—Blantyre, Zomba and Lilongwe. This was to provide business opportunities for Africans in rural areas, said Dr. Banda, 'but we are not chasing them away. They are part of the community, but they cannot play any significant role.'

The conference was peppered with Dr Banda's expressions of his personal philosophy and his views of government. 'It sometimes means doing harsh and unpleasant things, but that is how this world is.

'I am a practical and not a theoretical man. There is no use my going to Addis Ababa, London or New York making big speeches, posing as a champion of this and that. I must see to the economic and social condition of the peoples of Malawi first. They need food, second they need clothing, and third, a decent roof over their heads. To achieve this I have to devote 99 per cent of my time to the problems of my people.'

On one occasion he came close to losing his temper. One correspondent misunderstood something he said, and asked if he would let the press examine prison conditions. Banda worked himself up to a furious pitch, saying in effect that no country in the world allowed this, and when contradicted nearly popped. At this point, the extremely nervous party secretary general tried to close the proceedings, but Banda insisted that it continue unless all questions had been asked.

At the press conference, and on other occasions, we got a very good idea of how he dominates his government. Ministers and officials hardly dare let their bottoms touch their seats, hovering nervously in a squatting position in expectation of either having to recite statistics about latest agricultural production, or confirm any of Ngwazi's claims. When he calls on them, they behave like anxious schoolboys declining verbs for an authoritarian Latin master. At the press conference, the unfortunate sec. gen. stumbled over his recitation of tobacco crop figures; he was told to sit down, and the responsibility passed to the equally nervous secretary to the cabinet.

The personality cult is overwhelming by any standards, even allowing for the anniversary celebrations. I think one of the most bizarre sights I shall ever witness is His Excellency the Life President, Ngwazi (the conqueror) Dr Hastings Kamuzu Banda, homburg, dark glasses, three-piece suit and ivory cane, perched on the back of a slowly moving Land Rover, surrounded by hundreds of buxom women, dressed in prints carrying Ngwazi's face.

Not only was it bizarre, but one feels such an outsider, so remote from such a display of strange power. This diminutive, aging (late 70s) figure twitches his whisk in curious jerky movements, every now and then bending from the waist and waving the whisk over their heads as if sprinkling holy water. The expression on his face is indescribable: not a smile quite, but a slightly self-content, self-absorbed acknowledgement of homage—yet smart enough to know when the cameras were on him and obligingly flick his whisk—or so it seemed to me. The women chant and sing accompanied by drummers, a refrain of praise, shuffling, bending, waving.

At every ceremony, the women dance, and Ngwazi joins them. He enters the circle they form, and then one almost loses sight of him. He is not a vigorous dancer, not surprisingly—I think he has a stiff hip—but he does his best, a rather creaky shuffle, and the same jerky movements of the whisk. The outsider is then presented with a phalanx of shifting broad bums covered by material cut carefully so as to avoid putting Ngwazi's image on the posterior. All the time singing, the women bend from the waist, carrying their torso parallel to the ground, arms swinging loosely, moving from foot to foot.

At intervals they pull themselves upright, chant a chorus, and down they go again and in the middle the flywhisk twiddles away. Every now and then Kamuzu sings, a high, quavering craw. On the outskirts of the group stand bodyguards, and at least one minister, whose job it seems is to lead Ngwazi back to the podium. Accompanying Ngwazi all the time is a lady termed the Official Government Hostess, Miss Cecilia Somethingorother.[18] She is a large, handsome woman, whose duties may be exactly that. Apparently she was a nurse in his Blantyre practice, and has accompanied him ever since.

The dancing fascinates me, but no more: it's the sight of him on the Land Rover, waving his flywhisk, that appals me. I am tempted to say it looks evil.

We saw him in action three times: at the press conference, at the opening of the trade fair in Blantyre the next day, and at the main celebrations in Kamuzu Stadium, Blantyre, on Thursday.

Sunday was spent reading bits and pieces on Malawi, Monday doing the rounds of diplomats, Tuesday writing a piece for the FT. Wednesday was delightful. Three of us were taken into the country, first south to the foot of Mount Malanje, and then back to Blantyre and north (I think is the direction) to Zomba and on to the plateau.

It was a valuable trip because we frequently stopped, partly to take photos and partly to drop in on the village stores: if they are well stocked it says something about the state of the economy, I think. And they invariably were; further, the departure of Asians from the rural businesses has not caused much damage, at least in the south. (Asians I spoke to in Blantyre, by the way, said they were concerned it was the best country in Africa: no import limits—true—ample emigration and holiday allowances; the Goans, they said unkindly, had behaved very foolishly.)

Malawi is a very poor country indeed: but it does seem that under Banda, who is also Minister of Agriculture, crop production has greatly increased and all aid officials I spoke to are very impressed. Aid money is well spent; if money is left over on a project, it is returned to the donor, almost unheard of in Africa! There is no corruption.

---

[18] Cecilia Tamanda Kadzamira was the official hostess of Malawi during the reign of Kamuzu Banda and served as his first lady for several years.

The police are unarmed, perhaps the only case in Africa, and crime is low. The towns—Blantyre, Limbe, Zomba—are clean and attractive; the celebrations, in particularly the stadium gathering, were superbly organised.

Zomba was extraordinary. I've read of Indian hill stations which seem isolated from change, and that is how Zomba struck me, admittedly during a very short visit. Marvellous old colonial houses, green corrugated iron roofs, two storeys with a wide balcony running along the level of the upper floor, large well-maintained gardens.

The residence used by the governor in the 1890s is marvellously preserved as a government hotel. I hope my photos do it justice: high ceilings, polished floor, huge bay windows opening on to lovely gardens, stream running through. The only thing neglected was the tennis court, with ant hills, sprouting weeds and a rusting roller.

I walked on to the court and felt almost lost in time: I could imagine tennis parties and cucumber sandwiches, and an era when the governor and his staff dominated a country which must be as big as Britain.

From Zomba we drove up to the plateau along a road cut into the sides of the mountain. The Ku Chawe Inn is on the edge, and from some of the bedrooms one looks out over a steep if not sheer drop in the valley below. I think the scenery surpasses Vumba and Nyanga.

Although we didn't arrive till after two, the kitchen offered us the full menu. Meals out are seldom memorable for me—too many omelettes—and on this occasion I simply had cheese sandwiches with salad, accom-panied however by a lovely dry white wine from Germany —but the circumstances made this one exceptional.

Thursday: we were at the stadium by 9 and were expected to remain to festivities' end, after 8pm! Fortunately I was able to point to my 5pm flight to Lusaka and crept out at 2.30.

I must now write it all up—pieces for the *Scotsman*, *Economist*, Associated Press. Gabrielle leaves August 7 and it turns out she gets a stopover in Budapest as well as Moscow. I still plan to leave 21 August, also via Budapest, arriving London about 24/25.

All my love,
Michael

Ian Smith torturers exposed

Rhodesians arrest priests in bid to suppress shock report
The Observer, 4 September 1977

The Rhodesian special branch has arrested four officials of the Catholic Commission for Justice and Peace in Salisbury, apparently in an attempt to suppress a report alleging that the Rhodesian army is continuing to torture black civilians.

The report will be published in London this week by the Catholic Institute for International Relations.*

The officials arrested are the chairman, John Deary, the organising secretary, Brother Arthur Dupuis, the press secretary, Sister Janice MacLaughlin, and an executive member, Father Dieter Scholz who was last month ordered to leave Rhodesia by mid-September.

They are to be charged tomorrow under the Law and Order (Maintenance) Act and the Official Secrets Act. Sister Janice, I understand, is being held at present outside Salisbury. The others have been released on bail.

The commission, which has published two earlier reports on alleged army brutality and the conduct of the four-year guerrilla war, may now be forced to close. Last March, its president, the Catholic Bishop of Umtali, the Rt. Rev. Donal Lamont, was deported.

Reports of torture by the military forces 'continue to be the rule rather than the exception,' says the commission, a point made by the leaders of the patriotic front, who are insisting that the Rhodesian forces be disbanded under any settlement.

Two examples are documented with photographs, although names have been withheld to protect those involved.

On 21 December 1976 Mr. P.M., who had been working on the land with his wife and children, was questioned by two white members of a

24-strong army unit about the presence of gorillas. He was beaten on his lower back with a large stick 'until he fell and was then bound by his wrists with wire and tied to a tree.

'Meanwhile the other soldiers (who were black) had been preparing to eat and have made a fire in which some beer was boiling. One of the European soldiers then poured 15 cups over Mr. M.'s head and about five cups over his shoulders. After the meal the same soldier poured the boiling beer countless times over Mr. M.'s feet.' After nine weeks in hospital, Mr. M. had still not fully recovered.

In another incident on 29 June this year Mr. F.S., aged 21, was taken to an army camp for questioning by two white and two black soldiers. He denied any knowledge of a guerrilla presence. The report alleges that nevertheless 'the soldiers made him remove his clothes and attached an electric device to his ankles which he said gave a "terrible pain".

'They made him lie face down and beat him on his shoulders, back and buttocks with something which Mr. F.S. described as "a rubber fanbelt". The process went on for a very long time until Mr. F.S. began to lose consciousness. The soldiers said they were going to kill him if he didn't tell the truth. He was released the next day and spent the following month in hospital.'

Schoolchildren, says the report, are often brutally questioned. One method, according to a headmaster, is to cover the suspect's face with a towel, which is then saturated with water to simulate drowning.

Priests and sisters have also been beaten during questioning, the commission claims.

Over half a million tribespeople, double the official figure, are now held in 'protected' villages, the report says.

Protected villages (PVs)—fenced and patrolled hamlets in which Blacks have been regrouped—were first introduced in 1973 in an attempt to isolate tribespeople from guerrillas.

There are now 203 PVs, says the report, mainly in north-east and south-east Rhodesia, corresponding to the main operational areas of the war, but others are being established in the north-west.

On the basis of first-hand reports, mainly from missionaries, the commission estimates that there are 590,000 people who have been compulsorily removed. It claims that in one incident in the Tanda Tribal Trust Land (TTTL) last July, Rhodesian forces burned six villages whose 2,900 occupants had refused to move.

Residents say that conditions in most PVs are bad. Space is often limited to 13 square metres per family, toilet facilities are generally inadequate and water is bad. The families moved received no compensation for their abandoned properties. A strict dusk-to-dawn curfew in the villages means that fields—often some miles away—are vulnerable to raids by wild pigs and baboons.

The commission has received reports of hunger in many villages (grain stocks were often spoilt, if the move took place during the rainy season). There is a 'desperate need' for proper sanitary facilities in some of the Chiweshe PVs which house 120,000 people and there are reports of malaria in the Dande TTL villages in the north.

The policy of isolation is not working, says the report: 'In many areas the guerrillas move in and out of the villages.'

Officials of the Ministry of Internal Affairs, which is mainly responsible for the PVs, have come under frequent attack from guerrillas. Between January and June this year, 114 ministry officials were killed, 25 went missing or were abducted, and 243 were wounded. There have been at least 70 attacks on the villages in the first five months of this year.

The report doubts the accuracy of the government's figures on war casualties. According to military communiqués, between January and July this year 254 black civilians were killed by the army (curfew breakers and recruits caught in the crossfire) and 129 members of the military forces died. Guerrillas are alleged to have killed 248 civilians, all but 12 of them black. The commission believes that the true figures are higher, and gives examples of unreported deaths. It claims that when the army burned six villages in the Tanda TTL in July, nine soldiers died when they came under attack by guerrillas. The incident was never mentioned in official communiqués, and the names of only two soldiers were released the following week as having died in action.

Unreported black civilian deaths at the hands of the military, claims the commission, include a schoolboy who died following beatings, and a 'curfew breaker' shot 50 yards from his home. The deaths of mercenaries, and African and coloured soldiers, are often kept quiet, says the report.

The commission also questions some of the official versions of incidents in which civilians die. Three children and a teacher who were killed at Kandenga School on 18 April did not, says the report, die in crossfire between guerrillas and the army, as the communiqué claimed.

Children and teachers at the school maintained there were no guerrillas in the grounds. The killings, they say, were carried out by three white soldiers who landed at the school in two helicopters and opened fire indiscriminately.

The report also analyses government propaganda and details the constraints under which journalists work.

One example of the propaganda is a series of illustrated leaflets circulated to rural Blacks, carrying a basic message: carers are Communists—'murdering mad dogs'—who are responsible for kidnapping children, beating their recruits, spreading venereal disease and wanting to 'destroy the people with sickness and death, so that their evil Communist masters may come from their hiding places in Mozambique and steal a country from the people.'

*'Rhodesia: the propaganda war,' published by the Catholic Institute for International Relations, 1 Cambridge Terrace, London NW1.

In search of the missing M form

Financial Times, 18 June 1982

We travelled in mini-procession down noisy, bustling Broad Street in the heart of Lagos, side-stepping huge puddles left behind after torrential rain, in pursuit of a missing M form. This is the story of a search for that vital piece of paper—and five copies—which any businessman in Nigeria wishing to make a foreign exchange application must complete and submit to the country's Central Bank. It is the key document which amounts both to permission to import a particular item, and permission to pay for it in foreign exchange.

The story begins on March 23 when the Central Bank suspended the opening of letters of credit and processing of M forms as the first step towards assessing and reducing the country's level of imports, which were far outstripping earnings from oil exports. This was followed on April 20 by the announcement of wide-ranging austerity measures, including import curbs, hefty import deposits, and the need to revalidate all old M forms.

The full effect of those measures has yet to become clear: the past two months have been a grace period in which exporters to Nigeria have scrambled to beat the deadline for old orders to be delivered. But the Nigerian intention is to cut its import bill by one third, from N1.2 billion (£1 billion) to N800 million (£660 million) a month. For a major exporter like Britain, that would mean a cut in its annual export trade of £500 million from last year's £1.5 billion of goods sold to Nigeria.

For Alhaji Mahmud Umoru, Chairman of Ceramic Manufacturers (Nigeria) Ltd, the M form change was critical. His N17 million plant, in which Jouffrieau International of France holds 8 per cent of equity and Netzsch Freres of West Germany 12 per cent, is due to be commissioned in September. The plant, which will employ 1,750 people and produce 5,250 tons of sanitary wares a year, is in the process of installing equipment worth 30 million French francs (£3 million), imported of course under an M form.

Also required are the raw materials for the plant, including chemicals, acrylic bath tubs, taps, cisterns and siphons. All these have been ordered from British companies, are worth just over £1 million and require separate M forms. Without the rest of the equipment and the raw materials, the plant will not open as scheduled in September.

So Alhaji Umoro, an accountant and banker who took a marketing diploma at Harvard, arranged through the Kano Branch of the Société Générale Bank (SGB) to resubmit his forms, in compliance with the new regulations. This was in late April. By the beginning of June Alhaji Umoro was getting worried. He had heard nothing further. Time was running out. So on June 8 he flew the 750 miles from Kano, in the north of Nigeria, to Lagos to investigate the matter personally.

His first stop was the Broad Street branch of SGB. Yes, he was told, the forms had indeed been sent on to the Central Bank but nothing further had been heard.

From SGB Alhaji Umoro dropped in on the offices of the Manufacturers Association of Nigeria, on whose board he sits. Its director, Dr Eleazu, gave an account of the difficulties manufacturers were facing.

'The measures were well-intentioned,' he said, 'but there have been difficulties in implementing them.' The Central Bank, he went on, was seriously short of skilled staff and had had difficulty coping with the old system. 'Yet the new one is even more complex.'

Delays in M-form-processing are forcing some firms either to close for lack of raw materials or to go on to short-time working. Dunlop Nigeria, for example, is critically short of carbon black, an essential import for its tyre plant.

'The bank,' said Dr Eleazu, 'is inundated by M form applications and it seems that anything for over N500,000 is shelved.' Further, the new import duties announced in the austerity package had some serious anomalies. Raleigh Industries, which manufactures bicycles requiring some imported components, but with a 65 per cent local value added, was harder hit than firms which assembled CKD ('Completely Knocked Down') bicycle kits.

It should be said, however, that some observers believe the bank is making considerable efforts. 'Obviously there are going to be teething problems,' said one experienced businessman, 'but from the governor downwards the bank is trying to put its house in order.'

Meanwhile, Dr Eleazu did his best for Alhaji Umoru. He rang Mr. Nwarache, director of exchange control at the Central Bank, and made an appointment. So Alhaji Umoru and I set off from the Unity House offices of the manufacturers' association into the cacophony of steamy Lagos, dodging the yellow taxis and threading our way between the street vendors.

The first stop was the main Central Bank building in Saka Tinubu Square. Wrong place, it transpired. Onwards. A bank messenger was delegated to escort us, for Alhaji Umoru, who seemed to know every other person in the street, is what one would call here 'a big *oga*'—i.e., a man of influence and substance.

We made our way along Broad Street: first the messenger, then the oga, elegant Northern robes flowing, followed by your correspondent, equipped with a green and white umbrella carrying a picture of the national football team, the Green Eagles, and a notebook.

On the eighth floor of Mandilas House we were ushered into the office not of Mr. Nwarache but a senior manager in the 'comprehensive import supervision scheme, exchange control department'.

He listened patiently as Alhaji Umoru explained his predicament. He had some comfort to offer. The M form covering the import of plant and equipment remained valid—as the new regulations he read out made clear—for it involved a project already under way.

As for the M forms applying for foreign exchange for raw materials: when was it sent to the bank? Late April, was the reply; perhaps, Alhaji Umoru said hopefully, it lay in the very pile on the desk in front of him.

The official, a model of patience whose phone rang constantly with callers asking about M forms, made two observations.

If it had been submitted in late April it would not be in the pile: those forms were dated May. 'But we sometimes find that banks tell their customers that they sent the form off weeks ago, but in fact they have only just got round to it, and we are blamed for the delay.' He smiled sadly.

No doubt, said the official, SGB had acted promptly in this case. But if Alhaji could return to his bank and get the date of submission, it would be easier to trace the form M at the Central Bank.

And so Alhaji Umoru and I set off for SGB. The appropriate staff member, alas, was 'not on seat'—he was at lunch. But we were directed to the man who safeguarded the ledger in which all M form transactions were recorded.

A lengthy search ensued. No record of the M form. 'There was great confusion in April,' said an embarrassed official by way of explanation. And while the search continued he told us that the Central Bank appeared to be giving priority to applications for raw materials. 'We have N100 million outstanding in other categories, and we're only a small bank.'

The forms submitted by Ceramic Manufacturers could not be found. We had reached the end of the road. 'In future,' suggested the official, 'we think you should arrange for form M to be delivered directly to us and not through our branch.'

This is easier said than done. Communications between Lagos and Kano are poor. Telex and phone links usually do not work, and mail can take weeks. So if Alhaji Umoru has essential business in Lagos he has to make the journey himself—costing N155 for the return ticket and N208 a day for hotel, meals and car hire.

Alhaji Umoru, who in the course of the day has never raised his voice in anger or frustration, makes one observation: 'The delay costs us money. To recover this we have to charge higher prices for our products—and this is one of the reasons locally made goods can be more expensive than their imported or smuggled counterparts.'

It also means that Alhaji Umoru has to start all over again. He has no alternative but to submit fresh M forms, which will, if he is fortunate, take some six weeks before they re-emerge from the Central Bank. The raw materials for his plant will almost certainly not arrive in time and its opening will be delayed.

The strains begin to tell

Financial Times, 6 January 1983

It is almost as if a nightmare is returning to Zimbabwe, nearly three years to the day after a formal ceasefire came into effect, ending the country's seven-year guerrilla war and in turn leading to independence elections.

The recent brutal killings in Matabeleland highlight the insecurity in the south; a crude form of fuel rationing has been reintroduced to cope with a dire petrol shortage; the draconian security laws inherited from Mr. Ian Smith, the former prime minister, are applied so forcefully that indemnity legislation has had to be reintroduced to protect members of the security forces from prosecutions; and the ruling ZANU-PF of Mr. Robert Mugabe exerts its authority over the media with almost as much rigour as the former Rhodesian Front of Mr. Smith.

The morale of the dwindling white community—whose skills remain vital to the economy—is falling, while tensions between the Ndebele-based ZAPU party of Mr. Joshua Nkomo and the Shona-based ZANU-PF of Mr. Mugabe are heightening.

Potential foreign investors look on askance, and Western governments anxiously follow events in a country which has a key geopolitical position in southern Africa.

The question that must be asked is whether these are the growing pains of a country still scarred by war, whose protagonists are sometimes slow to accept Prime Minister Mugabe's election victory call for reconciliation, or whether something more serious is afoot.

The evidence of several senior and respected Zimbabweans, from differing political and ethnic backgrounds, has two things in common: they all agree that Zimbabwe is not simply slipping back to the bad old days of the civil war; but they are all deeply uneasy about the future.

A leading Shona businessman who worked in the country throughout the Smith years expresses embarrassment about the empty rhetoric and lack of realism of the recently-published development plan, and bemoans the lack of understanding for his problems in the ministries he has to deal with.

A senior civil servant in a sensitive ministry is more concerned about the external threat. Every one of the white officials who have left his ministry have gone to South Africa, he says. 'We had trusted them, we let them sit in on top-level meetings here and abroad.' He points out that a senior white intelligence official responsible at one stage for the security not only of the prime minister but of visiting heads of state, actually defected to Pretoria.

A white Zimbabwean who has long maintained black nationalist sympathies is now cynical, as he cites cases of high living, corruption and incompetence among what he sees as a new elite. While professing socialism and egalitarianism, its members do little more than tinker with the institutions they inherited, he maintains.

To put the current events in perspective, it is well to remember that at the peak of the war some 500 people a month were dying and hundreds of thousands were either forcibly confined to fenced villages or living as refugees. Eventually, 40 per cent of the country's budget went on military spending. Much of the then Rhodesia became no-go areas, many roads were unsafe at night, and on some main routes one travelled in a military convoy. Around 100,000 men and women, black and white, Shona and Ndebele, were carrying arms.

The white minority represented no one but themselves, one in around 25 of the population.

The end of that conflict remains a remarkable achievement and has paved the way for a better society. School enrolment has more than doubled, for example, and health care is reaching far more people.

Yet Zimbabwe's problems now threaten to overshadow these and other successes. The division between Black and White has taken second place to a rift between Black and Black. Mr. Smith's old ally, South Africa, is accused of destabilising the region, with catastrophic effects for Zimbabwe and its neighbours. And as these strains mount the Government is falling back on an intolerant, often brutal treatment of opposition, real or imagined.

The difficulties are compounded by the black economic prospects for 1983 (after two years of extraordinary growth), caused in part by poor export prices and the world recession, which will inevitably frustrate post-independence expectations.

Of all the stresses and strains the government is under perhaps the most painful, and ultimately the most dangerous, involves South Africa. Its apartheid system is bitterly opposed by the Zimbabwe Government but Mr. Mugabe must maintain his practical links: the Republic's ports handle 75 per cent of Zimbabwe's trade, and South Africa is Zimbabwe's largest export market, especially for manufactured goods. As in the days of Mr. Smith, Pretoria can exert its influence through rail and fuel supplies—and once again Pretoria's hand is on the petrol tap.

The origin of the current fuel crisis, with motorists queueing all night for petrol, lies in the December 9 sabotage of fuel tanks at the Mozambique port of Beira by the so-called Mozambique Resistance Movement (MRM). It was the latest in a series of attacks on road and rail routes—and on the Lonrho-owned oil pipeline itself, running from Beira to Mutake on Zimbabwe's eastern border.

The main aim of the MRM, allegedly with covert support of South Africa, is the overthrow of President Samora Machel of Mozambique. But in the process they are undermining both Mr. Mugabe and the other black states of the region, who are trying to reduce their trade and transport dependence on Pretoria through the Southern African Development Co-ordination Conference (SADCC).

Although information remains sketchy, fresh fuel supplies via Beira and the pipeline are unlikely to arrive in Zimbabwe before mid-January. In the meantime, the Government has been placed in the embarrassing position of bringing in extra fuel through South Africa, from Maputo in Mozambique. It may yet be forced to buy its oil supplies direct from the Republic.

Mr. Emmerson Munangagwa,[19] Zimbabwe's minister with responsibility for security, has no doubts about Pretoria's intentions. 'The South African Government has taken it upon itself to destabilise the region,' he said in an interview last week. 'They are using two instruments: military and economic.'

On the military front, he accuses South Africa of, amongst other activities, establishing four military camps holding some 4,000 recruits from Matabeleland, infiltrating them in groups into Zimbabwe where they pose as Nkomo supporters, 'commit crimes, make roadblocks and kill people.'

---

[19] Mr. Munangagwa's name is now spelled 'Mnangagwa'.

On the economic front, he says, 'South Africa attacks us indirectly by supporting the Mozambique resistance movement and instructing them to blow up the railway lines to Beira and Maputo, and the oil pipeline from Beira to Mutare,' as well as the fuel tank farm at Beira.

In an effort to protect its supply route, which has been sabotaged in the past, Zimbabwe is being drawn into its neighbour's conflict. Since November, according to diplomats in Harare and visitors from Mozambique, Zimbabwean troops at battalion strength (700–800) have been posted at strategic points such as at pumping stations on the 174-mile oil pipeline. Mr. Munangagwa, however, maintains that they have been sent simply to protect repair gangs and have stayed no longer than two or three days at a time.

The country's national army is also occupied on the domestic front in Matabeleland, where Mr. Nkomo's ZAPU won all but one of the 16 seats at stake in the 1980 elections (to give a total of 20 in the 100-seat parliament).

The security problems—hit and run attacks on farms, stores and buses—are carried out mainly by former members of Mr. Nkomo's ZIPRA[20] guerrilla force, who have deserted the integrated national army. Some 100 people have been killed over the past year, including more than a dozen Whites.

The desertions go back to early 1981 when ZIPRA units fought in Bulawayo and elsewhere with ZANLA, the guerrilla army of Mr. Mugabe. The uneasy truce between ZAPU and ZANU began to crumble and the integration of the two forces into a national army was jeopardised.

The discovery of arms caches on ZAPU property in February last year led to a further deterioration between the parties, including the sacking of Mr. Nkomo from the Cabinet, and the rate of desertions increased.

The number of deserters is now put at anywhere between 2,000 and 4,000 of whom several hundred, armed with AK47 rifles, are living off the Matabeleland countryside, sometimes taking refuge across the border in Botswana.

Villagers in the province have been subjected to tough and often brutal interrogation by the security forces in their search for bandits. They are caught between the demands for food and shelter of armed 'dissidents', common bandits (and possibly South African-backed

[20] See Footnote 2, page 25.

infiltrators, as Mr. Munangagwa alleges) and the equally forceful demands of a ZANLA-dominated army seeking information.

Mr. Nkomo, a backbencher since his sacking, is in a predicament. The younger members of his party resent what they see as their exclusion from senior government positions, and from jobs in state corporations, the civil service and diplomatic posts, and feel that Mr. Nkomo's leadership is lacking. Older members of the party tend to feel resigned to the inevitability of a one-party state, canvassed by Mr. Mugabe last year. They believe that ZAPU has little choice but to co-operate in its own demise.

There are other worrying domestic developments. Military spending, though now reduced to about 12 per cent of the budget, is nevertheless nearly five times the allocation to the ministry responsible for what is probably the most sensitive medium-term problem facing Mr. Mugabe: the resettlement of some 162,000 peasant families and the need to persuade their children to live on the land and not to add to the growing pool of urban unemployed.

Progress is painfully slow: perhaps 12,000 families have been resettled so far, while scores of thousands of squatters take the law into their own hands. The demand for individual plots, however, simply cannot be satisfied, for there is not enough land.

Within ZANU-PF itself, there is a continuing jockeying for authority between what might be termed the radical and pragmatic groups.

Some of the consequences of these internal divisions are reflected in apparent contradictions in government policies, and their application. Mr. Mugabe heads an avowedly socialist administration which regularly condemns capitalism, imperialism and associated governments and institutions. Yet the West is being wooed for, and is providing, most of the aid and the little foreign investment that is coming in.

The recently published three-year development plan is one example of a certain confusion. Misgivings about the government's technical abilities are aroused by a plan which sets unrealistic targets, contains anomalies, and is studded with jargon which raises doubts about the influence of pragmatists in the economic and planning ministries, such as Dr Bernard Chidzero, the minister himself.

It is difficult to find anyone who believes that the projected growth rate of 8 per cent a year over the plan period is realistic. (Growth last year is put at 2–3 per cent and is likely to be around nil this year.)

Whatever shortcomings there may be in the plan, or in the construction and implementation of government policies, arguably the most serious problems facing Zimbabwe remain political tensions within the country and in the region as a whole.

Zimbabwe is discovering its vulnerability as a front-line state, and an unfriendly neighbour can exploit those tensions. As long as Pretoria and black Africa are at loggerheads, Mr. Mugabe's government, along with other states in southern Africa, will pay a high price.

Julius Nyerere
Unpublished, c. 1995

Recently, a speaker at a Nairobi conference chaired by the Tanzanian president offered the following unconventional tribute: Did he know that Ian Smith, leader of rebel Rhodesia, had once described him as 'Africa's evil genius'? As back-handed compliments go, suggested the speaker, what better testimony could there be to Nyerere's influence on the continent?

For a split second there was silence, as delegates wondered how they should respond. Even then, more than 10 years after his retirement from the presidency in 1985, Nyerere, was held in something approaching awe at African gatherings. Invariably he is deferentially addressed as 'Mwalimu', the Swahili word for 'teacher'. Whatever the final verdict on his stewardship will be, he has won respect on the continent, and beyond its shores, as a decent, honest man who has done what in Africa was unprecedented. He has not, like so many of his counterparts, enriched himself through high office; and he voluntarily stood down as president.

Nyerere himself broke the tension, exuberantly laughing aloud, for he neither lacks a sense of humour, nor is he ever pompous.

Yet history may judge him harshly. Despite these and other fine qualities, he presided over one of Africa's most disastrous experiments in social engineering, enforced by an autocratic, one-party state.

Some 14 million peasants and their families were compulsorily moved under the socialist banner of *ujamaa* (familyhood), put into practice through the communal villages at the heart of Nyerere's vision. The ill-planned exercise, implemented by the army and authoritarian bureaucrats and party officials, disrupted agriculture, created environmental problems and set back an economy whose potential was as great as any in the region.

On the other hand, he scorns the grandiose lifestyle, is often his own harshest critic, and was almost alone among African leaders to condemn the Ugandan tyrant Idi Amin.

It is this combination of vision, albeit flawed, and charm, coupled with his keen intelligence and persuasive, witty, speaking style that won over a succession of aid donors, led by the World Bank itself. They turned a blind eye to Nyerere's faults, and turned Tanzania into one of the world's leading recipients of aid, on which it became more and more dependent.

Born in Butiama, on the shores of Lake Victoria, in 1922, Julius Nyerere was educated first at a government school and then at a mission, where he became a Catholic. After taking a teaching diploma at Makerere University College in neighbouring Uganda in 1948, he won a scholarship to Edinburgh University, where he read history, philosophy, political economy and constitutional law.

From the time he launched the Tanganyika African National Union in 1954 (later renamed Chama Cha Mapinduzi), leading the campaign for independence from Britain, until his resignation as chairman in August 1990, he dominated the country's politics.

It was in 1967 that he set out his political and economic credo in the Arusha declaration, in which he proclaimed socialism and self-reliance as the country's twin goals.

Initial gains in literacy, primary school enrolment and life expectancy in the post-independence era seemed to have validated Nyerere's approach. But by the mid-1970s several things were becoming clear: Tanzania was living beyond its means; aid projects were seldom self-sustaining; the state-dominated agricultural sector was increasingly inefficient; and agricultural production, the mainstay of the economy, was falling.

External factors—the mid-1970s rise in oil prices and deteriorating terms of trade—were partly to blame. But the prime responsibility lay with Nyerere's pursuit of a flawed ideology, indulged by donors who became complicit in the exercise. They, too, share at least some of the blame, as a World Bank report belatedly accepted. A confidential internal analysis, drawn up the agency in 1990, acknowledged that loans exceeding $1 billion over three decades since independence in 1962, helped sustain 'a poorly thought-out socialist experiment'. Between them, the bank and other donors provided more than $15 billion in aid during the first 30 years of independence, with comparatively little to show for it.

The document suggests that what it sees as Nyerere's well-meaning but impractical socialist vision was indulged by senior bank officials, an implicit reference to Robert McNamara in particular, the former US defence secretary who was bank president from 1968 to 1981.

The report criticises what it calls a stance of uncritical support for government policies. It pointed out that 'Tanzania's unprecedented access to concessionary flows of external capital has allowed it ... to maintain a high rate of largely ill-conceived and uneconomical industrial investment.'

'It was not until 1981 that the bank acknowledged that the situation was getting out of hand,' continued the report. Until then it had 'remained an apathetic observer and an impotent bystander ... as Tanzania became the testing ground for an allegedly unique socialist experiment and one that was poorly thought out at that.'

History may judge Nyerere severely in other matters. Tanzania's role in the overthrow of Uganda's Idi Amin proved costly for both countries, for the invading Tanzanian troops wrought great damage. Nor was the upshot satisfactory, for the restoration to office of former Ugandan pres-ident Milton Obote, with the assistance of Nyerere, triggered another costly war.

The break-up of the East African economic community in the mid-1970s was due as much to Nyerere's pursuit of socialism as any weaknesses in the structure of the community; and his role in nego-tiations over Angola, Namibia, Zimbabwe and South Africa has often been less than constructive.

It is a measure of Nyerere's personal appeal that his record at home, and in the region, has not prevented him from playing the role of pundit and statesman abroad, serving as chairman of the North-South Commission, and remaining in great demand as a chairman and speaker.

He continues to be a sharp and perceptive critic of the weaknesses of the international financial institutions, and a persuasive lobbyist on behalf of developing countries, but he would have been far more effective in these roles had his credibility not suffered irreparable damage when the world belatedly took stock of Nyerere's *ujamaa* legacy.

Medicine too harsh for a frail patient [21]

Financial Times, 15 February 1988

The optimism three decades ago that greeted Ghana's independence, marking the start of the post-colonial era on the continent, has vanished. It has been replaced by despair. Debt and drought, dissidents and disease, have left millions of people in misery.

Where did it go wrong? And how can Africa recover? The sad record of the independence years, disfigured by over 70 coups, the emergence of military regimes and authoritarian one-party states, and a steady economic decline, dominate impressions of contemporary Africa. The colonial era recedes into history, less easily recalled. And when it is, the period is often given a Eurocentric gloss, seen as a time when the colonial powers played a 'civilising' role in the 'dark continent'.

From an African perspective, the reality was very different. The colonial era, and earlier contacts with the West, left scars which mark the continent to this day. Africa's crisis is deep-rooted, and in those roots lie at least part of the explanation of some of the problems of today. When the *Financial Times* first appeared on the streets of London the continent's most traumatic experience was only just coming to an end—the traffic in slaves to the West Indies and the Americas, sometimes described as Africa's holocaust.

It was, as Basil Davidson writes in his book about the slave trade, *Mother Africa*, the greatest forced migration in the history of man. Between 1650 and 1850, the period when the trade flourished, some 12 million slaves were landed in the Americas, according to one estimate. It is calculated that two million perished on the journey and seven

---

[21] This article appeared in an FT supplement marking the paper's 100th anniversary.

million died before embarkation. The experience left African communities shattered, villages bereft of the able-bodied, and ethnic states and kingdoms destabilised.

Yet as slavery was coming to an end another traumatic experience was beginning. In what became known as 'the Scramble for Africa', Britain, France, Germany, Portugal, Belgium, Italy and Spain all staked territorial claims, in the process usually disregarding the boundaries of the indigenous nation states of Africa and overturning the societies they encountered.

'One of the most serious consequences of European colonisation in Africa,' writes the historian Ali Mazrui,[22] in his book, The Africans, 'has been the destruction of Africa's own legitimate institutions and structures of authority.' He continues: 'The initial military triumph of European power over the local rulers was itself enough of a strain on the historic prestige of indigenous monarchies and institutions of governance. But that initial European military triumph was followed by decades of Europeans' overlordship, with policies deliberately calculated to change the nature of Africa's political processes for ever.'

Africa's post-independence failure to develop durable and democratic political systems and institutions—an important factor behind the continent's current malaise—is at least in part explained by this upheaval from which the continent has yet to recover.

But the colonial system left its mark in other ways, not least in the area of peasant agriculture. As Professor Michael Crowder points out in a recent essay on Africa's colonial inheritance, local farmers were often, through taxation, compulsory crop cultivation, forced labour and requisition, made to produce 'cash crops that the big companies overseas required, even at the risk of impoverishment of the land and famine'. Colonial government marketing boards were used as a means of taxing further the potential earnings of the farmer, Professor Crowder adds, and wryly notes: 'Yet critics of the independent African regimes seem to suggest that this neglect and exploitation of the farmer was new, rather than a major legacy of colonial rule.'

Other features of the colonial legacy have an impact to this day. Britain cannot be proud of the fact that Northern Rhodesia became Zambia in 1964 with barely a dozen university graduates. Belgium's failure to prepare the Congo (now Zaire) for independence and abrupt departure

---

[22] Ali Mazrui (1933–2014), was a Kenyan-born academic, historian and political writer on African and Islamic studies. He taught in Uganda and from 1974 in the USA.

after 75 years of exploitation helped plunge the country into chaos from which it has never really recovered. Portugal's record was no better. Forced in the 1970s to surrender power to guerrilla movements in Angola and Mozambique, they left behind an illiteracy rate that exceeded 90 per cent.

Yet for all the burdens and problems inherited from the past, black Africa was imbued with optimism and enthusiasm as the roll call of independent states rang out in the 1960s. Kwame Nkrumah, independent Ghana's first leader, summed up the mood of African leaders, transposed from humble back-street offices where independence had been plotted, to State House: 'Seek ye first the political kingdom and the rest shall be added thereto.' Ironically the country that was once an inspiration to Africa became a symbol of what was to go wrong. Nkrumah encouraged a personality cult, muzzled the press and introduced draconian security laws.

An ill-defined, broadly socialist philosophy took Ghana down a disastrous path of burgeoning state-controlled corporations, prestige projects and unrealistic schemes for industrialisation. Peasant farmers took second place to mechanised state farms, and inevitably production of cocoa, the country's vital export, fell. The same crowds who greeted his accession in 1957 took to the streets to acclaim Nkrumah's overthrow in 1966.

There were exceptions to the Ghanaian model—among them Kenya, the Ivory Coast and Botswana. But for the most part Africa's new leaders espoused unrealistic ambitions and impractical policies, often abetted by Western bankers who were later to discover that they had lent unwisely, or aid donors who frequently had their own commercial interests at heart.

Sometimes the vision was pursued with integrity, as in the case of Julius Nyerere in Tanzania, who regrouped several million of his people into socialist villages for which it was easier to provide social services, but which severely disrupted traditional agriculture.

Some had high hopes, such as President Kaunda in Zambia, striving for a humanistic society but failing to reduce his country's unhealthy dependence on copper and suffering when the price of the mineral slumped in the 1970s. Others, such as President Mobutu in Zaire, merely cloaked the avarice of the ruling elite with socialist or nationalist rhetoric.

All, in varying degrees, failed: neglecting or mismanaging the vital agricultural base, creating inefficient state-owned corporations, cushioning their growing urban populations with subsidies, discouraging the private sector and in most cases spending heavily on the very armies that were to oust many of Africa's civilian leaders.

Few African leaders were equipped to handle a major blow to their aspirations: the economic buffeting which began in the 1970s as oil prices rose, prices for Africa's exports fell, and the cost of post-independence external borrowings became unbearably high as interest rates climbed.

The crisis set in train a profound reappraisal of what had gone wrong, on the economic front at least, since independence. And appropriately enough, it was Ghana that was among the first group of African states, now exceeding 30, that started taking the medicine prescribed by the two institutions that today loom large over the continent—the World Bank and the IMF.

Africa itself belatedly recognised that a false economic start had been made when in 1980, heads of state drew up the 'Lagos Plan of Action', the first blueprint for reform. But the toughest appraisal came from the World Bank, which in 1981 produced the first of a series of reports on Africa bluntly setting out the scale of the continent's predicament. The record of the past two decades was 'grim'. External factors, over which African leaders had no control, had indeed done severe damage. But the Bank pinpointed shortcomings closer to home: output of export crops had been stagnating and food production lagged behind population growth.

The Bank's reports have painted a bleak picture. Death rates on the continent are the highest in the world, and life expectancy is the lowest.

Nearly a fifth of black Africa's children die by their first birthday.

Barely a quarter of the sub-Saharan Africa's half-billion people have access to safe water.

If Africa is to recover, the Bank and the IMF have been arguing, its governments must press ahead with fundamental reforms: devaluation of over-valued local currencies, improved incentives for farmers, an overhaul of state-owned corporations, an end to subsidies including those on foods, an end to most price controls and strict limits on government spending.

Even self-proclaimed Marxist states such as Angola and Mozambique are coming under the umbrella of Western-inspired reforms.

Yet this medicine may well prove too harsh for frail patients. Some leaders, such as President Kaunda, argue that the measures are often inappropriate, the conditions too inflexible: 'Like a doctor who prescribes quinine, whether you have malaria, a cold or a broken leg,' Dr Kaunda complains.

Most observers believe that the reform programme is in jeopardy. The main reason, argues Mr. Javier Perez de Cuellar, the UN Secretary-General, is that the Western countries who have long urged Africa to change its policies are not backing the reforms now under way with sufficient additional assistance.

In particular, he says, they have not grasped the largest nettle: the need to ease the burden of the continent's $200 billion external debt (amounting to almost 54 per cent of black Africa's GDP) by agreeing to concessional rates of interest.

Economically debilitated, often politically unstable, unable effectively to challenge the military and economic muscle that South Africa exercises in its region, Africa faces a further trauma: AIDS (Acquired Immune Deficiency Syndrome) is now prevalent in several central, southern and east African states, and it is spreading. Health workers fear that one million people could die in the next decade, many from among Africa's skilled urban class—civil servants and factory workers, miners and politicians—on whom the implementation of recovery programmes greatly depends.

It adds up to a mounting tragedy of devastating proportions. Most disturbing of all, perhaps, is the possibility that Africa no longer has the adequate institutional capacity to help itself. The one-party systems and the military regimes have wrought terrible damage. The civil service has become subservient to presidential decree and is seldom a source of independent advice. The integrity of the judiciary has been eroded or eliminated. Trade unions have been emasculated. National assemblies often do little more than act as a rubber stamp. The political parties that were formed in the fervour of nationalism have ossified, and for the most part are incapable of inspiring loyalty or galvanising disillusioned citizens into action. And the post-independence generation of Africa is cynical, sad and debilitated.

Africa's resilience in the face of its ordeal remains remarkable. The stoical endurance of its people is extraordinary. But the continent has been generally ill-served by its presidents and generals. Today's crisis requires more than a programme of economic reform, new resources and debt relief. It also needs a new generation of leaders, a fundamental reappraisal of flawed political institutions, and a revival of the nationalist fervour of 30 years ago if an African resurgence is to get under way.

Kinshasa: As time goes by

Unpublished, c. 1988

I want to go back, just once more, to Kinshasa. I want to find out whether the pig-tailed piano player still works the cocktail bar at the Intercontinental Hotel, on the bank of the Congo river. And if he is still there, will he recognise me, and once again play 'As time goes by'?

There was the air of the survivor about him even then, for Zaire in the early 80's was in terminal decline. The lobby of the Intercon was a rendezvous for diamond dealers and coffee traders and men with Armani suits and gold bracelets, reading the *International Herald Tribune*, drinking espresso coffee and eating pastries.

The serious business took place around the swimming pool, or in the cocktail bar. The piano player made his entry in mid-evening: diffident, but with a nod of recognition here and there. I never caught him coming into the bar. One minute the stool was empty, the next minute he was there, slicked black slightly crinkly hair pulled back tight over his forehead and tied in a short pony-tail.

I asked my companion what she would like him to play. '"As time goes by",' she said, and smiled. She assumed a cultural heritage shared; but it was lost on me.

I had never heard of it; perhaps that would have been impossible. I surely must have heard it, even as muzak in a lift, but the title meant nothing to me. I had no idea that there was a film called *Casablanca*. Indeed, I had no idea that the two had something to do with each other. So I asked him, and he played it, and I thought it was a pleasant tune, and the opening bars stayed with me ...

Kinshasa. It's the river as much as anything, deep brown, languorous, originating in the heart of Africa, clumps of hyacinth drifting on a 500-mile journey to the sea. On the other bank, Congo-Brazzaville. A ten-minute ferry ride for the locals; for a foreigner like myself, as close and as inaccessible as an image in a mirror. Visas were hard to get, for the river marked an ideological divide. Kinshasa, a staunch Cold War ally of Washington; Congo Brazzaville, in the enemy camp. No visas. It was easiest reached by flying from Kinshasa to Paris, and flying back to Brazzaville.

The heat. Heavy, humid. And the atmosphere, even then, had a feel of anarchy. I say 'even then', but Zaire has always had an air of anarchy, past or impending, if not actually seized by it. But anarchy need not only be the conventional image of mobs roaming the street, or the army out of control.

Anarchy can be ordinary. The mobs stop roaming, the army stops killing and people go about their business. But there is nevertheless a quiet, calm, deceptive, frightening anarchy that can reign. When a capricious policeman or customs officer or immigration official embodies authority without a higher court of appeal. It's when he does not care that I know the president or the minister of defence, for their writ does not matter.

Zaire is also the Congo of the 1960s for me, a trauma embedded in the collective white psyche of a generation of white southern Africans. It was anarchy of the conventional sort—mercenaries and refugees and Moïse Tshombe[23] and Patrice Lumumba,[24] and the Cold War and the UN … and black hands on white thighs.

So I have mixed feelings about revisiting Zaire, in search of a pianist. But I have been to Kinshasa since that evening in the cocktail bar. I returned, three years later. The hotel was nearly empty and the management put me in a suite on one of the upper floors where I stood, alone this time, with a panoramic view of the river, curling past below my window.

The cocktail bar was almost deserted: ice cold beer and the air conditioning on high removing every trace of the heat, Africa kept at bay, no one at the piano. And then suddenly he was there, tinkling away.

---

[23] Moïse Tshombe (1919–69) was the president of the secessionist State of Katanga from 1960 to 1963 and Prime Minister of the Democratic Republic of the Congo from 1964 to 1965.

[24] Patrice Lumumba (1925–61) was the first prime minister of the independent Democratic Republic of the Congo (then Republic of the Congo) from June to September 1960.

I steeled myself and was about to go over to and ask him to play but he caught my eye. And slipped easily, silkily, into 'As time goes by'.

By then I had seen *Casablanca*.

Namibia: A long war draws to a close
Financial Times, 16 November 1988

The cordial gathering of diplomats, intelligence officials and generals in a Geneva hotel last Friday night turned out to symbolise the breakthrough that was to come in the south-western Africa peace talks.

The enmity of the war in the region was put on one side. Although nearly four days of sometimes fraught bargaining between delegates from Angola, Cuba and South Africa lay ahead, the atmosphere at a reception to mark Angola's 13th anniversary of independence suggested that independence for Namibia was at last within reach.

The key protagonists—President P.W. Botha of South Africa, Fidel Castro, the Cuban leader and President Eduardo dos Santos of Angola —seem finally to have been convinced that a settlement is in their best interests.

Pressure from the superpowers, the growing cost of the war in northern Namibia and southern Angola, and the existence of a UN plan for Namibia's independence agreed in principle almost a decade ago all played their part.

The package agreed by negotiators in Geneva yesterday has something for everyone. If it is ratified by the respective governments, Cuba will be able to claim that its force played a decisive role and its men will go home with honour. Angola will be closer to the peace it desperately needs. South Africa will lose a colony but will claim that it forced the Cubans out of southern Africa. The South West Africa People's Organisation (SWAPO), the guerrilla-backed Namibian independence movement, will almost certainly win office, although its authority will be severely constrained by economic dependence on South Africa. The US will take credit for a diplomatic triumph.

Only two groups will have misgivings. The African National Congress is likely to have its guerrillas excluded from both Angola and Namibia; the UNITA opposition guerrilla movement in Angola led by Dr Jonas Savimbi will lose Pretoria's military support under the deal.

But Cuba, Angola and South Africa all have something to gain. Thus at a series of press conferences in Geneva yesterday, the three delegations made clear that the protracted series of talks which began in London last May had produced agreement in principle, to be endorsed by the three governments in the Congolese capital Brazzaville within the next few weeks.

Although full details have yet to be revealed the broad outline of a regional package is already known. A seven-month countdown to UN supervised elections in Namibia is scheduled to begin early next year, coinciding with the phased departure of Cuban troops from Angola and South African forces from Namibia.

Assuming the settlement goes ahead, it will have profound implications for a region which has not known peace for over two decades. It will reduce, if not end, superpower tensions in the area.

Non-aggression pacts between South Africa and Namibia and Angola, which form part of the package, reduce the risk of further conflict. The agreement raises hopes for a negotiated end to Angola's civil war, because the fall-off in Cuban support for government forces, and an end to South African support via Namibia to UNITA, is expected to give impetus to discreet peace talks already under way.

The main obstacle to an agreement between the delegations—the terms of the Cuban troop withdrawal—appears to have been overcome during the Geneva talks when Dr Crocker[25] apparently won agreement on compromise terms for a withdrawal which the delegates will take back to their government for ratification.

The details of this have not yet been disclosed. It seems likely, however, that Cuba has said that it will carry out a phased withdrawal of its 50,000 troops from Angola over the next 30 months. At least 4,000 of them will go before the seven month transition to Namibia's independence begins.

Barring hitches, the 1.4 million people of Namibia will vote in independence elections in mid-1989 which most observers expect will be won by SWAPO, led by Mr. Sam Nujoma, which has been waging a guerrilla war since 1966.

---

[25] Dr Chet Crocker, US Assistant Secretary of State.

By early 1991, the last of the Cuban troops will have left Angola, although the majority will depart by the end of next year. Within the next few weeks, according to African diplomats, talks between Luanda and UNITA could get under way.

As part of the regional package, Angola's President dos Santos will request the ANC to close its guerrilla training bases in his country. Mr. Nujoma has already made it clear that while he supports the ANC, he will not allow the organisation military training bases in Namibia, nor permit guerrilla infiltration of South Africa through the territory.

At the same time, Mr. Nujoma has been softening his party's ostensibly Marxist stand, pulling back from pledges to nationalise the country's vital mining sector, assuring white farmers that their land rights will be respected, and urging the business community to stay on in a black-ruled Namibia. Mr. Nujoma has also accepted, for the time being at least, South Africa's legal right to ownership of the enclave of Walvis Bay, Namibia's main port.

Three main factors paved the way for the resolution of a regional conflict which has cost billions of dollars and scores of thousands of lives and which has seen the superpowers in conflict by proxy.

The first, and perhaps most critical, is what Dr Crocker calls the 'convergence of interests' between the US and the Soviet Union during the Gorbachev era. Both Washington, which helps arm UNITA, and Moscow, the main weapons supplier to the Marxist government in Angola, decided that it was in their mutual interest to extricate themselves from a regional conflict which served no useful purpose for either.

From the beginning of the initiative, Dr Crocker has sought the support of Mr. Anatoly Adamishin, the Soviet deputy foreign minister, and the ministry's Africa expert, Mr. Vladillen Vasev. The most tangible indication of Moscow's co-operation was the declaration earlier this year that the Soviet Union was prepared to be a co-guarantor of a regional pact.

This superpower cooperation took place as it became increasingly clear to Angola and South Africa that neither was likely to emerge the victor in an increasingly costly battle.

Angola, backed by a Cuban force which numbered in the hundreds in 1974–75 and steadily increased to the current level of 50,000, gradually concluded that, while they might contain, they could not defeat the combination of UNITA and its South African ally, whose forces dominated much of southern Angola.

At the same time economic factors began taking their toll. The government's tentative efforts to reform the economy needed the resources that only Western governments and institutions such as the World Bank and the International Monetary Fund could provide.

Washington effectively vetoed Angola's access to the IMF and the Bank. The economic screws were tightened as Angola, which gets 90 per cent of its export earnings from oil, watched world prices fall.

A combination of economic and military factors was also at work in Pretoria. Since 1985, when foreign banks refused to roll over its loans and precipitated a debt crisis, the South African economy has been in severe difficulties, compounded by the low price of gold which accounts for 60 per cent of export earnings.

On the military front, the past 18 months have seen the largest number of white South African deaths (more than 50) since the conflict began. The turning point, militarily and psychologically, came in 1987. An Angolan offensive in September and October against the UNITA stronghold of Mavinga proved disastrous. South African forces subsequently laid siege to the strategic Angolan town of Cuito Cuanavale.

Yet the military balance began to shift against Pretoria. Cuba responded by reinforcing its contingents and began moving units south to the Namibian border, protected against South African Mirage aircraft by a combination of Soviet-supplied radar and their own pilots.

The loss of 12 white South Africans during a joint Angolan-Cuban action last June at Calueque dam provoked no retaliation from Pretoria. As Gillian Gunn points out in a recent study for the Center for Strategic and International Studies in Washington, the incident highlighted 'the new balance of force in southern Angola'.

'The Angolan-Cuban forces now had a significant edge in the air war and could give the South African Defence Forces a good run for its money on the ground. If South Africa had retaliated it would have lost more planes and men than President P.W. Botha was willing to accept,' she wrote. These changing realities helped to produce the first tangible benefits of the Crocker negotiations.

Last August, Angola and Cuba signed a ceasefire with Pretoria which allowed a 600-strong South African force to withdraw from Angola. Both sides consolidated their positions on either side of the Namibian border.

Knowledge of the increased stakes in the conflict allowed the ceasefire to hold as Dr Crocker moved on to the second phase finally realised in Geneva—the terms of the withdrawal of the Cubans from Angola and South African troops from Namibia.

As Moscow exerted its influence and the realities of war took their toll on the participants, Dr Crocker was able to draw on the third factor in favour of a settlement: the fact that the framework for Namibia's independence process had been set out in a 1978 UN resolution and accepted in principle by South Africa.

Resolution 435 provides for a seven-month transition to independence elections, monitored by a 7,500-strong UN force. A constituent assembly, elected on the basis of proportional representation, would then draw up the country's constitution.

Two obstacles stood in the way: the insistence by Pretoria, with the backing of the Reagan administration, that implementation be linked to a Cuban withdrawal; and the reluctance of South Africa to drop what it saw as an alternative strategy—an 'internal settlement' in which a coalition of politicians drawn from local white parties and disaffected former members of SWAPO won domestic and international recognition.

At the heart of this strategy was Pretoria's unrealistic hope that the internal settlement could be based on a constitution that took account of ethnic differences—a code phrase for leaving power in the hands of the territory's 80,000 white community.

When a group of parties in the coalition last year put forward a constitution which envisaged majority rule, it was promptly vetoed by Pretoria. The internal settlement lost any vestiges of credibility, and power, for now, is in the hands of the South African-appointed administrator general in the capital, Windhoek.

The collapse of the internal strategy was probably not decisive when President Botha assessed the pros and cons of surrendering the territory South Africa has held for 73 years. But taken with the military and economic issues, it underlined the bankruptcy of Pretoria's policy in Namibia. For President Botha the prospect of President Nujoma running Namibia is galling. But he will draw consolation from the fact that SWAPO's concessions carry some major benefits.

After the settlement, the ANC will be denied military training facilities in a buffer zone of African states neighbouring South Africa, running from the west coast of southern Africa to Mozambique in the east.

The prospect of tougher western sanctions may recede as Britain and the US will doubtless use the settlement to argue that negotiated change is shown to be possible. And should the settlement be followed up by the release of Mr. Nelson Mandela, the detained ANC leader, Mr. Botha will be better equipped to pursue his diplomatic forays into black Africa.

Don't trust those statistics

Financial Times, 14 December 1989

The old aphorism about statistics should be borne in mind when reading about Africa. Four million people face starvation in Ethiopia, aid agencies warn. Africa's population is set to double in 20 years, from 500 million to 1 billion, claims the World Bank. Black southern African economies would have grown at a rate of 5 per cent a year were it not for South African destabilisation, says the UN Economic Commission for Africa. Over 30,000 children and 60,000 adults in Africa contracted AIDS in 1988, says the World Health Organization.

Really? How do they know? Of the 45 states that make up sub-Saharan Africa, barely a handful have reliable national statistics. Many of the figures about Africa are little better than guesses.

It is certainly true that Africa is in crisis. But no one really knows the scale because there are so few reliable figures. And if there are no reliable figures, how do donors or recipients draw up an efficient relief operation, plan the cities of the next century, or calculate the hospital beds or classrooms that will be needed in the 1990s?

Some examples: About one in five Africans is said to live in Nigeria. But how many Nigerians are there? The country's last census was in 1963, 'and even then there may have been an overcount,' a government paper acknowledges. Officials believe that the growth rate is 'most likely' increasing by 'more than 3 per cent per year'. The World Bank puts the mid-1987 population at 106.6 million. The government forecasts a population of around 163 million by the year 2000. Billions of dollars are going into Nigeria's economic recovery programme. But its architects do not know how many people they are planning for.

AIDS, say medical experts, could well decimate the population of several African countries. Uganda (population said to be 16 million) may already have 1 million people with HIV, according to a government statement this month. The World Health Organization says that 2.5 million people in Africa have AIDS. By 1992, said a recent report by the Panos Institute, 250,000 African infants will have been born with HIV since 1980.

The figures may be true. They may be underestimates; they may be exaggerations. But no one really knows. Governments of some of the worst-affected countries conceal information. Some run-down health services are simply unable to obtain and collate the information needed.

A UN report last October claimed: 'South Africa's military aggression and destabilisation of its neighbours cost the region $10 billion in 1988, and over $60 billion and 1.5 million lives in the first nine years of this decade.' It may well be true.

Yet two of the countries worst hit, Angola and Mozambique, have rudimentary statistical services. Further, the UN calculations include the cost of lost opportunities. This blithely assumes that the governments of a peaceful southern Africa, which, as well as the avowedly Marxist regime in Angola, includes Zambia, where Kenneth Kaunda pursues his idiosyncratic version of Socialism, would all have followed productive, efficient policies if left to their own devices.

What explains these dramatic but unverifiable figures?

In the mid-70s I was on hand for the first political rallies to be held by the newly released black nationalist leaders of Rhodesia (now Zimbabwe). I wrote about the enormous crowds of up to 100,000. The politicians' supporters were outraged. More like a million, they claimed. I was baffled by the gap, until one day I asked: 'What is a million?'

The answer, in effect, was a great many people. 'Million' was the only word that could do justice to the size of the crowd. Something of the same thing may be happening today, as those concerned about Africa's crisis attempt to convey the scale of the continent's plight to a sometimes indifferent outside world.

The tragedy is real, but we do not know enough about it. Helping Africa develop a reliable statistical base is as necessary a response to the continent's crisis as sending food to Ethiopia.

The 1990s

Facing up to the ethnic issue
Financial Times, 26 July 1990

Africa's advocates of multi-party democracies have the same problem as Pooh Bear had with his song 'Ho! for the life of a bear'. Readers may recall that Pooh managed the first line without any difficulty, but was then stuck for ideas. 'Perhaps if I sing the first line very quickly twice over,' he mused, 'the rest will just come to me.' He did but it didn't.

The first line of the democracy song can be heard on the streets of Abidjan, Lubumbashi, Lusaka, Nairobi and elsewhere. Out with whatever authoritarian figure has been in power for decades, and in with a multi-party system, goes the opening line. The second line, if there is one, starts with a call for a bill of rights and a free press, and then tails off.

This is splendid, as far as it goes. But the questions that need to be asked cannot be heard above the applause from a western audience finding doubtful parallels with the revolutions in eastern Europe.

Why did the multi-party system in Africa fail in the first place? What additional checks and balances can be introduced to curb executive power, given that the usual ones, such as an independent judiciary, were so rapidly and easily eroded?

As Nigeria's former military leader, General Olusegun Obasanjo, pointed out in a speech last November, he presided over a return to civilian rule in 1979 after multi-party elections under an admirable constitution. But the military were back in power after four years of corruption and mismanagement by political parties 'stratified on a tribal basis'.

How *does* Africa cope with the fact that many of its boundaries were drawn either arbitrarily or strategically, leaving pre-colonial nations divided? What role is there for chiefs and traditional spiritual leaders? Above all, how does Africa deal with that most sensitive issue, tribalism? As long as voters feel a primary loyalty to tribe rather than ideology, there is the likelihood that political parties in Africa will reflect ethnic divisions.

Undoubtedly Africa's imagination has been caught by events in eastern Europe. Many of its governments are as a result shakier, losing important allies. It is developments in South Africa, however, which will have the most impact on the African upheaval that may be under way, and be most relevant to the continent's future.

Apartheid has done appalling harm in the Republic. The defenders of apartheid have wrought great damage on their neighbours, using economic muscle or military might. But the malign influence has spread even further. It has helped stifle legitimate debate in Africa and elsewhere about ways in which ethnic, cultural, linguistic and religious differences can be accommodated, and about how minorities can protect themselves.

Apartheid made public debate of these issues if not taboo, then highly sensitive. There seemed to be an overriding concern that no shred of intellectual comfort should be given Dr Verwoerd and his successors, however bizarre and irrational might be the link between recognising and accommodating ethnic tensions, and white subjugation of black South Africa.

That may be changing. A senior official in an African one-party state, where the government is under growing pressure, recently spoke frankly (and in private) about the difficulties of introducing a multi-party system when Africa's post-independence history had shown that a winner-takes-all system had failed. Ways had to be found, he said, to ensure that the legitimate interests of tribes or minorities were represented at all levels of government, without too much dilution of executive authority.

A few days earlier, a cabinet minister in Cape Town made remarkably similar points. But it was the black African and not his white counterpart who made the assertion: 'Ethnicity and how to cope with it will be the issue for Africa in the 1990s.'

It is time Africa's leaders in the wings brought this concern into the open, and moved on from the opening lines of their song.

Between reform and more decline

Financial Times, 13 August 1990

Liberia's slide from dictatorship to anarchy is terrible, even by the standards of a continent used to upheaval. But far from being an aberration, Liberia could prove to be just the first of several states to collapse under the weight of economic mismanagement and ethnic tensions, compounded by policy failures on the part of the superpowers and aid donors.

Other wars in sub-Saharan Africa highlight the continent's fragility: Angola, Mozambique, Sudan, Somalia and Ethiopia are torn by conflict; Uganda has yet to recover from Idi Amin; Chad and Libya may again come to blows. Senegal and Mauritania keep an uneasy peace.

Almost wherever one looks, from Mali to Zambia, the ossified political structures of post-independence Africa are cracking.

From across the continent come calls—endorsed by western govern-ments, aid donors and lending institutions—for a multi-party system. Political adjustment is catching up with the economic adjustment programmes being introduced. But the cry for democracy is as much a moan of pain caused by the economic failures over three decades of independence, and Africa is delicately poised between reform and further decline.

'Good governance', the World Bank's term for better management and democracy, is essential to recovery from disaster. But it will not be the engine of growth for a debilitated continent.

The causes of the upheaval are complex. The most frequent explanation invariably couples the renewed search for freedom in Africa with the revolution in eastern Europe.

'The wind blowing from Europe has begun to sweep Africa. We

should not moan over it, we should even rejoice over it,' as President Mitterrand put it in a recent speech.

France, like Britain and the US, is encouraging the process by linking aid to democracy. 'France will link its contributions to efforts designed to lead to greater ... democracy,' Mr. Mitterrand told African leaders at the francophone summit last June.

Even the Organisation of African Unity, that club of autocrats so tolerant of each other's failings, last month conceded that it was necessary 'to democratise further our societies and consolidate democratic institutions'. But there are more important influences than eastern Europe that are driving Africans to the barricades.

France is reappraising its relationship with francophone Africa. The superpower rapprochement has reverberations in southern Africa and the Horn of Africa in particular, as well as leaving several African leaders anxious about their dwindling foreign patronage.

Aid-dependent regimes have become uneasy as the World Bank and increasing numbers of western governments have moved towards demanding political reform as a condition of aid. South Africa's search for a constitution which accommodates the aspirations of the majority, while coping with the fears of minorities, is gripping the attention of the rest of Africa. Above all, a decade or more of sharp economic decline has made impoverished citizens throughout the continent angry with their rulers, and impatient to find leaders with alternatives.

Certainly, eastern Europe's revolution encouraged opposition movements. It further undermined belief in centrally controlled economic systems—though the examples of Tanzania and Zambia had already done that. And as regimes in East Germany and elsewhere collapsed, the governments in Angola, Mozambique and Ethiopia lost reliable allies.

(South Africa is *sui generis*. Government officials there acknowledge a two-fold impact which proved decisive in persuading President F.W. de Klerk to embark on radical change. The spectacle of mass demonstrations against elitist governments evoked the worst white South African nightmare. And the collapse of Communism as an ideology encouraged Pretoria in the belief that it was safe to unban the South African Communist Party.)

But there are critical differences between the experience of eastern Europe and the process under way in Africa which limits the appropriateness of any comparison. The former has an industrial proletariat with considerably more muscle than that of the peasants in

Africa's predominantly agricultural economies. Essential to the success of the eastern European revolution was the fact that the region's metropolitan power—the Soviet Union—was preoccupied by its own domestic crisis, and made clear it would not intervene.

For Africa, this process took place two to three decades ago, when Belgium, France, Britain and Portugal decided that the price of the colonial relationship was too high.

Post-independence Africa then enjoyed a brief period of democracy, before voters discovered that the district commissioner had been replaced by the party apparatchik, and the parastatal bureaucrat. The latter are proving far more difficult to dislodge.

Alone among the colonising powers, France has kept up a willingness to intervene militarily and financially if a former colonial protégé is in trouble. This willingness may now be in doubt, a factor that will prove far more significant to political change in francophone Africa than anything that happened in eastern Europe.

Although France retains an extraordinary historical and cultural link with Africa, it is finding the financial responsibilities of underwriting the CFA[26] franc increasingly onerous.

The CFA Franc, the common currency used by France's 14 former colonies, has been pegged to the French franc at a rate of 50 to one since 1948. It proved of mutual benefit for a while but is now becoming a financial burden which is pushing France into a reassessment of its African ties.

France is also giving notice that its military involvement in Africa may be more limited than in the past. Mr. Mitterrand again: 'Our role ... is not to intervene in your internal conflicts. In that case France, in agreement with African leaders, will watch over the protection of its citizens but does not intend to arbitrate the conflicts. The prospect of losing the military umbrella—some 9,000 troops are based in Francophone Africa—is as disconcerting to current leaders as it is encouraging to their opponents.'

The impact of the superpower rapprochement is still being felt. The obvious benefit has been Namibia's independence, and the boost given to the peace process in South Africa.

---

[26] The CFA franc was the franc of Colonial French Africa and is now the franc of the Financial Community of Africa. It represents the west African CFA franc, used in eight West African countries, and the Central African CFA franc, used in six Central African countries. The French treasury guarantees both currencies.

As Namibia begins independence with a multi-party constitution, and the world demands the same from South Africa, opposition leaders in the region are asking: Why not us?

But détente has implications beyond southern Africa. Aid and security have long been linked. As Africa ceases to provide cockpits for superpower conflicts by proxy, so aid to certain countries will decline.

It has already in Somalia. Leaders of countries such as Zaire, who adroitly played on tensions between Washington and Moscow to bid up aid levels, are now getting less support, while their opponents receive a sympathetic hearing.

The rapprochement has also left a potentially dangerous power vacuum. In the Horn, this could well be filled by Israel—which is almost certainly supplying arms to Ethiopia's president, Mengistu Haile Mariam[27]—or by one or more of the Arab states. This would exacerbate rather than resolve the conflicts.

Last November, the World Bank added another element to the pressure on African governments. In the most searching examination of Africa's problems ever published by the Bank, the continent's largest donor called on leaders to become 'more accountable to their peoples'.

'Many governments are wracked by corruption and are increasingly unable to command the confidence of the population,' said the Bank, warning that without democratic reforms, many countries' structural adjustment programmes will fail and external aid will fall.

Most African governments are resigned to the prospect that in future, aid will have political as well as economic conditions attached. Neither the Bank nor governments such as the US and Britain, which have endorsed this approach, have so far drawn up formal political criteria. But on such a list would be issues ranging from the state of the local press to whether a recipient is a one- or multi-party state.

One of the first countries to face such a test has been Kenya, where opposition leaders have been detained and President Daniel arap Moi has entrenched the authoritarian ruling party. During last month's unrest, Washington made clear that aid flows could be reduced if reforms did not take place. Britain issued a similar message, *sotto voce*.

Whatever the roots of the African unrest, one thing is clear. Despite World Bank-supported economic reform progmmmes adopted in

---

[27] Mengistu Haile Mariam (born 1937) led Ethiopia from 1977 to 1991, first as chairman of the governing Derg, Ethiopia's socialist military junta, from 1977 to 1987, and then as President of the People's Democratic Republic of Ethiopia from 1987 to 1991.

varying degree by about two-thirds of sub-Saharan Africa, the continent remains in deep economic crisis.

The Bank's report on Africa pointed out that the region's economies must grow by at least 4 per cent to 5 per cent annually for a 'modest improvement in living standards. This target requires a 4 per cent a year increase in real terms of official development assistance, together with further external debt relief.

'(African) leaders will watch over the protection of its citizens but it does not intend to arbitrate the conflicts.' The prospect of losing the military umbrella—some 9,000 French troops are based in francophone Africa—is as disconcerting to current leaders as it is encouraging to their opponents.

It represents a gross Overseas Development Agency requirement of $22 billion a year at 1990 prices by 2000, the Bank estimates.

Many economists believe this underestimates Africa's needs, but even this comparatively cautious goal may be hard to attain.

Donor fatigue has set in since the 1980s, when the high point of compassion was Band Aid in 1984. Nor are aid flows helped by the spectacle of the World Bank and the Economic Commission for Africa, the UN body that acts as the continent's think tank, quarrelling over the type of medicine the patient needs.

There are growing doubts that the Bank's 'model patients' are in fact going to recover after seven years of external assistance running at an annual rate of about $500 million. Ghana, for example, is still a long way from passing the key test: can growth be sustained without substantial aid? And even if the patient pulls through, will there be sufficient external support for the 40 or more sub-Saharan countries that need varying degrees of help? It seems unlikely. Private investment is negligible, and the aid needs of eastern Europe overshadow Africa's. Meanwhile, the voice of the Africa lobby carries less and less weight.

Africa now beckons neither high-flying diplomat nor thrusting businessman.

Pretoria and perhaps Lagos rate highly. But the biggest career lure comes from Asia, Europe, and the US. Businessmen note that Africa's share of world trade has fallen in the past 30 years from 3 per cent to 2.5 per cent. They say that investing in south Asia costs roughly half as much as investing in Africa, and produces many times the return.

Africa, almost as impoverished today as it was 30 years ago, but now burdened by a $135 billion external debt that equals the continent's GNP, will probably get poorer.

More will feel the pain as the years go by. Africa's population is expected to double to about 1 billion over the next 20 years, unless fertility rates drop or AIDS wreaks the havoc that some observers fear.

Africa's marginalisation is not just its own affair. In an inter-dependent world, all places are vulnerable to each other's misfortunes.

African deforestation may contribute to global warming and plants which could provide important genetic material for crop or medical research may be lost; diseases such as AIDS know no boundaries. Muslim extremism in Africa, a potentially destabilising issue in Nigeria, could pose a new terrorist threat.

These may seem to be problems that can be addressed in the fullness of time.

But the 'multi-party' signals from Africa should be treated with caution: the continent may not be waving, but drowning, with more than Liberia soon to go under.

Step ahead, leap back

Financial Times, 2 November 1991

Africa marked the end of an era this week. The West abandoned Zaire to its fate, severing links forged in the Cold War. Almost simultaneously, neighbouring Zambia began what optimists hope will prove to be Africa's trail-blazing transition to democracy, as voters enjoyed a choice between parties for the first time in 20 years.

African leaders will be pondering their futures as they look on these two poles of the African crisis: revolution and reform.

While troops from France and Belgium prepared to pull out of Kinshasa this week, ignoring pleas from opposition leaders that they should stay, outside observers were arriving in Lusaka to scrutinise Zambia's first multi-party election in two decades.

Two authoritarian leaders, one brutal and the other benign, their careers spanning a quarter of a century, battled for political life in the face of the new realities that are forcing change on the continent.

The end of the Cold War, the collapse of Communism in the Soviet Union and eastern Europe, Africa's dismal post-independence record, and the search for economic recovery have driven electorates across Africa to the barricades and the ballot box.

African dictators such as Zaire's Mobutu can no longer shelter beneath superpower umbrellas, skilfully exploiting tensions between Moscow and Washington. They find themselves having to choose between making a last-ditch stand, deserted by their erstwhile allies, and putting their popularity to the test in multi-party elections, as demanded by their electorates and international aid donors.

The Zambian example, some diplomats believe, could give impetus to the democratisation of Africa. A stable handover from the reign of

Kenneth Kaunda to his presidential rival, Frederick Chiluba,[28] could encourage the delicate peace processes in Mozambique and Angola, where parties that have ruled since independence have been forced to concede multi-party elections.

Zambia's change of government at the ballot box could also serve as a precedent for advocates of multi-party democracy in Zimbabwe and Malawi. Even further afield, in countries such as Kenya, where President Daniel arap Moi clings to a one-party system, Zambia's example could prove salutary.

But that may be only part of the picture, and a rose-tinted view. There is another, more cautious assessment of events in Zambia. And developments there could be eclipsed by the looming anarchy in, and international indifference, towards, Zaire.

Although the Zambian elections have so far gone remarkably smoothly, African leaders pondering a similar process may justifiably suggest that the real test of Africa's new wind of change is yet to come.

The point the optimists have to answer is: how much of a structural change has really taken place, even in countries which have apparently moved towards multi-party democracy? Most African states won independence on the basis of a democratic constitution. But the various checks and balances—such as an independent judiciary, a bill of rights, and the authority of parliament or national assembly—were soon dismantled, by military coup or diktat.

There is, say the sceptics, nothing in Zambia's new constitution that can in itself prevent an authoritarian government re-emerging. Ethnic and regional rivalries will return, they warn, to provide the rationale for a one-party state once more.

Optimists and sceptics agree, however, that Africa's fragile democratic process needs a healthy environment in which to take root. It is here that anxiety about Zaire and the West's role may overshadow the cautious optimism that has greeted developments in Zambia.

Zaire's seemingly inevitable slide into chaos threatens destabilisation at the heart of Africa. Conceivably this could have been avoided if Washington, helped by its allies, had convened a peace conference, as the US did for Ethiopia earlier this year.

It is difficult to imagine, for example, a flourishing Zambian copperbelt—source of over 90 per cent of the country's export earnings—if there is a repeat of past secessionist insurrections in Zaire's Shaba

---

[28] Frederick Chiluba (1943–2011) was Zambia's second president from 1991 to 2002.

province just across the border. Similarly Uganda's search for recovery will grow more intractable if Zaire's neighbouring eastern province becomes ungovernable.

Nine African states are contiguous with Zaire and exposed to its malaise.

What most worries African diplomats is the sense of a power vacuum on the continent. 'Of course the end of the Cold War brings us benefits,' says one.

'But it is also contributing to our marginalisation in world affairs. Instead of superpower rivalry, we could have superpower indifference.'

Adds a west African observer: 'We've got disintegrating states such as Liberia, Somalia, Sudan and now Zaire, and the superpowers seem hardly to care. The United Nations stands aside, and the Organisation of African Unity doesn't have the resources.' Thus it may well be that Zaire's decline into ungovernability—'Liberia writ large,' as one African diplomat puts it—will in the months ahead outweigh the good news from Lusaka. If so, the decision by the US, France and Belgium to jettison President Mobutu while making little if any attempt to fill the resulting power vacuum may prove a tragic landmark for Africa.

In many ways Mr. Mobutu is a creature of the West who thrived during the Cold War. Post-colonial military intervention began soon after Zaire's independence from Belgium in 1960, when an army mutiny prompted Brussels to send soldiers to protect and evacuate Belgian nationals. UN troops followed, after a provincial rebellion against central government. In the further turbulence that followed, foreign troops and US arms were vital in defeating other rebellions, notably in mineral-rich Katanga, now Shaba.

When President Mobutu took over in 1965 he did so with the covert backing of the US Central Intelligence Agency, which considered him a force for regional stability and a bulwark against Communism.

For the next 26 years, Mr. Mobutu skilfully played on western concerns about the communist threat to Africa, seen then as a vital source of strategic minerals. The takeover of Angola by the overtly Marxist MPLA movement in 1975, with the assistance of Cuban troops and Soviet arms, increased Mr. Mobutu's importance in the eyes of the West.

In the late 1970s and early 1980s Washington increased its assistance to President Mobutu in return for being allowed to build an airbase to supply arms secretly to UNITA rebels in Angola. Since 1962, the US has given Zaire $960 million in aid.

Western assistance to Mr. Mobutu has taken other forms. Throughout the 1980s, Washington and Paris used their influence to press for debt reschedulings and assistance from the International Monetary Fund and World Bank, despite evidence of widespread corruption and Zaire's persistent failure to make promised economic reforms.

All this time Zaire was being run as Mr. Mobutu's fiefdom, enriching him and impoverishing the country's 35 million people. Only in the late 1980s did the West begin to distance itself from Mr. Mobutu, who was becoming an embarrassing relic of the Cold War.

The countries that helped Mr. Mobutu retain office are today being beseeched by Zaire's opposition parties to send troops back as peace keepers, while the politicians attempt to resolve the country's seemingly endemic crisis.

So far they have been turned down. Historians may well look back on a week in which Zambia took a modest step forward in Africa's recovery, but Zaire took a giant leap back.

A continent at stake [29]

Introduction to the *Financial Times* 'Africa Survey', September 1993

Not since the end of colonial rule, some three decades ago, has Africa been gripped by such a fundamental struggle. At stake is the fate of a continent battling for economic recovery against mounting odds.

Over the past handful of years, the old order has collapsed or is on its last legs. Apartheid has crumbled. Dictators have been overthrown, democracy has been sought and state-controlled economies have succumbed to the market.

As the world itself changed, African presidents lost the patronage of Moscow and Washington, and donors demanded 'good governance' from previously tolerated corrupt or mismanaged regimes.

From Lagos to Lusaka, the mood of the continent has altered drama-tically as Africa has entered a new era. Africans have fewer inhibitions about criticising their governments, and they speak out more confidently for human rights and against corruption.

Above all, they debate what is critical to their future: structural adjustment—as powerful in its impact as any ideology the countries of sub-Saharan Africa have adopted. Drawn up by the World Bank, endorsed by other official donors and the IMF, criticised by many non-government organisations, and often bitterly attacked within the region itself, it shapes the lives of more than 600 million Africans.

Yet some 10 years after its inception, the results are modest. As articles elsewhere in this survey suggest, the business environment in Africa has changed for the better. But in its crucial forthcoming review of adjustment in Africa, provisionally entitled *Progress, Payoffs and*

---

[29] The author's original draft, before being edited by the *Financial Times*.

Challenges, the Bank is expected to warn that progress falls short of expectations.

Implementation by governments has been weak, the obstacles formidable, the time required longer than expected, and elements of the programme flawed.

The report is guarded in its conclusions. But the insights it provides, together with the experiences of FT writers on the ground, point to a sombre conclusion: structural adjustment, while essential to Africa's recovery, is not sufficient. The African crisis is outpacing efforts to resolve it.

For millions in the region, the new era is associated with pain. Factories have been closed, food subsidies eliminated and social services cut as governments seek to live within their means. The poor are the first to suffer. 'Structural maladjustment is even more painful than adjustment,' observes Dr Kwesi Botchwey, Ghana's long-serving finance minister. He is sympathetic to their plight, but that is scant comfort.

Even in the most successful of the 30 or so countries in various stages of structural adjustment, relief is modest and the road ahead long and arduous.

At present growth rates (5 per cent for GDP, 3 per cent for population) it would take 20 years for Ghana to join the ranks of lower middle-income countries. The less successful have longer to wait: 'With today's poor policies it will be 40 years before the region returns to its per capita income of the mid 70s,' says a Bank official.

In the meantime, Africa is being left far behind by countries which have made better use of their resources and compete more vigorously for capital.

In 1965, Indonesia's GDP per capita was lower than Nigeria's; today, it is three times higher. Thailand's income per head in 1965 was lower than Ghana's; now it is one of the fastest-growing economies in the world.

Equally striking is Africa's declining share of developing-country exports of food and agricultural products. It halved between 1970 and 1990 (from 17 to 8 per cent) with Asia increasing its market share.

'Can Africa's decline be reversed?' asked the Bank in its latest important study of the continent's plight: 'The simple answer is yes. It can be and it must be. The alternative is too ghastly to contemplate.' Four years later, the region remains racked by disease, disaster and debt: the question becomes more compelling, the alternative creeps closer. The Bank's hopes, back in 1989, that African economies could grow at a rate of 4 to 5 per cent proved optimistic. Growth has been barely half that, well below the region's 3.2 per cent annual rise in population.

Today, more people in Africa are poorer and more children are dying. Other signs of stress are apparent, beginning with the distressing list of countries that have effectively ceased to function as modern nation states: Zaire, Somalia, Liberia, Sudan, Angola. Hopes raised by the end of the war in Ethiopia, the peace agreement in Mozambique, and a fragile peace pact in Liberia, are offset by renewed civil war in Angola, Nigeria's steady decline, and strife in Sierra Leone and Rwanda.

Former 'success' stories and 'role models' in the 1970s have since become cautionary tales. Kenya struggles to implement economic reforms which erode the patronage on which the ruling Kanu party has been so dependent. Cote d'Ivoire moves deeper into difficulties that cannot be addressed until the CFA franc is devalued, an obstacle that holds up effective economic reform in the 13-member CFA bloc.

The collapse of the settlement in Angola and continuing violence in South Africa raise doubts about whether, in the short term at least, southern Africa can be the engine room for regional growth.

Most disturbing of all, perhaps, is the concern that Africa no longer has the adequate institutional capacity to help itself. The technological gap between Africa and the world has widened, and the continent's management is weak. Many schools and universities are without teaching materials. Civil services have been neglected or politicised. The integrity of the judiciary has been eroded.

Meanwhile, Aids takes its terrible toll. More than half of the world's 15 million sufferers are in Africa. The virus has already killed about 1.2 million Africans.

An estimated 14 million will be infected by 2000; many will be from the skilled urban class on which the implementation of reform greatly depends.

Hopes that the emergence of multi-party politics would prove a simple stepping stone to good governance have proved premature. Opposition parties have turned out to be weak, fractious and susceptible to patronage, owing more to ethnicity than policy for their support.

For the industrialised world, the will to help may emerge only when an ailing Africa is seen as a threat to self-interest, in the form of immigration to southern Europe, a rise in Muslim extremism, growth in drug-trafficking or health risks posed by a continent that cannot be ring-fenced, or when it is stimulated by the loss of flora and fauna with medicinal value, or environmental concerns.

Self-interest or humanitarian imperative, UNICEF's poignant warning is timely: 'The abandonment of hopes for the continent would mean the writing off of the talents, aspirations and potential of one eighth of mankind, both now and far into the next century.' From Africa must come a new generation of leaders, committed to reform and tapping the same spirit that brought freedom 30 years ago. Angered by the failures of corrupt and autocratic leaders, frustrated by economic policies that did not deliver, impatient to recover their lost civil rights, and worn out by wars, Africa's people are striving for a fresh start.

Long snakes and short ladders

Unpublished, 15 March 1994

Unseen hands play Snakes and Ladders across sub-Saharan Africa. Democracy fitfully emerges in South Africa, is denied in Nigeria. Civil war revives in Angola, Zaire slides towards anarchy, a fragile peace pact holds in Mozambique.

News is as unpredictable as the throw of the dice. Snakes marked 'Drought', 'Corruption' or 'Civil War' writhe across the board; ladders appear as 'Debt Rescheduled' or 'World Bank Loan'. Short ladders, long snakes … and loaded dice.

As the latest World Bank Sub-Saharan Africa report published at the weekend makes clear, the destination labelled 'Recovery' remains out of reach. A decade of structural adjustment, and net aid flows of $170 billion (£113 billion), have stemmed the region's decline but not launched a revival.

'Current growth rates among the *best* [emphasis added] African performers are still too low to reduce poverty much in the next two or three decades,' warns the Bank.

Whoever is to blame, the policy at the heart of relations between Africa and the West is failing. 'Good governance', the concept which links aid to Africa with economic reform, human rights and democracy, has not got to the heart of the continent's predicament.

Admirable in principle, complex in practice, today the policy appears confused. Increasingly the West is placing responsibility for Africa on the World Bank, but providing neither adequate mandate nor clear guidance.

Once enslaved, later colonised, and marginalised in the 1980s, the continent faces a continuing crisis in the 1990s—but with a new dimension. Africa is not only in danger of losing the battle, the world is losing interest. The countries that led the scramble for Africa's resources some 100 years ago are now disengaging.

'If only the West cared enough to want to recolonise us,' an African diplomat ruefully observes. 'But we're hardly an attractive proposition.' At one level, the West continues to respond positively. Sub-Saharan Africa's share of global aid is up to 38 per cent in 1991 from 17 per cent in 1970.

But the critical link between economic and political reform is being neglected, and aid is ineffective.

Under the auspices of the World Bank's economic recovery programme, Africa's governments were expected to cut budget deficits, curb inflation and monetary growth, introduce competitive exchange rates, reform tariffs and revive agriculture. The good news, says Mr. Kim Jaycox, the Bank's vice-president for Africa, is that the formula works: 'The six countries that improved their policies the most (over the period 1987–91) saw their GDP growth per capita jump about two percentage points per annum between 1981–86 and 1987–91.' The bad news is that this is not nearly enough. The Bank's claim in a 1989 report that African economies could grow at a rate of 4–5 per cent has proved optimistic. Growth has been barely half that, well below the region's 3.2 per cent annual rise in population.

Part of the reason for Africa's failure is made clear in the report.

Implementation of the World Bank structural adjustment reforms has been poor, political will lacking, and management resources scarce.

But essential to the success of economic reforms, donors have argued, is a matching programme of political reform. Transparency, accountability and democracy are vital to sustain development, they maintain. The World Bank report agrees, but it does not address how it can be achieved in practice, or assess the part political problems have played in Africa's failure to reach economic targets.

The only reference is to 'a strong social consensus on the need to improve governance'. Corruption is not mentioned, nor military spending, nor is there any discussion of a central issue: how to reward reformers, punish laggards.

Yet the experience of Bank representatives across Africa is that this is precisely the area which needs attention.

'Structural adjustment means reducing state patronage,' explains a Bank official in west Africa. 'Reducing patronage undermines the ruling party.

'Unless the president is prepared to risk political suicide, there is not enough I can do to force him down a path of reform, whether it's the big stick or the big carrot.' The reason for the report's reticence on 'good governance' issues is hard to find. The Bank, officials privately point out, is constrained by a mandate which precludes it from a political role and its mandate is determined by the directors—'none of whom wants to rock the boat'.

The board's third-world appointees tend to reflect the views of their leaders, who would be the last to support tougher measures, say their domestic critics. Developed country directors may be reluctant to jeopardise commercial or security interests.

But the misgivings of directors representing the biggest donors about applying tougher pressure on reluctant African reformers stem from a further, more understandable concern: the generally poor performance of Africa's opposition parties.

After the high hopes of the 'new wind of change', the wave of democratisation that swept through Africa in the late 1980s, opposition parties have turned out to have most of the weaknesses of the regimes they oppose: ethnically based, few carefully worked out policy alternatives and likely to be as corrupt if ever they won office.

'Who can blame us for our reluctance to follow through a policy that could destabilise Nigeria, with its 80 million people and huge problems, and where the opposition seems as incompetent as the army?' asks an irritated European diplomat.

The report leaves further questions unanswered. If democracy is essential to sustained growth—the assumption that underpins the concept of good governance—how can the position of Ghana, under military government until 1992 but the leading reformer, be explained? As long ago as 1981 the Bank called for 'a new kind of social compact, an agreement within the world community that the struggle against poverty in Africa is a joint concern which entails responsibilities for both parties'.

World Bank officials and aid workers argue that Africa's need for such a compact is overwhelming. But until the West renews its interest in Africa, resolves the anomalies in its policies, and gives the Bank and other donors a clearer mandate, the compact will remain a pipe dream.

Who, me? A racist?
Financial Times, 21 January 1995

I am starting to miss apartheid. I can no longer get a room at the Mount Nelson, or a compartment on the Blue Train. Flights are full, and my dream of a cottage at Hermanus is receding as rapidly as prices are rising.

I stood in the immigration queue at Jan Smuts airport, cross and exhausted after a ten-hour flight, and reflected on these tribulations. But at the heart of my discontent was something more profound.

I was missing the tension of a township funeral. I recalled the electric atmosphere at the Johannesburg Market Theatre during the brutal decade of the 1980s. Just being part of the audience, watching a Barney Simon production about contemporary South Africa, seemed to be a political statement. But it was more than this. I missed the stress that bonded the friendships forged by adversity.

As I stood, the queue hardly moving, I realised that Nelson Mandela's inauguration marked the day they shot my fox. Apartheid was the issue which allowed moral certainty, the glorious conviction that right and wrong was black and white. These are now grey days in South Africa, thank goodness. The euphoria of the election has faded, and those certainties, those moral absolutes are harder to define.

In their place are admirable plans to build a million houses a year, or bring electricity to the townships. But 'Forward with the Reconstruction and Development Plan' does not have the same ring as 'Free Nelson Mandela'.

When apartheid was swept away, we journalists made the best of the good news. We exchanged anecdotes at the Ritz, the northern suburbs restaurant that served as an informal press club, its entrance guarded by a man with an Uzi (although his colleague preferred a sawn-off shotgun). To the secret regret of some of us, it was the closest we got to violence.

Nelson Mandela's inauguration was marked with a celebratory dinner and a poem written in honour of the occasion:

> O what joy to be a hack,
> As power shifts from White to Black!
> O what bliss to be alive,
> When a British pound can buy rands five.

So I miss apartheid. Perhaps the immigration officer detected my malaise, as I stood in the queue at Jan Smuts. The queue was black, for most of the passengers had come off a flight from Angola. Only two desks were open at the immigration counter. A third was marked 'SA passport holders only'.

A white immigration officer stands, arms folded, in the hall, surveying the scene. I catch his eye, and thus a conversation begins. It is conducted in the sign language of *mzungus* in Africa, expressing their frustrations and impatience. Gone are the days when such irritations could be expressed aloud.

But through the silent changes of expressions, a lifted eyebrow here, a fleeting grimace there, a twitch of the shoulders, an upward glance to the heavens, we exchange views. I catch his eye. 'See?' his expression is saying. 'This is what happens. Let one in, and then they all want to come.'

I gave a discreet 'Bit of a nuisance, this' gaze at the heavens.

His lips pursed a fraction. 'We've got to live with this. ... Alright for you, you are just a visitor.'

But colour bonding was having its effect. A split-second tilt of his chin in the direction of the South Africa passport holders' desk spoke volumes. 'Join the other queue,' the gesture said, 'it will be quicker.'

I dislike racists and queue jumpers with equal passion, but ten hours in economy class, sandwiched between fellow passengers with whom I had lost the battle of the arm rests, drained my patience and undermined my principles.

But I needed reassurance. I made a quick side to side glance as if to say 'Who, me?'

He maintained eye contact. 'Get a move on, before someone sees us.' I had hesitated too long. A terrible suspicion was growing in his mind. But for both of us, it was too late to turn back. I had picked up my bag, avoiding eye contact with the patient travellers in front of me. My fractional hesitation, however, tells him volumes.

Twenty yards now divides us, as I move to the shorter, adjoining queue, but his upper lip has a momentary sneer. I look away.

'Aagh you liberals.' I almost hear a contemptuous rolling of the Rs, the more pronounced for having unwittingly assisted someone whom he thought might be sympathetic.

'Aagh you liberals. Full of talk.'

Robert Mugabe's legacy[30]
Reserve obituary, unpublished, 1995

It is all too easy to dismiss Robert Mugabe as a ruthless despot who held Zimbabwe in his thrall for more than three decades. Or to portray him as a caricature of a dictator, complete with toothbrush moustache, and inviting derision.

While responsibility for the tragedy that enveloped Zimbabwe rests on his shoulders, history suggests that Britain, the colonial power, should take some of the blame; and that white Rhodesians, now scattered around the globe and reminiscing about 'the best years' of their lives, might consider a grim possibility: that the man they loathed and feared as a 'Communist terrorist' was a creation of their racist policies. And one does not have to believe in conspiracy theories to wonder whether three critical decisions in which Whitehall played a central part, and which helped equip the Whites for war, were the product of calculation rather than coincidence.

Make no mistake. Robert Gabriel Mugabe was a very nasty piece of work. He subjugated the southern province of Matabeleland, slaughtering thousands of civilians in the process; he condoned the use of torture by the police and the secret service; he intimidated political opponents and systematically abused human rights; he evicted white farmers from their land, allowing invading mobs to go unchallenged; and for three decades presided over the pauperisation of the state and its 14 million citizens, at least a million of whom fled to the comparative safety of South Africa.

---

30 In common with many newspaper obituaries, this obituary was written in advance of its subject's death.

Yet the same man began his 37 years in office with a speech as magnanimous as it was pragmatic. He brought Whites into his cabinet; he retained Ian Smith's intelligence chief, sought the advice of Lord Soames, Britain's departing governor, and enjoyed chats with Margaret Thatcher during his visits to London.

It is not enough, then, to dismiss the man as no more than a ruthless dictator. Was he not also a product of the empire, moulded and shaped by his reaction to colonial rule? And should he not be seen as as much a victim of the racist values of the era as the perpetrator of the abuses with which he is associated today? What, in short, made Robert Mugabe tick?

Part of the answer lies in the weakness of the structures he inherited on becoming prime minister in 1980 and almost immediately began to exploit: a state-owned press and media that for years had served the interest of the white minority; a judiciary that compromised and abandoned its integrity when it treated as lawful Ian Smith's illegal declaration of independence; a trade union movement that had been battered by decades of anti-union legislation; and a church that lost its moral compass—with the honourable exception of the Roman Catholics.

Without these checks and balances, social as well as constitutional, and inheriting the structure of a one-party state from his predecessor, Robert Mugabe had a free hand.

Furthermore, unlike Nelson Mandela, who was constrained by a vigorous media, a powerful trade union movement, influential academics and inspirational church leaders and by the democratic values and structure of a party nearly 100 years old, Mugabe led a young organisation. It was authoritarian, wracked by ethnic divisions and ill equipped to stand up to the destabilising tactics of Pretoria which defended apartheid by waging wars in its neighbours' territory.

Robert Mugabe needed all the help he could get. Not only did he face a threat from South Africa, he was up against a formidable legacy, three developments that dated back to the 1950s and 1960s, and which helped buttress white minority rule.

WHEN ROBERT MUGABE was studying for the seven degrees he was eventually awarded—I like to think that the process got under way when he was briefly detained at Gwelo jail—he could hardly have failed to register the significance of these events, all of which would play a crucial role in the outcome of the guerrilla war that was to lead to the liberation of Zimbabwe: the location of one of the world's largest hydro-electric power stations, completed in 1959; the breakup of the Central African Federation and the distribution of its assets among the three member countries—Southern and Northern Rhodesia and Nyasaland—in 1963; and the British government's effective veto of newly independent Zambia's request for World Bank funding for a route to Dar es Salaam.

At the break-up in 1963 it was Britain that approved the allocation of the bulk of the federal armed forces to white-ruled Rhodesia. This gave the regime of Ian Smith the muscle to make a unilateral declaration of independence two years later in 1965, and to wage war against black nationalist guerrillas.

It was Britain that effectively vetoed landlocked Zambia's request in the early 1960s for World Bank funds to build a railway that would link it to the east African port of Dar es Salaam. The decision forced continued dependence on trade routes through apartheid South Africa—and rebel Rhodesia.

Responsibility for the most contentious of the three—Kariba—is not clear-cut, but as Britain was the colonial power at the time, and much of the money for the project was raised in London, Whitehall must have been heavily involved.

Two factors provoked concern about underlying political motives: the location of the plant was switched from a site on Zambia's Kafue river to the Kariba gorge on the Zambesi river, and the operations room was located on the Rhodesian side. It meant that a hostile white Rhodesia controlled the supply of power to the copper mines of the newly independent Zambia.

Mugabe has further reason for resentment. He argues that Britain reneged on the spirit, if not the letter, of a provision in the Lancaster House settlement intended to tackle the worst feature in the legacy of white rule: half the land was owned by Whites. The UK contributed (in real terms) to the buyout of 5,000 white farmers in Zimbabwe, just over half the amount it had provided for a similar exercise in Kenya in the early 1960s—although its former East African colony had barely a thousand white farmers. No one suggests that Robert Mugabe does not shoulder the bulk of the blame for today's tragedy. Nelson Mandela has shown how leadership can transform a country. But any judgment of Mugabe's performance would be incomplete if it failed to acknowledge colonialism's role in his making.

Apartheid and the power of rugby
Michael Holman and Mark Suzman
Financial Times, 20 May 1995

In the shadow of Table Mountain, in the Cape that cradled apartheid, one of the biggest sporting events in the world is about to start. It will include an image as potent and poignant as sport has provided since Jesse Owens won four gold medals at Hitler's Berlin Olympics in 1936.

Just as, almost 60 years ago, the black American sprinter shattered the myth of Aryan invincibility and conveyed a message that transcended sport, so the scene is set for a similarly momentous occasion at Cape Town's Newlands stadium on Thursday. In the presence of Nelson Mandela, South Africa's president, and in the green-and-gold colours of the Springbok team, Francois Pienaar, a descendant of the Afrikaners who journeyed into the African hinterland, will lead his team mates onto the turf of Newlands Stadium.

These children of apartheid, born in the dour 1970s, at school during the revolution that was the 1980s, and for whom the world opened up in the 1990s, will take part in an event which would have been unthinkable a few years ago.

They will join in the singing of the hymn of southern Africa's liberation movement, *Nkosi Sikelel' iAfrika* (God bless Africa). Then, accompanied by Mandela, the man their fathers imprisoned, the moving words of South Africa's original anthem, *Die Stem*, will carry from Newlands stadium across the land, to the frontier towns of the northern Transvaal, the dorps of the Orange Free State and into the hearts of the white tribe of Africa.

In an atmosphere charged with as much *hwyl* as a crowd in full voice at Cardiff Arms Park, and with all the defiance and challenge of the New Zealand *haka*, the Springboks will take to the field in the opening game against Australia, marking the beginning of the four-week-long competition for the mantle of rugby union world champions.

Sixteen national sides, from countries as diverse in their cultures as Western Samoa and Japan and Argentina and the Ivory Coast, take part in a contest which has grown rapidly since its inception eight years ago. It may well be for the last time in this form, for media tycoon Rupert Murdoch's plans for the game could well transform it, sweeping away the difference between amateur and professional players.

But before sponsors tally their exposure and publicity, and before the world discovers just how much 'amateurs' earn, and before 35,000 visiting fans discover whether South Africa's hotels and aeroplanes can take the strain, the world might pause for a few moments and marvel. Not simply at South Africa's continuing and remarkable peaceful revolution that is transforming a country, but to consider how extraordinary it is that the sport that the architects of apartheid embraced with the passion they brought to religion and politics could became a force for change.

The same passion became part of their Achilles heel. The world was to discover that cutting off Afrikaners from their rugby, and white South Africans in general from most international sporting contacts, was almost as important as economic sanctions in the battle against apartheid. For Afrikaners above all, being granted the opportunity to host the event signals their return to the outside world, and the formal embrace of a game they love and which for so long excluded them. But nowhere did this game, created by the English—a race for whom Afrikaners have mixed feelings—take hold with greater fervour and passion than in South Africa, and in particular among Afrikaners.

Their roots go back 350 years, and it all began not far from the site of the stadium where the opening match will be played. It was here in the Cape that old South Africa was born when Jan van Riebeeck established a settlement.

'The fairest Cape in all the world' could be also called the cradle of apartheid. It was the fertile land, glorious beaches, imposing mountains, that sheltered and nourished the first white settlers. In time they were to become known as Boers, who developed the language that gave them the name Afrikaners.

Chafing under the British, in 1836 they began the Great Trek that led to two great wars of liberation: the Boer War, and the war for democracy, which they lost. It was in 1948 that the National Party won power, which they only relinquished more than 40 years later, in the meantime imposing the cruel social engineering known as apartheid.

If the Dutch Reformed Church was seen as the National Party at prayer, the Springbok scrum was its cabinet in conclave: heaving solidarity in battle against the 'kaffirs' and a hostile world. War was diplomacy for apartheid South Africa, as it tried to hammer its neighbours into submission, and rugby was diplomacy by other means.

It was during this period that *Nkosi Sikelel' iAfrika* became the anthem of black liberation, funerals and political rallies—so often the same thing during black southern Africa's struggle to overthrow white rule. Hundreds of thousands, indeed millions, died on the battlefields of Angola, Mozambique, Zimbabwe, Namibia and townships, from bullets or war-induced famine and disease.

It is a long way from the darkest days of the sport, when in 1961, Hendrik Verwoerd, the father of apartheid, banned Maoris from the visiting New Zealand team. Indeed, to international rugby's shame, during the heyday of apartheid in the 1960s and 1970s, the Springboks happily toured the world and accepted visiting teams, albeit not without raising widespread disapproval and dismay.

For many New Zealanders, South Africa's notorious 1981 tour remains an unhealed wound that tore apart families and split the cabinet, resulting in one of that country's most painful political traumas since the Second World War. And when the International Rugby Board finally caved in and extended the sports boycott to South African rugby in the mid-1980s (25 years after the country had been expelled from the Olympics and 15 years since the same had happened in cricket and tennis) it was regarded by white South Africa as the last straw.

For many Whites, it was the most painful of all international sanctions and it was followed shortly after by the sustained black unrest of the mid-1980s and international disinvestment. The rugby ban was a potent and poignant symbol of the country's global isolation under apartheid. Ironically, however, this resulted in rugby authorities contributing, almost inadvertently, to the beginning of national reconciliation between White and Black in South Africa. One of the first Afrikaner visitors to the African National Congress headquarters, in Lusaka, Zambia, was none other than Dr. Danie Craven, the long-time doyen of South African rugby, to plead for a relaxation of the boycott.

The ANC, which swept to power in last year's elections, refused. But a line of dialogue was opened that would, a decade later, culminate in the joining of F.W. de Klerk, South Africa's former president, and Nelson Mandela in a government of national unity. And while the team may be all white (through an injury to one of the Springbok's most exciting players, the charismatic wing, Chester Williams), for most of the 15 players on the pitch, and the supporters, the pleasure of being part of a new South Africa, while tinged with regret for a past in which they were undisputed masters of the land, is genuine.

Rugby may have been slow to change, and even today some of the sport's extensive development schemes to try and wean soccer-loving black youths to the oval ball have an air of reluctance. Yet the undeniable underlying fact is that change, as in every area of South Africa, is irrevocably under way.

Fifty years from now, there will still probably be a few unreconstructed Afrikaners sadly waving the old orange, white and blue South African flag from the grandstand, in much the same way that white southerners in the US have retained the stars and bars as a symbol of past power. But, with luck and patience, the next time South Africa hosts the world cup, both the team on the field and the supporters packing the seats will be a closer reflection of South Africa's demographic reality. And this week, even if black South Africa then ignores the rest of the tournament, for a few moments at least, as the strains of the two hymns of South Africa fill the packed stadium, sport will transcend itself as the Springboks sing the two anthems.

That rousing hymn of African nationalism *Nkosi Sikelel' iAfrika: Nkosi sikelel' iAfrika, Maluphakanyisw' uphondo lwayo, Yiva imithandazo yethu, Nkosi sikelela, Thina lusapho lwayo. Yihla Moya, Yihla Moya, Yihla Moya oyingcwele.*[31] And the stirring sentiments of *Die Stem: Ons sal antwoord op jou roepstem, ons sal offer wat jy vra. Ons sal lewe, ons sal sterwe—ons vir jou, Suid-Afrika.*[32]

Boer and Bantu, Afrikaner and African, shoulder to shoulder and in full voice: *Jislaaik*, as they say in southern Africa, it will be a helluva game, man. Hendrik Verwoerd will be turning in his grave.

---

[31] 'God bless Africa, let its banner (or spirit) be raised, hear our prayers and bless us, your family. Descend, O Spirit, descend, O Spirit, descend, O Holy Spirit.'

[32] Literally: 'We will answer your call, we will sacrifice what you ask. We will live, we will die—we for you, South Africa' but sung as 'At thy call we shall not falter, firm and steadfast we shall stand. At thy will to live or perish, O South Africa, dear land.'

Patensie, Eastern Cape

Sunday Independent, Johannesburg, June 1995

Grumbling good naturedly, Espie Ferreira, Afrikaner, farmer and president of Patensie rugby club, sets off for the township in search of the first team's missing black player.

A couple standing outside the *shebeen* blink in the powerful head-lamps of Espie's Mercedes as it noses its way down the rutted dirt track. Drifting up from the valley below, carried on the chill night air, come the sounds of boot on leather, and the grunts from players.

Patensie is preparing for Saturday's big game against the Port Elizabeth Harlequins, the league's top team. But Manie Nelson is missing, and Espie is determined that practice should not go ahead without him.

I join him as he drives from the field, up the hill and into the township, an Afrikaner patriarch in search of a protégé. And as we drive, Espie talks of how rugby has become a force for change and tolerance in a small town in the heart of conservative, Afrikaans-speaking South Africa.

It was after Nelson Mandela's release in 1990, but two years before the election that brought him to power, that Espie Ferreira warned his members that what was once unthinkable had become an imperative.

As South Africa embarked on its political revolution, Patensie had to undergo its own traumatic changes. The town's all-white rugby XV had not only to play in black townships but to open its ranks to black players, a delicate process that was charted in a moving BBC television documentary last year.

Stand on the terrace of Espie's home high above the valley and the symbols of Afrikaner power and the white tribe's way of life seem as potent as ever. Immediately below the house is the whitewashed police station, under a clump of blue gum trees.

Behind a desk in a room that is more like a parlour sits Marius de Klerk, Patensie police chief and rugby club secretary, with the build of a prop and the eyes of the big city detective he once was.

Beyond the police station, halfway up one flank of the valley, stands the Dutch Reformed Church, its spire like a solitary goalpost.

Just up the tarred road that runs below Espie's house is the Tolbos farm produce store, where farmers' wives sell traditional Boer delicacies: *koeksisters*: syrup-soaked plaits of deep fried dough, fruit preserves called *konfyt*, *biltong* and rusks, *melktert* and mango chutney. Beyond the Tolbos is the tiny commercial centre, with the Volkskas bank, the garage and the Ripple Valley Hotel with red polished *stoep* (veranda).

And in between all these landmarks lie neat citrus orchards, 400 acres of which are farmed by Espie and his three sons. Speckled with ripening oranges, the trees stretch as far as the eye can see, into the foothills of the mountains that cradle the fertile valley.

But the most evocative sight of all, nestling in the bend of the Gamtoos river which winds through the valley, is the rugby field.

For generations, Patensie's social life revolved around its rugby club, with its modest pavilion and modern club house. So strong a hold has the sport exercised that in the past it has been able to field four teams from a white town and farming community of a couple of thousand families. Here in the eastern Cape, however, rugby is not a white preserve.

The history of black and coloured (mixed) enthusiasm for what is seen as the national sport of the Afrikaner goes back more than a hundred years, born on the playing fields of mission schools when the Cape was a British colony.

In Patensie this tradition survives in the form of the United Barbarians Rugby Football Club. But this poor relation is out of sight in Patensie township, opposite the church but concealed behind the brow of the valley, home to the coloured citizens of the town.

And home to Manie Nelson, who looms out of the night when he spots the Mercedes' searching beam, greets Espie in Akrikaans and climbs into the car.

We drop Manie at the club and Espie takes me home for dinner with his wife Hilda. Over rusks and coffee, rugby and politics become intertwined, and it is late in the evening when I risk teasing my host: 'So you're a *Kaffir boetie*.'

Kaffir-lover. An epithet reserved for those who would betray the *volk*, deny their heritage, and expose their womenfolk to unspeakable acts by *swart mans*—black men.

For a split second I thought Espie might have taken offence. But he chuckled and repeated the phrase, rolling it around his palate, implicitly correcting my English-speaker's pronunciation. 'I'm a United Party supporter,' he said; 'I always have been and always will be.'

It was the party of Jan Smuts, defeated in the 1948 election by D.F. Malan, the first National Party prime minister, whom Espie holds in contempt. 'A stupid man, he started all the nonsense.' Espie's anger at what apartheid has done to South Africa comes to the surface and the mood in the kitchen changes.

We return to rugby and talk about the days he played for Eastern Province, in the 1950s, sporting credentials that I suspect compensated for his *verligte* (enlightened) stance.

Rugby memorabilia line the walls of Espie's den and it is here that I talk to Manie the next day. Fluent in Afrikaans, he is less articulate in English, but enough to convey the pain of the insults at the hands of some white players when he first joined the club some 18 months ago.

'They called me a *Kaffir*,' says Manie, but I suspect the term was embellished. What did he call them in return? I ask. Only when I press him does Manie tell me.

'*Boertjies*', he says, not looking me in the eye, as if embarrassed by an obscenity. 'Little farmers.' It doesn't seem very offensive to me, but Manie assures me otherwise: 'It made them very cross,' he says and giggles. The insults stopped, however, after Espie and Marius intervened, and effectively expelled the three worst offenders.

Manie relishes the higher grade of rugby and the friendships now established but hints at his hurt at teammates' failure to invite him to join in excursions after away games.

As I spend more time in Patensie, it becomes clear that the club has to appeal to young men like Manie if it is to flourish. Turnout at practices is not what it was. Television and the city lights lure the youngsters. And many of the white supporters have been deterred, it seems, by the changed atmosphere at hometown games. They complain that black supporters are raucous, rude or undisciplined, and that the stand is no longer a place to take wives and girlfriends and children.

It is all part of Patensie's transition. For the sons who have followed in their fathers' farming footsteps, change is especially difficult and delicate. One young farmer recounts a familiar tale of how he and the sons of labourers grew up as playmates, exploring and hunting together. Then by the early teens came the parting of the ways. Apartheid determined that the relationship as adults should be master and servant. Learning to come to terms with the farm workers as political equals is an awkward, slow process.

Later that morning we drive back to the coloured township to meet Johannes du Plooy, the president of United Barbarians and a teacher at the coloured township's primary school.

Espie says he has offered to share the committee posts equally with Barbarians. But Johannes, who is also chairman of the township branch of Nelson Mandela's African National Congress (ANC), does not seem reassured. 'Our members' voices will not be heard,' he says.

Amalgamation seems an intractable problem and we depart—but not before Espie and Johannes have made arrangements for the collection of keys to the Patensie club facilities. The Barbarians' own field, recently ploughed and reseeded, is still not fit to play on.

Driving back, Espie shakes his head in frustration. 'I know Johannes well,' he says. 'His father worked on the farm.' Later Espie tells me how he made his home available to Johannes for his wedding reception.

On Saturday morning we set out on the 90-minute drive to Port Elizabeth. At Adcock stadium, the Harlequins' ground, spectators chant and cheer to a background of booming loudspeakers as the home team, nearly all Coloureds, knock the stuffing out of the visiting farmers, all of whom but Manie are white.

Halfway through the game, their attention is diverted. The crowd rises to applaud as four white men in green-and-gold blazers take their seats in the stand. It's Morne du Plessis, former Springbok captain, and three players from the South African world cup squad.

The game over, we leave for the Rugby World Cup game between South Africa and Canada that's being played in the city that night, but my thoughts keep turning back to the conversation with Johannes du Plooy. The day before, while driving around Patensie, I had told Marius de Klerk and Espie the story of a politician who was puzzled by an opponent's bitter attack on him in parliament.

'Why does he dislike me so much,' the puzzled politician asked his aide: 'I've never done him any favours.'

Marius gave a throaty chuckle. Espie was silent, seemingly lost in thought.

Welcome to the Hotel Milimani

Unpublished, c. 1995

It sits hunched on a hill, in slow, idiosyncratic decline, a 1960s concrete block, brooding and scarred like a retired boxer, remembering old glories and lost in the past.

Welcome to the Hotel Milimani, my Kenyan home from home. With each successive stay, I have got to know the Milimani better, adapting to its ways, and learning how to tolerate its eccentricities. I have learnt how to jiggle the key to get into my room. I have mastered the manipulation of the handle required to flush the toilet. I have come to terms with the mysteries of the hot water system. I now hardly notice the stains on the green-grey carpet and no longer speculate about their origins. And when my bed collapsed in the early hours of the morning, I soon got back to sleep.

True, I have not tracked down the source of a curious smell from one of the cupboards, and some late-night noises have been alarming. I have yet to discover whether those wires that trail by my door are live or how the television works.

Nevertheless, I feel at home in Room 339. It has not always been thus. First I had to overcome my fear of the room's carpets and cope with a journey that once made me squeamish.

Bed to bathroom is but a few early-morning barefoot steps but it was not just the variety of stains on the threadbare carpet that deterred me. It was its ingredients, trodden in by many guests over many years: a mulch of skin flakes and toenail cuttings, gravy from countless takeaways and cigarette ash, crumbs and crisps—a veritable compost in which exotic varieties of athlete's foot and other fungi surely flourish.

At first I took the coward's way out. Rather than expose my naked feet to these horrors, I travelled over the uncarpeted parts of the floor: from bed corner to stool, stool to desktop, and a final leap to bathroom threshold, using my strategically placed socks, positioned the night before as a stepping stone.

These days, however, I tread that carpet boldly, having been brought to my senses by a nasty fall 'tween stool and desk, while my soles are protected by a daily application of tea tree cream, which I hope will keep verrucas at bay.

It is just as well that I have overcome my fear. This is where I am trying to finish the sequel to my first novel, *Last Orders at Harrods*. Just off State House Road, the Milimani is ideal for me: close to the heart of Kenya's capital and within reach of Kibera, east Africa's biggest slum, where both novels are set.

And it's cheap: £15 a night at the once up-market hotel that now caters for a different clientele.

There are the occasional backpackers from Europe but most of the guests are Kenyan or Somali business travellers; some come with families and rent long-stay apartments. The sound of their children frolicking in the hotel's outdoor swimming pool carries up to my third-floor balcony and in the early morning I usually spot a hawk, circling the garden, eyeing up the skinny cats that prowl the grounds.

Bathed and shaved, I begin the day, and take the ancient, creaking lift, buttons rubbed smooth by generations of fingers. Only long-term residents like me prod the panel with confidence. One morning the fellow occupant is an untutored overnighter and despite repeated button pushing, the lift doesn't move.

I intervene with a self-deprecating cough and with the nonchalant air of a Milimani veteran and confident forefinger, I press an anonymous button. The lift wearily descends. I wave my hands to demonstrate that he had been pushing the Door Open button.

'A mistake easily made,' I say magnanimously, but he does not respond, startled by the thump as the lift hits the ground floor.

It is here, in the lobby, with a fading colour photo of tourists at the coast (it's a good 40 years old to judge by their demure swimming costumes), that my status as a resident is acknowledged. I look into a reasonably-sized broom cupboard and greet Tony, the shop's proprietor, sitting under his brave red-lettered slogan: 'Everything You Need We Have'.

And from a shelf above the toothpaste and the shampoo, chocolate and condoms, biscuits and batteries, sodas and mineral water, he pulls out the daily papers which he has reserved for me. I hand over my 70/- (UK 50 pence) and sneak past the dining room. I am not prepared to discuss yet again with the reproachful chief waiter why I avoid the hotel breakfast, and slip through the back gate on my way to an internet café down the road.

En route, twenty pence buy me a cob of sweet tender maize, roasted over a charcoal brazier, but I resist the appeals of the shoe cleaner and the curio sellers, and at my destination read the papers over a cup of hot chocolate and a honey pancake.

Back at the Milimani, my working day begins. I slide open the balcony door, and the sun and the sounds of the city pour in. On Sundays the local church is always in fine voice. Its hymns drift through the morning air, up to my desk. Inspired, I start to type.

'Africa sings like the rest of the world breathes.'

A hotel at the peak of its decline

Financial Times, 14 October 1995

It is a hotel at the peak of its decline, but I will not tell you where it is. I want to keep it to myself. The billiard room smells musty and the cues are neatly stacked and the last person using the table must turn out the lights. The residents' lounge has deep chintz-covered armchairs and Dornford Yates on the shelves of the glass-fronted bookcase. 'Key obtainable from reception,' but the key has long gone missing.

You were expected to write your name and room number in the note-book, with a pencil attached by a piece of string. But things have got slack and no one bothers any more. Or perhaps no one reads Dornford Yates any more.

The French doors of my room open onto the lawn and I sit on the steps and write these notes. Africa begins beyond the encircling flower bed and then stretches for miles until you reach Mount Kenya, and on a clear day you can see snow on its peak. When it rains, I smell the earth, tangy, acrid and smoky, and if I stand downwind I can smell the rain coming.

It is a hotel where you wake to the clink of thick crockery rattling on the trays carrying early morning tea, with the sugar in bowls and not in sealed paper packets, and a jug of hot water comes with a pot of strong tea.

You know that if you doze off, there is no danger of missing breakfast (served between 7 am and 8.30 am, except on Sundays, when it is from 7.30 am to 9 am) for you will wake again when the verandas get their daily red-wax polish.

The dining room floor creaks, wooden beams cross the ceiling and the food is British colonial. The menu for each table is typed on the receptionist's Remington, which also taps out the bill at the end of your stay.

A faded map in the lobby shows the walks you can take but I have never gone beyond the garden, acres of lawn and shrubs and flower beds, with benches beneath trees. I always mean to take the river walk but I haven't got round to it, just as I have yet to play the adjoining golf course. Nor for that matter have I used the squash court, just across from my room. I have never seen anyone on it but it is nice to know that it is there if you want it.

The breakfast menu has 'Good Morning' without an exclamation mark and there is no sign saying 'Please wait to be shown to your table.'

The waiters are not servants but retainers, in bow tie and black jackets and starched white shirts, and they expect you to be at your supper table between 7.30 pm and 8 pm. They want to serve you coffee by 9.30 pm because they like to leave for the village by 10 pm.

The ceilings in my room are high and geckos come out in the evening. I lie beneath a mosquito net and watch the flames from the fireplace flicker on the ceiling, and when I awake the embers still glow. I do not know if the radio in the old wooden cabinet by my bed works because I have never thought to turn it on.

The bathroom is as big as some modern hotel bedrooms and has a deep, enamelled tub and an Armitage Shanks lavatory, substantial and solid on its porcelain plinth. I distrust those bowls that project from the wall with no visible means of support.

At night the sky is clear and the stars lie low, and the sounds of the village drift up from the valley, where the cooking fires flicker, and my cigar smoke hangs in the air.

If you are patient and wait around the hotel watering hole, you may spot an Old Buffer coming for his evening drink. The barman, as old as he is, places it in front of him without being asked, and watches out of the corner of his eye as the mzungu (white man) leaves, unsteady on his pins.

I sit by the pool and am the last to leave. I watch the steward lock the changing room and close the bar and fold the chairs. And after he has poured chlorine from a sawn-off plastic bottle into the deep end of the pool, he picks up his newspaper and bids me good night.

No key-cards here, just mortice locks and long-shanked keys, attached to blocks of wood, polished by handling over the years.

As I say, it is a hotel at the peak of its decline. No doubt someone will decide to improve it. Then I will not stay there any more, and I will tell you where it was.

The sultan's band no longer plays outside the English club
Financial Times, 7 October 1996

The sultan's band no longer plays outside the English Club in Zanzibar. It is 25 years or more since you could take the river steamer down the Nile to Nimule. It's ages since the S.S. *Robert Coryndon*[33] plied Lake Albert, from Butiaba to Pakwach. And the last flying boat from London touched down on Lake Malawi many years before I started travelling to and around Africa.

You can, however, fly from Heathrow to Johannesburg in about ten hours or from Paris to Nairobi in eight hours and I suppose that's progress.

For all its trials and tribulations, Africa has opened up to the world dramatically, as political and economic reforms have taken hold and modern technology, from jumbo jets to mobile phones, shrink distances and make the lives of business travellers easier.

Visas are easier to obtain, tiresome regulations which required travellers to declare their foreign currency on arrival at airports have been dropped, credit cards are widely accepted and, more likely than not, your hotel will have CNN.

Getting there

Because I always fly from London, I always travel on British Airways, partly because I am hooked on air miles but also because I think that their service is the best on the routes to Africa. However, the FT buys my tickets and open return tickets are not cheap. Otherwise, I would be doing bucket-shop deals with Kenya Airways, KLM and Alitalia and

---

[33] Named after Sir Robert Coryndon (1870–1925), a former secretary to Cecil Rhodes and one of the most powerful colonial administrators of his day.

hoping that when Virgin starts flying between London and Johannesburg this month it will force BA and SAA to bring their prices down on what is one of their most lucrative—and overcharged—routes.

Domestic and regional travel

For all the headlines about crime in Johannesburg and armed robbers in Lagos—admittedly serious problems in both cities—I still find Africa a remarkably safe, friendly and courteous continent. (Yes, even Nigeria!)

In many years of travelling around Africa, I am hard-pressed to recall anything having gone seriously wrong. I have never been mugged. I have not lost a suitcase *en route*. Nothing has been stolen from my hotel room. I have always managed to get a seat on a plane—provided I wanted it badly enough. I haven't been in a car crash. And I have not suffered from malaria.

That is not to say that I am not careful, for Africa in general is getting more hazardous as economic decline takes its toll, whether in the form of airports where navigational aids do not work, cars with faulty brakes, jobless youths taking to crime, or aircraft that are poorly maintained.

So I take a taxi for the six-block journey from the Carlton Hotel in central Johannesburg to the FT office. I don't walk alone after dark on the beach across the road from Dar es Salaam's Oyster Bay Hotel; I leave my wallet in my room when venturing out from Nairobi's Inter-continental; and only in Asmara, capital of Eritrea, do I walk the streets at night without a qualm or a care for my safety.

I try not to travel on Africa's roads after dark, for too many people I know have ploughed into the back of a truck or car parked on the side of the road without a warning reflector.

In most countries I stick to bottled water; in nearly all countries I take my anti-malaria tablets.

I also travel light: my crumpled cream linen suit (not really practical, but I cannot resist it); a pair of slacks; a baggy swimming costume that doubles as a pair of shorts; a shortwave radio; a bottle of bath oil; a penknife for peeling mangoes and tucking into avocadoes; sunglasses; and business cards. Oh yes, and a floppy hat and my Tandy computer, all of which fits into my carry-on case with wheels.

Air travel between countries in Africa is expensive and there is little that the traveller can do about it, for the routes are controlled by a cartel formed by the national airlines of the two countries concerned. Thus an open economy return ticket between Nairobi and Johannesburg costs about $1,100.

Car hire is available in most countries, but I prefer to strike a deal with a local taxi driver. They could not be more different from their European counterparts for they are singularly well informed and able to assess the merits of every cabinet minister, their chances of re-election and the extent to which they have their hands in the state till. Communications, I am sorry to say, are a lot better than they were and not nearly as good as they should be. I preferred it when it was all but impossible to get an international call.

Now I feel obliged to try and will pay a fortune when I succeed. In fact, calling abroad from most countries in Africa is usually straightforward; the problem comes when you try to make a phone call from one part of Africa to another.

Hotels

The same ambivalent view of progress applies to hotels: there are many more that boast five-star status but far fewer that are pleasant to stay in. Those wonderful establishments with red-polished verandas, rooms with high ceilings, residents' lounges with chintz-covered chairs and snooker tables are becoming a thing of the past. But one tip: wherever you may be planning to stay (unless it's the Mount Nelson in Cape Town), I suggest you take your own soap. Throughout Africa, local soap seems to be made of tallow obtained from the boiled-down fundaments of goats.

Reading

The *Rough Guide* series on Africa is excellent. Business travellers should take the Economist Intelligence Unit report on the country of their destination (and the latest FT survey), while the World Bank country reports are now readily available.

Money

While credit cards are widely accepted, they should be supplemented by travellers' cheques, and a stash of US dollars provides a universal currency.

One final piece of advice

Something is bound to go wrong at some stage in your travels: the aircraft will be over-booked; the hotel will not have your reservation; a critical appointment is not kept. Don't worry unduly. Be patient, keep your sense of humour, for eventually things will work out.

And if, when you get back, you are worried that you have, despite all precautions, picked up something mysterious and nasty, make an appointment at the London Hospital for Tropical Diseases, probably the best institution of its kind in the world.

Harry Oppenheimer, grandee of Anglo American

By Philip Gawith and Michael Holman

Financial Times, 7 November 1998

He has the demeanour of the Oldest Member of P.G. Wodehouse's legendary golf club, diffident and self-deprecatory but clearly delighted to have been consulted about the pin placings for a particularly successful tournament.

In fact, the courteous, bright-eyed gentleman behind the desk of his London office, head quizzically cocked, is one of the world's wealthiest men and he is talking about what is perhaps the most momentous event in the 81-year history of the $10 billion family firm.

'I'm pleased about it but I really played no part at all, except that I like vaguely to know what's going on, and my colleagues are very kind to tell me, more or less,' says Harry Oppenheimer, who turned 90 last week.

A few days earlier, Anglo American, the company which towers over the South African economy, had announced plans to merge with its offshore associate Minorco and to relocate from Johannesburg to the City of London and be listed as one of the top 100 stocks.

'We think, rightly or wrongly, that with the company being based in London, people will be more inclined to invest in South Africa.'

It has been 16 years since the man they call HFO handed over the reins at Anglo. Today he likes to give the impression of an elderly uncle allowed to potter around the business provided he does not get in the way. 'I go to the office, not for very long, meet my colleagues in the passage, and they are very nice to me.'

But Oppenheimer is no doddery old buffer. Every now and then the self-effacing manner drops, revealing a man used to being listened to and who still presides, ultimately, over a vast family business empire.

146 | POSTMARK AFRICA

Through Anglo and its associates, De Beers and Minorco, it controls the world diamond industry, is the largest gold and platinum producer, and much else besides.

The day-to-day running of the business is firmly in the hands of the current chairman, Julian Ogilvie Thompson. But although he retired formally from Anglo in 1982, and from De Beers in 1984, no one doubts that HFO remains a valued source of advice and wisdom. After all, he draws on a career that spans the growth of two great and enduring mining companies (Anglo and De Beers), spent 10 years in parliament, watched the rise and fall of apartheid, and has first-hand knowledge of African leaders, past and present.

He expresses no doubts about Anglo's London move. If the company wanted to be a global business, it needed the investment rating and profile which a London listing would offer, he says.

'I'm immensely impressed by the attitude the South African government has taken. They not only gave us permission, they've gone out of their way to say it is a very good thing for South Africa. Certainly, if we have a better position by what we've done, I think we owe it to them to use it the best we can to benefit South Africa more rapidly than we would have been able to do otherwise.'

He then adds, with all the authority of the company's largest investor and its guiding spirit: 'We are certainly going to think that way.'

The sentiments, of course, are not what you hear from your average FTSE 100 company chairman, but then Anglo is no ordinary company. Its sheer size has brought an inescapable political dimension to its activities. Indeed, Oppenheimer justifies his own stint in politics—he was a member of parliament for the United Party from 1948 to 1958—as almost a necessary part of the business apprenticeship.

'I hope it [Anglo management] goes on being very concerned about the environment in which we operate. I've always rather pompously said the best way to make money for a group like ours is to make the money as a by-product of developing South Africa. I feel strongly about that. I hope it goes on.'

A recent example of Anglo trying to 'do the right thing' was its attempt to put JCI, the mining house, into the hands of black South Africans. A combination of bad luck (the slump in the gold price) and bad management saw this exercise fall well short of expectations. JCI still has significant black shareholders, but it is a pale shadow of the company it was.

Oppenheimer is unfazed about this and other black empowerment setbacks: 'It was vital to make it possible for black people to control some of the big companies in South Africa. It was the right thing to do —part of a necessary response to the efforts for peace made by Mandela and his colleagues. You felt business had to match their efforts. We had to play our part too in making it a peaceful united country.'

One subject on which he is emphatic is the crucial cross-holdings between Anglo and De Beers. Together with the family's own stake, this confers control over both companies. It is an arrangement the City will not like but Oppenheimer says he cannot imagine them as separate vehicles—though he adds the caveat: 'You can't tell what's going to happen in the future.'

He explains the relationship: 'When I was chairman of De Beers [1957–84], in order to run the diamond business in the way we wanted, it was vital to have big interests outside of diamonds in bad times. You couldn't run [it] unless you had substantial interests outside diamonds. You could have said De Beers must have a great department to invest money itself but it really wasn't sensible to do that. We were closely associated with Anglo, my father was chairman of both companies, and it seemed only sensible that Anglo American would look after their interests outside of diamonds.'

The conversation turns to African leaders he has met. Mobutu Sese Seko, late president of Zaire (now Congo), 'was agreeable enough, but he was a thug, wasn't he? I remember lunching with him in his palace in Kinshasa. Behind you was a huge cage, extremely smelly, filled with leopards.'

Robert Mugabe, Zimbabwe's leader, is 'very clever and very articulate ... I think still a Communist.'

Tanzania's former president, Julius Nyerere, however, is 'a very attractive fellow. He was in the habit of reading Shakespeare.'

Malawi's Hastings Banda, who defied fellow African leaders by paying a state visit to South Africa in 1971, 'had a genius for public relations'. 'I remember him coming to Johannesburg and his car stopped at a traffic block. In a second he was outside the car with a white child under one arm and a black one under the other. That was when Vorster was prime minister.'

And what of President Nelson Mandela? 'We owe an immense amount to him. If it hadn't been for Mandela, we would not have had the peaceful transition,' he says, adding: 'Of course, when it comes to the practical day-to-day running of the country, I don't think that 27 years in prison is a very good introduction to that.'

Has South Africa's transition gone as well as he had hoped? 'Much better.' He goes on to tell the story of a trip to Russia, where he asked his young guide whether she thought things were better than they were.

'"No," she said, "they are very much worse." So I asked if she wanted to go back to the old days.

'"Not at all," she replied. "In the past, they could only get worse. Now they can only get better."'

The Oldest Member chuckles at the recollection. 'I thought that this was a very clever saying from one so young. I certainly apply it to my own country.'

Ideas of luxury

Financial Times, 2 October 2002

A hot shower, a cold beer, and a loo that flushes. That's my idea of luxury when I reach my destination at the end of a long and dusty day in the African bush.

If your idea of comfort under the same circumstances is a jacuzzi on the pool deck, a splendid menu with fine wine and an attentive butler, I know just the place for you: the Royal Malewane, in the heart of a private reserve embraced by South Africa's Kruger National Park.

If, however, you are prepared to rough it, and go without a jacuzzi and a butler—although you will have your own swimming pool—then Leopard Hills in the same part of the world will probably suit you better and cost you less.

You do not, of course, go to one of Africa's great game parks to sample the wine, excellent though it may be, and cheap though it is at 16 rand to the UK pound. At the end of the day, it is the animals that count, and I was bowled over.

Your sightings will depend on the skills of the tracker and the ranger who accompany you, and both lodges provide some of the best in the business. The tracker sits on a metal chair attached to the front of the four-wheel drive, reading the information from the dusty path unfolding before him with the ease with which you and I read out the headlines of the daily paper to our breakfast partners. The ranger offers an encyclopaedic knowledge of the animal and the terrain.

Having learnt more than I really needed to know, I watched rapt as a pair of lions mated, paying no attention to the vehicle and the headlights that illuminated their coupling.

Elsewhere, a quartet of lions demolished a giraffe. I looked on as a leopard separated her trio of cubs, quarrelling over access to their mother's kill. I had been riveted by the sight of a cheetah, gorging on a freshly caught impala. I had been astonished to see a rhino and its calf emerge from the bush. Just minutes before I had seen an elephant stripping a tree of its bark.

All this from a distance of a few yards. Sitting comfortably atop the open four-wheel-drive vehicle, I was close enough to hear the flesh tearing as the animals tucked in, the leopard cubs growling like angry kittens, the cheetah belching, the lions breaking wind. I had gone on the game-spotting trips, part of the package provided by each lodge, feeling ever so slightly superior to my fellow spotters. After all, I was brought up in Zimbabwe ... but if I set out as a sceptic I returned from the trips a believer.

But now for the more difficult part of the answer to the question: is it worth paying £300–£450 per person per night? If you choose to stay at Royal Malewane, your every need is catered for, by excellent staff: you can sit in your jacuzzi and watch the sun rise, go for a game ride, have a multi-course breakfast in the bush and return to keep an appointment with the in-house masseuse.

If you stay at Royal Malewane (where the number of guests is limited to 16) or at Leopard Hills (also limited to 16) the worst thing that can happen is to discover that your wine is corked.

There is none of the risk, that frisson of fear, that we old Africa hands relish; none of those uncertainties that give life on the continent its edge. There is no chance that your gin and tonic—whether served during the break in your daytime excursions or before dinner in the elegant dining room—will be without a slice of lemon, or ice. The greatest challenge might be the frustration of taking ages to read your email, for the system can be painfully slow.

And this is where I part company with the modern definition of luxury. I vividly remember, with sadness and regret, the time when I realised that one of my favourite hotels had entered the modern age. I was sitting on the grassy terrace, looking out over Lake Edward at the green hills of Congo, smoking a Davidoff, at peace with the world. A waiter approached, bearing a tray, carrying a piece of paper which his colleague presented to me with all the pride and aplomb of a maître d' offering the wine list. It was a fax and I knew that my hotel had changed for ever.

I also have some doubt about the merits of what is called exclusiveness. Another way of describing this intimate gathering is that you could be cooped up with a dozen or so other people who, to put it bluntly, are pains in the balubas.

My last area of doubt involves the link between taste and spectacle, and the circumstances under which they are enjoyed. Does the beer taste better if it is drunk from a frosted, crystal glass? Is that wild mushroom *vol au vent* really more delicious than a roadside purchase of sweet, tender young maize, roasted over charcoal, eaten with an appetite honed by hunger? It boils down to one question: if ITC Classics had not offered me a stay in two of the lodges it recommends to clients, would I have paid to go there? If I was someone with a great deal of money, and proportion-ately little time, the answer is undoubtedly yes.

Never have I been so pampered, so thoroughly spoilt, as at Royal Malewane.

Whether it is the real Africa, whatever that is, is another matter. But for half the cost of a week in these splendid lodges I would show you a different Africa. And be warned: in my Africa there are no jacuzzis—and certainly no aromatherapists.

And just in case, I would suggest that you bring along a towel and a bar of your favourite soap, because in most countries on the continent the local product is horrid. And to tell the truth, I could not even guarantee a hot shower. However, all that is for another day.

If that puts you off, then book in at Malawane or Leopard Hills and then you won't be disappointed.

From Gwelo to Soweto

From *Soweto Inside Out*, Penguin, 2004

I do not like Soweto. I know that it is almost *de rigueur* to sing its praises but I just don't like the place. Never have. I have never written a salute to what may be called its 'indomitable spirit' or hailed its 'indefatigable diversity' or praised its 'boundless courage'.

This township or suburb or slum, call it what you will, may well be a symbol of gutsy resistance, a grim symptom of apartheid, or deserve its portrayal as one of the worst legacies of white rule.

Not for me. Perhaps I am just being perverse. My friends have been known to call me bloody-minded. But for me there are other, more persuasive monuments to dark days, such as the soulless dormitory of Onverwacht, in the Free State, where black families lost hope, well out of the spotlight that focused on Soweto.

And on the scale of sheer human misery, Soweto lags behind the festering favelas of Luanda. Nor does it match the horrors of the slums of Lagos. Lagos: now there's a city to reckon with. Rough, tough, raw and powerful. Walk down Broad Street, once lined with banks which long ago migrated to the safety of Ikoyi or Victoria Island. Wander a block inland and you are in Jankari market. Follow your nose and you'll find the butchers' stands, awash in blood and offal. 'Like the Somme on a bad day,' said an irreverent colleague. But Soweto does not inspire me or intimidate me as Lagos does.

When it was in the front line of the struggle against apartheid I visited the place, but with no great enthusiasm. Duty took me there. I've accumulated no special anecdotes from the grim urban sprawl. Unlike nearly every journalist of my acquaintance, I have never been mugged, shot at or car-jacked there.

Today, I do not care to visit its *shebeens*, however sophisticated or fashionable they might be. I don't find Soweto's contrasts in lifestyles engaging, or its enthusiasms entertaining. I regard the ghettos of wealthy residents, with their expensive houses, not as a triumph of the entrepreneurial spirit but as conspicuous displays of dreadful architectural taste.

So I have had no reason to commemorate or celebrate Soweto—until, that is, some ten years after the elections that marked the end of apartheid.

It took place during one of those guided tours. I think it is a good thing if tourists find time in an itinerary of beaches and game parks to spend a few hours seeing the way many black South Africans live. And it was on such a tour that Soweto became indelibly associated with the day that I cracked.

Friends from London were visiting South Africa and we were a few minutes into a visit to the museum that commemorates Hector Petersen. He was the 13-year-old who was said to be the first to die when some 30,000 students took to the streets of Soweto, protesting against a government edict that all classes were to be taught in Afrikaans.

At the time of his death in 1976 I was a journalist based in Salisbury (now Harare, in Zimbabwe) and was soon to move to Lusaka in Zambia. The image of that young boy, carried dead or dying in his friend's arms, must be one of the most powerful to emerge from those grim, ghastly days.

But it was not this image, moving as it is, that triggered my distress and penetrated my professional carapace of detachment. If I were carrying emotional baggage associated with Soweto, I was not aware of it then. It was not this poignant photo that triggered memories of the past in a way that left me vulnerable. It was something mundane and banal.

We had entered the museum together but soon I was separated from the group. I lingered near the start of the display, fascinated as well as repelled, transported to the days of my youth in Rhodesia, as I listened to an interview. It was a filmed interview, on a loop, and so the images and the words recurred at regular intervals.

A white woman, in her mid-thirties, speaking with those clipped southern African vowels, was setting out her concerns about majority rule. I cannot remember any more detail. But in familiar codeword language, in a reasonable tone, quite matter of fact, as if spelling out the obvious, she justified an evil system. Over and over and over again.

It became the voice I had heard throughout my youth and beyond. I watched and listened, mesmerised by this voice from the 50s.

Then it hit me. I was overwhelmed by a great wash of sadness for generations lost during the scourge of apartheid. Not just for the millions who died, directly or indirectly, victims of war or preventable disease; but for the might-have-beens, the should-have-beens, the could-have-beens: the unread writers, the unheard musicians, the uncelebrated athletes, the talented and the ordinary—lost to Africa, lost to the world, sacrificed to prejudice.

Suddenly and unexpectedly, I was weeping. Or to put it bluntly, I sobbed. There was none of the dignity that can be associated with the word 'weep'. These were not discreet tears, not dignified drops, rolling down my cheeks. My shoulders shook and my nose ran copiously.

So why, I still wonder, was I so uncontrollably moved? For over thirty years I have been a journalist. I like to think that I am as hardbitten as the next hack. My notebook has recorded racism and its consequences all this time, drawing on my childhood in Gwelo, Rhodesia, the events that followed Ian Smith's unilateral declaration of independence, and the export of South Africa's battle to Angola, South West Africa and Mozambique. It was a grim and ghastly era, the 60s, the 70s, the 80s, until that loop was broken in the early 90s.

But when I visited the Hector Petersen museum in 2003 my guard was down. My notebook had been left behind, literally and meta-phorically. And over the years that notebook has served as the great anaesthetic. It has functioned as a mind-numbing filter through which tragedy is kept at a distance. It ensured that compassion takes second place to more pressing concerns: how much space for the story, how to write it, when to file it.

This time there was no deadline to distract me, no byline to seduce me, no dateline to add to my collection. For the first time in many years, I was off duty. And although the link may be tenuous, that is how I remember Soweto. The Hector Petersen museum. The place where I blubbed. But I write this dry-eyed. My memory has served as my notebook. The protective artifice of my trade still works.

Africa's Potemkin village is fooling the world

Financial Times, 20 January 2004

It is more than 200 years since Prince Grigori Potemkin is supposed to have created mock villages in the Crimea to persuade Catherine the Great that her empire was thriving. Although the techniques are different, the tactic is still in use. The victim is Africa and the perpetrators and benefactors are those who claim to be the continent's friends.

Behind a façade of bogus statistics, misleading language and misguided concepts lies sub-Saharan Africa, crippled by debt, disease and disaster. Wishful and self-serving thinking by western governments and aid donors conceals both the depth of the region's crisis and the ineffectual nature of policies intended to reverse its decline.

Africa's 'Potemkin deception' begins with statistics. It is accepted, for example, that Nigeria is the continent's most populous nation. But there could be anything from 120 million to 140 million Nigerians. The last reliable census was conducted by the British in the colonial era, some 50 years ago. Post-independence counts have been distorted by rivalry between the Christian south and the Muslim north, and tensions over the distribution of the country's oil wealth among the states: allocation is based partly on a state's population.

If we do not know something as fundamental as the number of Nigerians, who account for one in six Africans (or five, or seven) and we guess at their birth rate, every statistic about Nigeria confidently cited by its development partners is not a fact but an assumption, based on trends with questionable foundations.

And if this is the case with Nigeria, can we believe World Bank figures, often based on extrapolations that go back decades, for Mali or

Malawi or Mozambique, whether about radio sets per thousand households or literacy rates?

Language compounds the problem and abets the deception. We have words for participants in conflict—terrorists, guerrillas or freedom fighters, depending on the writer's sympathies—but none for the consequences of poverty. We have no words for schools that lack books, a collapsing civil service or for presidents of countries that have imploded.

Yet policy statements from Africa's western partners are too often based on the assumption that these words count, that they mean the same thing to a reader in New York and a nomad in Nairobi.

With the help of these misunderstandings, or deceptions, the policies that emerge are given a credibility they do not deserve. To demand elections without a census in a country that has never known good governance, where roads have returned to the bush, does not make sense. Yet this is what western governments urge Congo to undertake within two years.

One reason Western policymakers have got away with such delusions is the Potemkin factor. Africa's partners take a combination of thumb-suck statistics that are treated as facts and use misleading words to sell schemes that are insupportable—all wrapped in an unwarranted assumption that Africa is slowly, albeit erratically, 'getting better'.

I would be contradicting my own argument to claim the continent is slowly, albeit erratically, getting worse. I cannot use the statistics I deride, even if many of them bear out my case. Nor is my personal anecdotal evidence any more persuasive than that of the Afro-optimists.

The gap between us Afro-realists and the Afro-optimists may well be explained by the 'cocoon factor'. The conditions under which journalists, diplomats and aid officials do their job have certainly improved. Aeroplanes are more comfortable, computers and satellite phones make communications easier and hotels are more attuned to our needs. If you observe Africa from within this cocoon, it may well seem a better place.

But there is more to it than that. The difference between Afro-realists on the one hand and the optimists who speak for western donors on the other is that if our pessimism proves wrong, we merely end up with egg on our face. We have no failed policies or vested interests to defend, no constituents to answer to.

For overseas aid ministers and their ilk, the stakes are much higher.

If they are mistaken in their optimism, they have a tough question to answer: why have they got Africa so wrong, for so long? Two decades after the world recognised Africa's crisis and scores of billions of aid dollars later, the Potemkin façade is crumbling.

Lessons from Kenya

The Nation, Kenya, August 2005

It was a potentially explosive situation. A few hundred white farmers held over 8 million acres of the country's best land, and memories were fresh of a guerrilla war to dispossess them. Over 6,000 British troops had been sent out to protect the farmers and suppress the rebellion in which 37 settlers and more than 10,000 'terrorists' were to die.

The country's 6 million African majority, impatient for change, controlled parliament, full independence from Britain was only months away, and land redistribution was high on the agenda.

'Is European farming going to carry on?' asked an anxious writer at the time. 'Can the country keep going when it turns sound economic farms into subsistence units? Farming and expediency are at logger-heads,' he concluded gloomily.

The country was Kenya, the time was the early 1960s, and the parallels with Zimbabwe may yet prove instructive as London and Harare seek a way out of their impasse.

Forty years ago the British government of the day was prepared to be the main contributor to a £20 million land resettlement fund—worth £250 million at today's prices—to help pay for the redistribution of former white farms in Kenya.

By the time Zimbabwe won independence in 1980, however, the British government's purse strings were tighter, although Zimbabwe at independence had five times as many white farmers.

Britain's initial contribution to Zimbabwe's land resettlement programme was £30 million—£75 million at today's prices. And while a further £14 million was provided, and an additional £36 million has been promised conditionally, in real terms the total UK contribution has been well under half the support given to Kenya. Yet the history of the two countries has many shared features.

Both countries were British colonies, and the white minority in each country—60,000 in Kenya, 275,000 in Zimbabwe at their peak—expropriated land at the turn of the century and dominated the economy. And both had to come to terms with the rise in African nationalism in the 1950s that was to mark the end of the colonial era. As in Zimbabwe, land was a sensitive issue in Kenya and at the heart of what became known as the Mau Mau rebellion.

Backed by the Kikuyu, Kenya's largest ethnic group at the time, it first surfaced in the late 1940s, and gathered in strength. A state of emergency which was to last until 1960 was first declared in 1952, and on the night of October 20 that year the first British battalion arrived. By May the following year there were two British brigades—over 6,000 men—supported by six battalions of the King's African Rifles and two RAF Bomber squadrons.

Britain—and the settlers—were convinced that the driving force behind the Mau Mau was Jomo Kenyatta, the man who was to become Kenya's founding president. Convicted of managing the Mau Mau, and banned by the colonial administration, he was held in detention for seven years until his release in 1961. It was he who paved the way to peaceful transition to majority rule when he addressed farmers in the 'white Highlands' and assured them of a role in independent Kenya.

But he also had to meet the demands of another constituency—peasant farmers seeking land. Land reform had got under way in the mid-1950s but more had to be done. 'At the approach of independence,' writes a contemporary commentator, 'rising pressures from the landless Kikuyu tribes for farms was combined with the run-down estates in the highlands owned by Europeans, many of whom were anxious to emigrate provided they could recover the capital they had invested in their land.'

Hence the launch in mid-1962 of what became known as the 'million-acre scheme' financed by Britain, with West Germany and the World Bank providing the balance.

A little over one million acres of land owned by 780 white farmers was purchased, and by the end of 1971, when the scheme was wound up, some 35,000 families had been settled on 1.2 million acres. After 1965 the government adopted a different approach. A special commissioner for squatters registered and settled squatters on 10-acre plots carved out of abandoned or mismanaged white farms which had been taken over.

By the mid-1980s, these squatter schemes, together with the million-acre scheme, had settled over 71,000 families on nearly 2 million acres of land—about 17 percent of all land original held by white farmers.

'Without such a plan undoubtedly there would have been a breakdown in race relations, and violence and theft on a very large scale and a collapse in the general economy,' writes the commentator. Resettlement not only defused political tension. It helped change the structure of Kenyan agriculture, with exports crops such as tea and coffee, previously a white preserve, for the first time being grown in quantity by smallholders.

The story of the intervening decades is one of mixed success, however. Although one third of the purchase price under the million-acre scheme was met by UK grants, the farmer had to repay the balance over 30 years. For many this proved too much, and they were replaced by larger farmers, businessmen or the urban political elite.

A few years after independence, Kenyatta made Kenya a one-party state, and corruption and mismanagement took their toll.

Meanwhile land remains at the heart of the country's politics: the size of plots is shrinking by the year under pressure from population increase, and the demand is increasing for the subdivision of the many large farms that remain in the hands of politicians and businessmen. Above all, the number of landless Kenyans is over 2 million and rising.

Nevertheless, Kenyans with long-enough memories must be looking back on their own history and giving thanks that they lived in times when Britain was able to offer a big carrot, as well as wield a big stick.

Peter Godwin: When a Crocodile eats the Sun

The Literary Review, March 2007

What is it about the experience of Whites in Rhodesia that readers and publishers find so fascinating? Peter Godwin led the field with his memoir *Mukiwa: A White Boy in Africa*. Then came Alexandra Fuller's *Don't Let's Go to the Dogs Tonight*, which she followed up with *Scribbling the Cat: Travels with an African Soldier*. Coming soon is Lauren St John's *Rainbow's End: Childhood, War and an African Farm*. And almost certain to repeat the deserved success of *Mukiwa* is Godwin's sequel, *When a Crocodile eats the Sun*.

This output seems a mite excessive, given the number of Whites: peaking at around 275,000 in the early 1970s, today it is fewer than 30,000. Does the interest in their old lifestyle reflect a concern about kith and kin? After all, most 'Rhodies' were British immigrants, and their fate seems to confirm Europe's worst fears about post-independence Africa: Whites are evicted from their farms, inflation at 1,200 per cent a year renders pensions and savings worthless, and Robert Mugabe replaces Idi Amin as the black man we love to hate.

Or perhaps there is a simpler explanation. White Rhodesians were a talented bunch. 'Surbiton in Africa', a visiting British journalist once sneered. As a Rhodie myself, I'm hardly unbiased, but: some Surbiton! The country produced world-class figures, from ballerinas to international businessmen, not to mention cricketers, tennis players, golfers, Olympic yachtsmen, and some outstanding writers who tapped a dark and nasty side of Rhodesia: the fact that the white minority was not only disproportionately talented, most of it was racist.

In 1962 the Whites elected a party which promised to entrench a Rhodesian version of apartheid. A farmer called Ian Smith put promise into practice. In 1965 he severed all remaining constitutional links with Britain and unilaterally declared the country independent. White Rhodesians thumbed their nose at UN sanctions, kept ancient Viscounts flying, steam locomotives puffing, old cars on the road—and the five million black Rhodesians firmly in their place.

It was, for Whites, a paradise until the guerrilla war that started for real in 1972. By the time Rhodesia became Zimbabwe in 1980, at least 30,000 people had been killed in the conflict, of whom 468 were white civilians.

It was in this society that Peter Godwin grew up, as he described so well in *Mukiwa*, a tender evocation of childhood in Rhodesia, where his British-born parents managed an estate, and his mother was the local government doctor. The sequel—*When a Crocodile eats the Sun* (a reference to a local legend that attributes solar eclipses to a celestial crocodile demonstrating his displeasure with Man)—deserves to rank alongside *Mukiwa* as an African classic. It begins in July 1996. Godwin is on journalistic assignment in South Africa; his mother calls: his dad is dying. Peter rushes to Harare, bringing the medicine that saves his father's life. For the next five years he shuttles between his home in New York and his parents' house, monitoring the health not only of his father, but of Zimbabwe—and coming to terms with the discovery that his dad is not British after all but a Polish Jew called Goldfarb. Each visit charts a further step in the country's descent into brutish madness. Godwin's pain and bafflement at the abuse of the country and its people permeate a book that brings little comfort and offers no answers.

In one poignant scene Godwin illustrates the predicament of many Whites. After his father dies, Peter tries to persuade his mother to leave Zimbabwe. She refuses, pulling out from her bookshelves a volume of Rudyard Kipling's poetry. Handing it to her son, she tells him to read the lament of a centurion ordered back to Rome with his cohort. The power supply has failed, yet again, and he does so by torchlight:

> I've served in Britain forty years. What should I do in Rome?
> Here is my heart, my soul, my mind—the only life I know.
> I cannot leave it all behind. Command me not to go!

Ironically, it is her son who is ambivalent about where his loyalties lie. Yet if any White belongs to Africa, it is Godwin: a fluent Shona speaker, born and bred in Rhodesia. His passion for the continent is the real thing.

He has experienced the pain of love, as well as the pleasure. 'A White in Africa,' he acutely observes, 'is like a Jew everywhere, on sufferance, watching warily, waiting for the next great swell of hostility.' Later, after discovering that what appeared to be a night ambush was in fact the mustering of a friendly neighbourhood watch squad, he writes: 'Africa does this to you. Just as you are about to dismiss it and walk away, it does something so unexpected, so tender. One minute you're scared shitless, the next you are choked with affection.'

Peter Godwin's is a wonderful book: a picture of a society gripped by madness; a portrait of remarkable parents, in love throughout their marriage, who represent the best of old Rhodesia; and an account of a man coming to terms with identity old and new, African and Jew. It is beautifully written, packed with insight and free of rancour.

Oliver Tambo

Oliver Tambo Remembered, Macmillan, 2007

They say no man can be a hero to his valet.

By the same token, it would seem unlikely that a politician can ever be a hero to a journalist.

Just as the intimacy enjoyed by a servant sooner or later psychologically disrobes the master and exposes hitherto concealed flaws, so should a journalist's innate scepticism penetrate all pretensions.

Above all, it should serve as armour against that dreadful possibility that one could end up admiring, and even—heaven help us—befriending, the man or woman we write about.

Some nevertheless break through this protective carapace and find a place in one's heart.

Alas, there was never the chance to find out if Oliver Tambo would have joined Nelson Mandela and Joe Slovo on my personal pedestal reserved for politicians I revere.

Tambo's disabling stroke came when the battle against apartheid was all but won, and thus his mettle was never tested to the full. We can never be sure that he would have made a success of the transition from opposition leader to head of government.

Nor did I know Oliver Tambo the way I like to think I knew Joe Slovo, the South African Communist Party General Secretary and African National Congress guerrilla commander. We forged a friendship when we both lived in Zambia in the 1970s and 1980s, and the ANC had its offices in the capital, Lusaka.

I stayed in a cottage in the grounds of the Twin Palms Road home of Harry and Marjorie Chimowitz, the exiled South African couple who opened their home to Joe, Mac Maharaj[34] and so many others.

Joe would regularly drop in for a swim in their pool or to watch football on an old black-and-white television set in the lounge of the main house, his enjoyment of the game overcoming the erratic reception, the result of an uncertain relationship between the set and its aerial.

Oliver Tambo made regular visits to Lusaka but not to Twin Palms Road, so I can offer no Tambo anecdotes from those years, nor claim to have shared a drink with him on the veranda of the Chimowitz's home. Indeed, I feel fortunate to be invited to contribute to this collection of tributes by many of his friends, for the truth is, I barely knew the man.

Yet I nevertheless hope that I qualify as a contributor to this celebratory volume on two counts. As a journalist, a good part of my career— first as the *Financial Times* Africa correspondent from 1976 to 1984 based in Lusaka, and then in London as the paper's Africa editor until 2002— has been devoted to following the fortunes of South Africa. And that, of course, meant following the ANC under President Oliver Tambo.

The second reason is more personal.

I came to admire the man and the example he set and the principles he stayed true to, for this helped to shape my own values. And this is an opportunity to explain how he came to play this role; and to say 'thank you' to a remarkable leader who had a crucial part in the forging of a democratic South Africa, and for which I believe he deserves more public credit.

I was brought up in what was then called Southern Rhodesia, the son of a South African mother from King William's Town, and a Cornish teacher who served in the Royal Air Force during the Second World War, based in Queenstown.

After a spell in Durban, the family moved north, and from the early 1950s we lived in the small town of Gwelo, now Gweru.

It was a golden period for us 'Europeans'. I was educated at Chaplin High School, where Ian Smith had been a pupil, a state school with all the facilities of a top English public school; as a boy scout I roamed the countryside fearful only of snakes; and an illicit beer or cigarette in the school bus on the cricket team's trip to a border school called Plumtree was as close as one got to drugs.

Yet challenging the Whites' sybaritic lifestyle of sundowners and

---

[34] Sathyandranath 'Mac' Maharaj (born 1935) is a South African politician linked to the ANC and was official spokesperson to Jacob Zuma while president of South Africa.

servants, there came the rumble of African nationalism that was advancing south. The Belgian Congo was disintegrating, with Moïse Tshombe seeking independence for the copper-rich province of Katanga, and white mercenaries recruiting for his secessionist cause.

Most white Rhodesians, however, believed they could halt nationalism's march at the Zambezi River, sheltering behind what their minority government liked to call 'separate development'—apartheid by another name.

As a politically precocious Gwelo teenager, I lived in awe of a pantheon of politicians who led opposition to white rule: Nyasaland's (Malawi's) Hastings Banda, detained without trial in Gwelo's jail, which I would cycle past, marvelling that the man who vowed to destroy the Central African Federation of Northern and Southern Rhodesia and Nyasaland (and duly succeeded) was detained behind its whitewashed walls; Kenneth Kaunda, who led neighbouring Northern Rhodesia to independent Zambia; Julius Nyerere of Tanganyika, soon to become Tanzania's prime minister—'Africa's evil genius' as Ian Smith, white Rhodesia's leader, later called him, in a backhanded compliment that Mwalimu relished; and Jomo Kenyatta, Kenya's first president.

All had an instinctive grasp of public relations. Banda had his dark glasses, pinstriped suit and flywhisk, a potent combination of Victorian values with a hint of voodoo. Kenneth Kaunda will be remembered for his ever-present white handkerchief, threaded through the fingers of his left hand; Kenyatta had his flywhisk. And Nyerere stood for modesty in his simple, open-necked safari suit never encumbered by a tie.

Missing from this group were men such as Albert Luthuli, Oliver Tambo and Nelson Mandela—partly because of my ignorance, and partly because they could not use those words, 'founding president', almost magical in their impact.

The triumph of Tambo and Mandela, the vindication of Luthuli was yet to come, and from my Gwelo perspective it seemed an impossibly long way off.

That era of relative calm was soon to be shattered.

In November 1965 Ian Smith unilaterally declared independence. Wars for the liberation of Angola and Mozambique intensified and the people of South West Africa struggled to become Namibia.

The 1974 coup in Portugal—colonial master to Angola and Mozambique for nigh on four centuries—was a seismic event for southern Africa. The guerrilla war in my homeland stepped up. By the mid-1970s white rule in Rhodesia was coming to an end.

In late 1979 I was at London's Lancaster House helping Bridget Bloom report on the negotiations that marked the conclusion of Mr. Smith's costly rebellion.[35]

It was during the Lancaster House talks that I went to interview the late Joshua Nkomo, co-leader with Robert Mugabe of Zimbabwe's guerrilla alliance, the Patriotic Front. When I entered his hotel room I barely noticed a figure sitting in the corner. Nkomo gestured towards his guest, who rose to greet me.

'Do you not know who this is?'

I took a further look. There was something familiar about him but, no, I could not place him. There was no Kaunda handkerchief, no Banda Homburg, no Kenyatta flywhisk, nothing that could jog my memory.

Nkomo gave a grunt of rebuke when I shook my head and introduced his guest: 'The next president of South Africa.'

I shook Oliver Tambo's hand and apologised for my ignorance. It was a long way from Gwelo.

---

[35] As a result of the Lancaster House conference, an agreement was signed on 21 December 1979 and independence elections were held in Rhodesia in early 1980. Bridget Bloom was the *Financial Times*'s Africa editor at the time. Subsequent Africa editors at the FT were Quentin Peel and then Martin Dickson, whom the author succeeded.

Desmond Tutu, 1931–
Reserve obituary, unpublished, 2007

This profile was commissioned by the Financial Times's *obituary editor following a scare about Archbishop Tutu's health. Thankfully the Archbishop has proved wonderfully resilient and the profile has not been required.*

Seldom has a public figure inspired as much universal love and commanded such worldwide respect as Desmond Mpilo Tutu, Archbishop Emeritus of Cape Town.

Alongside Nelson Mandela, South Africa's first democratically elected president and fellow winner of the Nobel Peace Prize, Tutu came to personify the battle against apartheid.

The loss of this hero of our time, modest and self-effacing, entertaining and courageous, will be hard for South Africa to bear. Once loathed by many Whites, it is testimony to Tutu's greatness that he will surely be mourned by all South Africans, whatever their creed, colour or conviction.

That battle against apartheid's grim legacy, however, is far from over. The journey to a fair society is taking much longer than expected; the roadblocks on the route to a decent democracy are proving hard to dismantle.

It was Nelson Mandela, compassionate and pragmatic, who dealt with the practicalities of political power in post-apartheid South Africa; it was Desmond Tutu who took on the role of conscience of the nation and spokesman for the underdog. In the years that followed the 1994 election that brought Mandela and the African National Congress to office, it became increasingly clear that overcoming the obstacles to a fair and just society—notably, the flagrant abuse of state resources, the cronyism that lies behind many a public appointment, the emergence of a selfish and corrupt elite—is proving almost as challenging as the fight against apartheid itself.

As Mandela moved out of the public arena after his retirement in

1999, it was Tutu who set the country's moral compass. He pulled no punches, yet often used his impish sense of humour, punctuated by an infectious giggle, to make his point and shame his target.

He attacked Mandela's successor, Thabo Mbeki, for his failure to tackle the Aids crisis, he berated Jacob Zuma, the current president, for his squandering of government assets. Further afield he condemned Robert Mugabe for his flagrant and frequent violations of human rights in Zimbabwe. He was supportive of women's rights and gay marriage, opposed Western intervention in Iraq.

His most harrowing task, one which strained his spiritual resilience, was to chair the country's Truth and Reconciliation Commission, which showed the world a new approach to the trauma caused by conflict. Rather than sweep the past under the carpet, or put the men respons-ible for apartheid on Nuremberg-type trial, South Africa opted for a third way. To those who had committed gross violations of human rights, it offered amnesty in exchange for public repentance and full disclosure of the truth about their crimes; for the victims it gave a chance to be heard, to express their pain and put their case for reparation.

Listening to the testimony of the perpetrators of evil, and to hear the stories of victims who lived to tell their tale, was a painful, gruelling experience. Looking back on the commission and its work, Tutu acknowledged that it has taken a heavy toll.

'Yes, I have been greatly privileged to engage in the work of helping to heal our nation,' he wrote in 1999, at the end of his account of the Commission's deliberations. 'But it has been a costly privilege for those of us in the Commission, and I have come to realise that perhaps we were effective only to the extent that we were, in that celebrated phrase, "wounded healers".'

His spiritual resilience was matched by physical courage. At a funeral service for four guerrillas in the township of Duduza, in July 1985, he put his life at risk. During the procession from a football field to the cemetery, a crowd of angry mourners turned on a man suspected of being a police informer. The man broke away from the mob and collapsed at the feet of Tutu, crying for mercy. The punishment that was imminent was known as 'necklacing'—a car tyre forced over the head of the victim, doused in petrol, and set alight—a barbaric practice that was a symptom of a sick society. Tutu pleaded for the man's life. The oppressed, he argued, should not sink to the level of the oppressor. The man was reprieved.

Desmond Mpilo Tutu was born in Klerksdorp, where his father was a teacher and his mother a cleaner and cook at a school for the blind.

'One day,' Tutu recalls, 'I was standing in the street with my mother when a white man in priest's clothing walked past. As he passed us, he took off his hat to my mother. I couldn't believe my eyes—a white man who greeted a black working-class woman!'

It marked the start of a friendship that was to influence him for the rest of his life. The white man was Trevor Huddlestone, then a parish priest in the township of Sophiatown, later to become a bishop and an influential anti-apartheid campaigner.

Initially Tutu wanted to become a doctor, but could not afford the fees. Instead he followed in his father's footsteps and became a teacher. But not for long. He resigned over the Bantu Education Act, in protest at the second-class system it entrenched.

After attending a theological college he was ordained as an Anglican priest in December 1961.

With his wife Leah Shenxane, a teacher, he travelled to London, studying for his bachelor's and master's degrees in Theology. Returning to South Africa in 1967, he became chaplain at the University of Fort Hare, going on to lecture at the National University of Lesotho.

Tutu's emergence on the international stage, however, began when he became the first black person to be appointed Anglican Dean of Johannesburg in 1975. He used this position to reach a new, wider, audience: 'I realised that I had been given a platform that was not readily available to many Blacks and most of our leaders were either now in chains or in exile. And I said, "Well, I'm going to use this to seek to try to articulate our aspirations and the anguishes of our people."'

In 1976, shortly after he was appointed Bishop of Lesotho, further raising his international profile, Tutu wrote a letter to the South African Prime Minister warning him that a failure to quickly redress racial inequality could have dire consequences. The letter was ignored.

In 1985, Tutu was appointed the Bishop of Johannesburg, and a year later he became the first black person to hold the highest position in the South African Anglican Church when he was chosen as the Archbishop of Cape Town. In 1987 he was also named the president of the All Africa Conference of Churches, a position he held until 1997.

Underpinning his faith was the concept of ubuntu, central to the African Weltanschauung, which, said Tutu, touches 'the very essence of being human ... so to say someone has ubuntu means they are generous, hospitable, friendly, caring and compassionate ... . It also means my humanity is inextricably bound up in theirs.'

Thus 'to forgive is the best form of self-interest. What dehumanises you inexorably dehumanises me.

'*Ubuntu* means that in a real sense even the supporters of apartheid were victims of the vicious system which they implemented and which they supported so enthusiastically.'

When apartheid officially ended and South Africans elected Mandela as their first legitimate president, Tutu was accorded the honour of formally introducing the country's new leader.

With his characteristic look of mischievous glee and the high-pitched chuckle that endeared him to millions, he recalled that, as he basked in the joyous event, he had whispered: 'If I die now it would be almost the perfect moment.'

Despite disappointments and setbacks, Desmond Tutu's essential optimism sustained his belief that South Africans would pull through, even if the odds seemed stacked against them.

'God,' he declared, 'does have a sense of humour. Who in their right mind could ever have imagined South Africa to be an example of anything but awfulness; of how not to order a nation's race relations and its governance. We South Africans were the unlikeliest lot and that is precisely why God has chosen us ... God intends that others might look at us and take courage. God wants to point to us as a possible beacon of hope ... and say "Look at South Africans. They had a nightmare called apartheid ... . Your nightmare will end too."'

Let the last word come from his old friend, Nelson Mandela: 'Sometimes strident, often tender, never afraid, seldom without humour, Desmond Tutu's voice will always be heard.'

Jonathan Lawley: Beyond the Malachite Hills

The Lady, July 2009

What bliss it was to be young, 'European' and idealistic in central Africa in the 1950s! For a decade that stretched into the 60s, the region was their oyster, or at least their vast social laboratory, where they searched for a decent alternative to the evil of apartheid.

Jonathan Lawley, born in India and educated in southern Africa, decided to 'do his bit', as he puts it, by signing up for the Northern Rhodesia colonial civil service, a nine-year posting that was followed by five years on a copper mine in southern Congo. Then came spells elsewhere in Africa, punctuated by visits to Southern Rhodesia (Zimbabwe since 1980), the country that was his first love.

Beyond the Malachite Hills, his wonderful account of these Africa years, is far more than the memoirs of a colonial veteran. Neither is it a conventional travel book, nor an autobiography, though we learn much about him.

Instead, imagine Swallows and Amazons written for adults and set in Africa, combined with a late 50s edition of the Guide to Southern Africa, without pretension, by a decent man who speaks his mind, is fond of food, enjoys his cars, and cherishes his friendships.

Take, for example, his account of a trip into the bush marking the end of his time in Northern Rhodesia (by then independent Zambia), packed with detail and as fresh as if it were yesterday.

Lawley and a friend—a former district officer from Kenya, who had become a first secretary in the British high commission in Lusaka—hatch a plan for a journey in what was Lawley's pride and joy, his 'nearly new Ford Cortina Estate'.

They drive from the Zambian capital to Livingstone, on the

Zambezi, and travel up river to Mongu, the capital of the province of Barotseland. After a night in Livingstone, they continue their expedition: 'Past the turn to Chief Sekute's village on the right and to Katombera reformatory on the left ... [we] crossed and re-crossed the famous Mulobezi railway line, where the trucks loaded with timber were pulled by the ancient wood-burning steam engines ... . I remembered my amazement the first time I had seen an old Anglia motorcar, fitted with metal wheels, zipping up and down at fair speed.

'The dust was bad, but we left that in clouds behind us, and we saw no other vehicles ... . We were making for a remote forestry department rest house, half way to Sesheke ... delighted to find a substantial house, double-storeyed and thatched, with a lovely view over the *dambo* (wetlands) and forest, and as isolated and deep in the bush as it is possible to be ... . We had steaks for the cook to prepare as well as beer, wine and some camembert.' Wonderful stuff!

Meanwhile the poison of racism is taking hold. Lawley writes about a spell as a teacher at an all-white school in Livingstone, during what we would now call a gap year. The children had been given an essay subject: 'What can be done to improve our town?'

'Get Blacks off the streets,' was the gist of most responses.

Using language more sophisticated but with a matching political agenda, Ian Smith unilaterally and illegally declared Southern Rhodesia independent in November 1965, and as Lawley points out, the consequences of this folly still contribute to Zimbabwe's current crisis.

Many of his views will outrage those for whom Robert Mugabe has become the black man they love to hate, not least his assertion that the country's white commercial farmers contributed to their own demise by ignoring the fact that their dominance of land in an independent Zimbabwe was both politically and morally intolerable.

And he suggests that President Mugabe, the man who began as a conciliator and ended up as a political thug, was shaped by the times, notably the values of those Livingstone high school children and their parents.

'Perhaps,' observes Lawley, 'the depth of Robert Mugabe's feelings really goes back to the days of old Southern Rhodesia when far too many Whites paid no heed to human dignity and went out of their way to humiliate and denigrate Blacks to help persuade themselves of their "superiority" and to justify their privileged status.'

It is in the nature of the author, one suspects, that his memoir should end on an optimistic note: 'What gives me most pleasure and confidence for the future is the emergence of growing numbers of young African entrepreneurs.'

But I still want to know: how did the camembert survive its long, hot and dusty journey?

The 2010s

Douglas Rogers: The Last Resort
A Memoir of Zimbabwe
The Literary Review, May 2010

Land has been at the heart of Zimbabwe's politics since the 1890s, when the first white settlers arrived. They came in the hope of finding a country of gold; but the gold they discovered was comparatively modest, while the land was fertile. At the end of the 1980s, Robert Mugabe launched a policy which invoked the anger of the West. Memories, however, are short. The white minority government had been as ruthless as Mugabe in enforcing the Land Apportionment Act, which divided the country into 'European' and 'African' areas. The most notable case was that of Chief Rekayi Tangwenya. He and his people were driven off their ancestral land on the border with Mozambique, not far from the resort run by the parents of Douglas Rogers. The review provides an alternative account.

There is something very odd, disturbing even, about the appetite for memoirs written by Whites who either grew up in Rhodesia or whose parents still live in what is now independent Zimbabwe.

What explains the sustained fascination with the lives of barely a quarter of a million settlers, of whom perhaps 10 per cent still live in the country? Is it the link of kith and kin? Or nostalgia for the colonial past? Has President Robert Mugabe, the black man Brits love to hate, managed to get under their collective skin?

Whatever the reasons, over the past ten years or so there have been at least a dozen memoirs. They have usually been about white farmers, either on the front line during the guerrilla war to end white rule or as victims of the land grab that benefited Mugabe's cronies and helped ruin a once flourishing economy.

One or two of these accounts are outstanding. Alexandra Fuller's description of her upbringing in *Don't Let's Go to the Dogs Tonight* transcends its location and becomes an engrossing tale of adolescence.

But it is Peter Godwin, another 'Rhodesian', with whom Douglas Rogers, author of *The Last Resort*, will be compared. Godwin produced two classics of their kind: *Mukiwa: A White Boy in Africa* (Picador, 1997), about his boyhood in Rhodesia, followed by *When a Crocodile eats the Sun* (Picador, 2006).

The latter is a masterly, moving account of his return to Zimbabwe to assist his dying father. While ministering to his parents, he observes and records the death throes of democracy under Robert Mugabe.

Like Godwin, Rogers returns to rescue his parents. As befits someone whose business is words (he is a journalist), he writes about it well. And he has an extraordinary story to tell. His parents, Lyn and Ros, a couple in their sixties, struggle to survive, as farmers across the country fall victim to thuggish intruders. Their home, Drifters, with a game park and backpacker lodge, slides into seedy disrepair. But it is still a prime target for the thugs. Instead of leaving, as their son pleaded with them to do, the Rogers load a shotgun and vow to stay on.

This formidable couple use some unorthodox measures to keep income flowing. One laughs out loud when Rogers discovers his father growing marijuana, the son remonstrating with his sheepish dad.

But for much of the book, the writer seems all too susceptible to white Rhodesia's selective amnesia and false memory syndrome.

Early on the author records his father's furious response to Mugabe's denunciation of white farmers as 'enemies'. 'Go back to Britain,' the President tells them, 'go back to Blair.' Watching the speech on television, Rogers senior explodes: 'Fuck me! I am not British. My people have been on this continent for 350 years ... My father fought fascism in Europe ... Who the fuck does [Mugabe] think he is?'

To imply that citizenship of Zimbabwe can be claimed on the basis of family links with South Africa, however far they go back, is arguable. Most Rhodesians, in fact, were immigrants from Britain, many of whom fled post-war austerity for the sunshine and servants of Rhodesia.

As for fighting fascism, certainly white Rhodesians can be proud of their brave volunteer role in the Second World War. What they seem to forget, however, is that thousands of their black fellow citizens also volunteered to 'fight fascism', serving with distinction in Malaya and elsewhere.

What is more, there would have been many thousands of additional African volunteers had their white comrades not opposed the creation of extra black battalions. As one historian put it, 'they feared that the inevitable result of arming and training a large body of Africans would be the extinction of the white man in Rhodesia.' Today, the black contribution is all but forgotten.

If, in his chronicle of his parents' wonderful, courageous, two-fingered defence of their property, Rogers had displayed a sharper awareness of his country's history, a good book could have been much better. After all, he did not need to look far.

I was once taken to a vantage point high in the mountains that mark Zimbabwe's eastern border with Mozambique. Sitting under a makeshift shelter, not many miles from where Drifters is today, a grizzled old man told me about his battle to keep the land that had been in his family for generations.

He recounted the daily harassment he and his family had endured. The police had come in the night and destroyed his home and confiscated his cattle. Appeals to the courts failed, for the judges supported the government.

The year was 1974. Ian Smith was prime minister. And the old man I interviewed was a black Zimbabwean, the late Chief Rekayi Tangwenya.

At the start of his memoir, Douglas Rogers quotes an extract from Graham Greene's The Power and the Glory. It ends: 'Even in danger and misery the pendulum swings.'

Indeed it does, indeed it does.

Nelson Mandela: Conversations with Myself

The Literary Review, December 2010

Conversations with Myself *is a collection of Nelson Mandela's letters, diary entries and other writing published in 2010 to amplify his 1995 autobiography,* Long Walk to Freedom.

Let's get one thing out of the way. Nelson Mandela is a great man. His compassion, his tolerance, his capacity for forgiveness and his wisdom broke a political logjam that threatened to engulf southern Africa and enabled him to preside over South Africa's transition from apartheid to democracy. Others, all extraordinary in their own right, played invaluable roles: Archbishop Desmond Tutu, President F.W. de Klerk, Walter Sisulu, Joe Slovo, Oliver Tambo, Thabo Mbeki. Without Mandela's magisterial, benign authority, however, South Africa would have remained at war with itself and with its neighbours.

But that is no reason to set aside doubts and misgivings about this fascinating albeit flawed volume, packed with titbits embedded in material that should be essential to the specialist reader. The problem is that these titbits, intriguing though they are, hardly warrant the purchase of this 450-page book; and historians and biographers need be wary, for what is promised is not always what is delivered.

In the words of Verne Harris, leader of the eight-member team responsible for the publishing project, Mandela has 'opened his personal archive'. Twenty-seven years in prison allowed him much time to reflect, and those reflections were smuggled out of jail in the form of an extraordinary range of letters and diaries, transcripts and journals, notes and memorabilia, going back to his Methodist Church card, dated 1930. The result, says Harris, reveals 'not the icon or saint ... Here he is like you and me ... [the book] gives us his own voice—direct, clear, private.'

Admirers can trawl the pages and discover the trivial, the intimate and the poignant, finding out what Mandela had for breakfast on the day he was moved from Robben Island to the mainland (bacon and eggs), how he coped without sex ('one gets used to that ... and it's not hard to control yourself'), and his reaction to the death of his mother ('I had never dreamt that I would never be able to bury ma,' he wrote in a letter from jail). We learn that Queen Elizabeth is 'a great lady, very sharp'; Pope John Paul II is 'humble, very humble'; Margaret Thatcher is 'warm ... charming ... I was tremendously impressed by her.'

But who is this book for? If *Conversations* was intended for the general reader, these insights, observations and homilies should have been halved in number. Even then, it would require a near obsessive interest in the minutiae of Mandela's life, for we already know much about the man.

We have his 400-page autobiography, *Long Walk to Freedom*; an authorised biography by Anthony Sampson; a sharp, unauthorised biography by Martin Meredith; the books by Allister Sparks; the account of the transition by Patti Waldmeir; and, if you still are not satisfied, his jailers' story.

Perhaps *Conversations* is intended for biographers and historians? It should be an invaluable source, and it would be churlish to deny that the two-year project is a remarkable achievement. But researchers cannot rely on these documents, for they have been 'winnowed', as Harris puts it—a polite way of saying they have been edited. Mandela's own role was limited. Although the book was produced with his 'blessing', writes Harris, Mandela 'indicated his wish not to be involved personally'. He has merely given the project his approval. So one must assume that Harris and his colleagues took it upon themselves to select the material that would be suitable for us to read.

This winnowing explains some important gaps and raises some questions. Does Mandela's first wife, Evelyn, whom he divorced in 1957, really warrant only two references? Should not Mandela have said something about allegations that he physically mistreated her? Why is there not a single indexed reference to the Iraq war, a subject he felt strongly about? Why is there no reference in his papers to Zimbabwe's Robert Mugabe? There may well be good reason to withhold sensitive material. But the failure to register the gaps in the record not only undermines the claim that Mandela has opened his life to public scrutiny, it blunts the cutting edge of what should have been an essential researchers' tool.

So what lies behind this book? Harris says it 'has its origins in the 2004 inauguration of the Nelson Mandela Centre of Memory and Dialogue as the core function of the Nelson Mandela Foundation'. I cannot help wondering if there is more to it than this. I suspect that the book was conceived not merely as an academic exercise but as a fundraising scheme by a foundation that has been in the forefront of a process that has been going for some time: the commercialisation of Nelson Mandela.

Whether it is his autograph or his lithographs, access or image rights or product endorsement, the touch of magic that comes from an association with the world's best known and most loved statesman is available at a price—and that price is often set by the Foundation, which is insatiable in its search for funds to continue its work, and imaginative in devising means of raising more money.

No doubt *Conversations* will make the Christmas bestseller list. For some, the knowledge that the Foundation will benefit from its sales—it holds the copyright to the material in the book—is reason enough to buy it. Others may be tempted to cut out the middlemen, write out a cheque for the price, and send it directly to an African charity of their choice.

Band Aid
Prospect, September 2011

Our hearts demand a generous response to the Horn of Africa famine. Our heads should now ask some tough questions. The UN general assembly, convening on 20th September, should be the venue for frank answers.

For all the calls from international aid donors for African 'ownership' of policies involving the continent, for all their pledges to ensure a role for 'stakeholders', for all their advocacy of 'community participation', one thing stands out: aid agencies have assumed leadership of the famine relief effort in east Africa and have taken decisions that will impact the region for years to come.

Far from providing a hand-on-the-policy tiller, and a voice at the planning table, Africa has sat back, watching from the sidelines the biggest relief operation on the continent since the Ethiopian famine of 1984.

Of course, operating in such a tough neighbourhood is a huge challenge. The drought embraces some of Africa's most troubled states: Eritrea and Ethiopia are bitter enemies; Sudan is a pariah; the newly independent South Sudan is a fledgling in world affairs; Somalia, the worst afflicted by famine, has no government; Kenya, where up to 3 million are at risk, is a byword for corruption.

But this does not justify Africa's absence from the operations room. Nor does it explain why a president or senior minister from one of the afflicted states, or a former leader, or at least a top official from the African Union, has not been chosen by peers to take responsibility for coordinating donor assistance and recipient needs.

Instead, Africa has twiddled its thumbs, postponing by a fortnight an African Union 'emergency' summit scheduled to be held on 9 August. Meanwhile, there has been no one to field some awkward questions.

Many lives have been saved by international intervention, but many have been lost by a late response to an obvious crisis; and many more will be affected by decisions made by aid donors after inadequate consultation. Why was the official announcement of the famine, and the appeal for help, made so late in the day? Children were dying of hunger in north-east Kenya weeks earlier, a fact underplayed at the time by elements of the Kenyan media. Who decided when to declare that the famine was leading to a catastrophe? Were African governments involved in the announcement? If not, why not?

It is unclear who is in charge of relief strategy in the Horn; who takes responsibility for decisions such as endorsing the role of Dadaab, the settlement in north-east Kenya, as a centre for relief operations and home to hundreds of thousands of Somalis fleeing the drought. With a population of over 400,000, Dadaab is one of Kenya's largest 'cities'. But catching up fast will be a second such camp: the result of pressure on a reluctant Kenyan government, despite the fact that the country's weak coalition doesn't have the governance and security capacity to absorb a huge flow of refugees to another site.

Africa's economic recovery has gathered pace in recent years, changing many countries dramatically. But decades of decline have left a grim legacy. In far too many places, the state is weak; its capacity to initiate change has shrunk. The reluctance or inability of African governments to play a part in the response to the famine marks yet another step in their surrender of authority and abnegation of responsibility—and the beneficiaries are the very organisations that play such a big role in disaster relief: non-governmental organisations (NGOs).

The power and influence of NGOs has grown dramatically since African independence 50 years ago. From a few thousand in the 1960s, controlling funds measured in the millions, there are now over 50,000 NGOs operating in South Africa alone.

Although the NGO record on development is mixed at best, the number of NGOs granted consultative status by the Economic and Social Council—the central UN forum for formulating policy on social and economic issues—has risen from 41 in 1948 to over 1,350 in 2008.

As their numbers have grown, they have helped to undermine what the character named Oldest Member, a crusty retired district officer who lives in Kenya and features in my latest novel, *Dizzy Worms*, identifies as the social contract.

In the novel, he asks himself: 'What if the government doesn't deliver? What if the chaps in the north east come to realise that although there is a "food deficit" every year, they won't starve? ... Why? Cos WorldFeed and Oxfam and their UN chums will chip in. All managed by foreigners. Tens of thousands of the buggers come out each year, catching the gravy train that chuffs its way around Africa ... If you are starving, the UN will feed you; if the mozzies are killing your kids, Bill Gates will provide a mosquito net; if your road needs rebuilding, DanAid will help ... So if the state can't deliver, why be loyal? Why pay your taxes? Instead you look to big-man politics, to your relative, to your clan, to the ethnic leaders or the regional boss.'

In other words, a vicious cycle has been created. As the state surrenders many of its core responsibilities to aid agencies, its capacity to manage deteriorates. In the process, it loses some of the country's brightest and best to the NGOs and UN agencies, who offer salaries that local employers cannot match.

Soon the aid caravan will move on, leaving the two biggest questions unanswered: where has Africa been during the crisis? And why have international aid donors not raised this question themselves? Generosity without accountability is no way to respond to Africa's gravest famine for 25 years.

Africa is rising—and Britain's bwanas are out of step

Financial Times, 28 February 2012

Africa is on the move: from basket case to a potential bread basket, from dodgy debtor to investor opportunity. Too bad that Britain risks remaining out of step and out of touch.

Last week's London summit on Somalia was remarkable for its high turnout and admirable in its good intentions. No one can dispute the damage done by piracy in waters used by international shipping, or the threat posed by extremists who shelter behind a collapsed administration. But safety at sea is dependent on economic recovery on land. And restoring a failed state means tackling poverty.

This needs a summit of a different kind, by all means endorsed by David Cameron,[36] but initiated by African leaders—and it should have preceded any gathering on Somalia.

Such a conference would not only have celebrated the start of a new era for Africa, it would have taken advantage of the continent's growing capacity to help itself, and invited pledges of international support for changes that give hope to the people of shattered Somalia and beyond.

There is much to celebrate. A market of nearly 1 billion people, about a third of them under 21, is making up for five wasted post-independence decades. From Johannesburg to Djibouti, from Lagos to Lusaka, something dramatic is afoot. Fuelled by booming oil exports, boosted by higher commodity prices, funded by cheap loans from China and by returning capital from the diaspora, as well as by foreign investment, Africa's social and physical landscape is being reshaped.

---

[36] David Cameron (born 1966) was British Conservative prime minister between 2010 and 2016.

But it is gaining more than new shopping malls and airport terminals and skyscrapers. The military by and large stay in the barracks. Human rights are higher on the agenda. And in a sign of the change afoot in a continent that had lost confidence in itself, there is a wave of creativity: novelists and artists, film-makers and musicians, designers and stylists, all are thriving.

Of course, huge challenges remain. Despite the hurdles, there is no doubt that the continent is at an exciting stage in its modern history. Yet something is missing.

To many African officials and business leaders, Britain—for so long Africa's traditional partner in Europe—has seemed slow to respond to the challenge posed by the new era and, unable to see the need for a fresh relationship, has failed to turn Commonwealth membership and the shared English language to commercial advantage.

Part of the reason may be the malaise that still hangs over the continent, a legacy from past disappointments. Many diplomats see Africa as life in the slow-career track; academics struggle for research funds; retired colonial civil servants take their knowledge to the grave; journalists drop in and move on; and business leaders who once forged careers on the continent now see a stint in Lagos or Luanda as a hardship post. The result? Contracts are lost, markets seek new suppliers, old ties count for little and old friendships go unnourished.

Another part of the reason goes back, I suspect, to Britain's colonial past—with an unexpected twist. For years UK ministers have lectured Africa's leaders on the need to rise above their colonial heritage. The continent has been urged to put aside old grievances and start afresh.

How ironic, then, that while a youthful continent breaks free of this legacy, welcoming new investors from Turkey, Malaysia and elsewhere, it should be Britain, not Africa, that at times seems burdened by the past.

Perhaps embedded in the national consciousness, seldom recognised and rarely acknowledged, are attitudes that continue to distort Britain's relationship with a continent it once dominated.

Too often behind official pronouncements lies a belief that Britain retains a right, indeed an obligation, to offer correctives to African governments seen to transgress. British aid agencies assume the right to shape local policy when natural disaster strikes. Increasing aid is seen as the path to economic growth and African entrepreneurs resent the assumption that the City of London, and not Beijing, will be their first port of call when seeking project finance.

Until recently Africa had no choice but to put up with this. After all, there was no denying postcolonial governments had been corrupt and incompetent. Weak economies had no option but to take the medicine from the International Monetary Fund.

Today the Fund has other matters on its mind, preoccupied as it is with saving European economies. And for the first time, loans from the World Bank to Africa—the reward for taking the IMF medicine—have been overtaken by soft loans from China. The stick once used with abandon is now little more than a twig.

As Africa changes, there arises a niggling question. Could Britain's response to the opportunities on the continent be influenced by memories of the days when the colonial *bwana* knew best?

Dambisa Moyo: Dead Aid

Why Aid is not Working and How There is Another Way for Africa

The Literary Review, August 2012

The international aid industry is surely one of the most successful lobbyists the world has seen. Its record after forty years of involvement in sub-Saharan Africa, funnelling a trillion dollars of assistance, is abysmal: the region is as impoverished today as it was at independence. Yet the worse the aid agencies' performance, the more money they ask for—and get. This is chutzpah on a truly grand scale.

It is hardly surprising that every year this gravy train attracts some 100,000 expatriate 'experts', ranging from the well-meaning to the self-serving. Many of them have been recruited by the multi-tentacled United Nations; others work for the official government development agencies; and the rest enlist in the thousands of non-government organisations that have sprung up since the 1960s.

Meanwhile 60,000 of Africa's best and brightest officially emigrate to Europe and North America. That is worrying enough. The continent can ill afford this annual brain drain. Equally disquieting, the inflow of aid funds is matched by capital outflows from Africa which end up in the West.

Clearly something is wrong. Dambisa Moyo,[37] Zambian-born, a string of degrees to her name, a two-year stint at the World Bank and eight years at Goldman Sachs under her belt, thinks she has the answer.

'The problem is that aid is not benign, but malignant; no longer part of the solution, it's part of the problem—in fact, aid is the problem.'

---

[37] Dambisa Moyo (born 1969) is a Zambian economist and author specialising in macroeconomics and global affairs, and has served on the boards of numerous international corporations and banks. Dead Aid was the first of her four New York Times bestsellers.

Ms Moyo, humming with anger and frustration, goes on to draw up a passionate indictment of all forms of Western aid, and official aid in particular. Whether during the Cold War, when donors courted dictators and sacrificed development, or the more recent efforts encouraged by celebs and pop stars, the consequences have been destructive, she argues. Aid projects have siphoned off scarce local talent. And most damaging of all, the social contract between the governed and the state has been eroded.

The answer, Moyo maintains, is a phased end to Africa's 'addiction' to aid.

Donors, she says, should put each and every country on formal notice that they have five years to find alternative sources of development funds. Further Chinese investment in Africa should be encouraged, especially in infrastructure; African governments should borrow on the international bond market; they should do more to promote domestic savings and to support micro-credit schemes; and a radical overhaul of land ownership is long overdue, turning property rights into security against loans, within the framework of an independent judiciary.

There would have been problems with these suggestions at the best of times. It would take more than a threatened aid cut-off to make venal and autocratic African leaders turn over a new leaf.

But the main weakness of the package lies in its failure to take into account the impact of the financial crisis that grips the credit-crunch world. The implications for Africa are profound. The commodity boom, at the heart of what many had hoped was a sustained African economic recovery, has ended. The call for fair and open trade faces renewed protectionist opposition. Remittances from Africans working abroad—a crucial source of foreign exchange for most countries—are falling as unemployment rises in the West; and it will be a brave investor who puts their money into an African government bond. Tanzania has postponed plans to issue a debut Eurobond of $500 million until market conditions improve; Uganda and Ghana have followed suit.

A wiser and braver publisher would have insisted that publication of *Dead Aid* be delayed while Moyo assessed the impact of these developments and then came up with fresh ideas. Instead she has been allowed to get away with no mention of the international economic trauma at all.

The author has, as Niall Ferguson writes in his enthusiastic foreword, 'quite a CV', which combines 'academic expertise and "real world" experience'.

Real world? Oxford, Harvard, the World Bank, and eight years of debt capital markets, hedge funds, global macroeconomics at Goldman Sachs ... . Ms Moyo may have been born in Zambia but she was bred in an ivory tower which she has been reluctant to leave.

No doubt she will be in great demand, invited to grace speaking platforms and attend book festivals around the country. I trust she will be alive to the danger that her arguments against aid will be used as intellectual fuel by those whose motives may be far from pure and whose concern for Africa may be less than genuine.

In the meantime, the continent could well be forced to look afresh at aid flows, but without the five-year cushion in which to find new sources of funding.

As the old adage has it, be careful what you wish for—it may come true.

Paul Theroux: The Last Train to Zona Verde

The Literary Review, June 2013

'I am not an Afro-pessimist,' writes Paul Theroux, looking back on a journey that has taken him from the slums of Cape Town to the *musseques* of Luanda. You could have fooled me. *The Last Train to Zona Verde* is imbued with a pessimism that verges on Afrophobia, peppered with sweeping, doom-laden conclusions about the state of Africa, triggered by a trip that takes in but a fraction of a vast continent.

Given the nature of most of the stops on Theroux's journey, the gloomy tone is not surprising. It begins with Khayelitsha and Guguletu, the Cape's two sinkholes of humanity; takes in northern Namibia, 'a land of drunken men, idle boys and overworked women'; includes a visit to the Kalahari home of what an eminent anthropologist calls 'the most victimized and brutalized people in the bloody history that is southern Africa'; and ends in Angola, a country cursed by its huge oil wealth, which has been siphoned off to personal overseas accounts by members of a regime as corrupt as any in Africa.

If the destinations are depressing, the manner of travel seems intended to make things worse. Theroux relishes his discomfort, which he wears like a hair shirt, chronicling nights spent in seedy dosshouses; hour upon hour in miserable buses with shouting, jostling passengers, peeing children and dying chickens; and unpleasant encounters with aggressive border officials.

His experience of Luanda, the noisome capital of Angola, proves too much. Something in Theroux snaps, and he lets rip. 'I seemed to be traveling into greater misery,' he writes: 'the misery of Africa, the awful, poisoned, populous Africa; the Africa of cheated, despised, unaccommodated people; of seemingly unfixable blight: so hideous, really, it is unrecognizable as Africa at all. But it is, of course—the new Africa.'

He had contemplated taking the train from Luanda to Malanje, some 265 miles inland, where a *zona verde* was said to be home to much of what remains of the country's wildlife. Theroux lets it leave without him. 'What am I doing here?' he asks, time and again.

Plans to end his journey at the ancient Malian city of Timbuktu are dropped. Travelling to 'squalid cities and fetid slums', he writes, 'requires all the skill and temperament of a proctologist ... deft in rectal exams ... staring solemnly ... up its fundament and trawling through its intestines, making the grand colonic tour ... [which] pretty much describes the experience of traveling from one African city to another, especially the horror cities of urbanized West Africa.'

This is schoolboy stuff, gratuitously offensive, a crude and ignorant portrayal of Africa as arsehole, refusing to acknowledge the many ways the continent is changing for the better. There's not a word on the new breed of African entrepreneur, the computer whizz kids, the spread of the mobile phone and its impact on democracy, no mention of the renaissance in art, literature, fashion and music, or the surge of foreign investment and the competition for Africa's minerals, oil and farmland.

It is an omission that undermines Theroux's credibility and the book's effect. This is a pity, because he does more than bemoan the current state of the continent; he also mourns the loss of an Africa long gone, which he captures in two poignant portraits. He is at his best when he describes the fate of the Kalahari people known as Ju/'hoansi. These former fleet-footed bush-dwellers have become sedentary town folk reliant on hand-outs, and face extermination through alcohol and Western mores. The other image is of a group of wretched elephants, rescued from captivity only to be prodded into servitude, providing rides for guests at a $4,000-a-day game lodge in the Okavango Delta. They represent the fate of Africa's fast-disappearing wildlife, destined for game parks that are becoming little more than glorified zoos.

Theroux, of course, is no stranger to Africa. His experience of the continent goes back to the 1960s, when he worked for six years as a teacher in Malawi and as a university lecturer in Uganda—'the freest period of my life'. In 2002, he travelled overland from Cairo to Cape Town. The result was *Dark Star Safari*, where his frustration and irritation with Africa were already apparent. His latest journey, almost certainly his last in Africa, ends on a bleak note, envisaging a continent whose population of one billion will—according to Theroux—double in four years, doomed to subsist in slum cities and burnt-out villages, ill-governed and insecure.

He used to travel, he writes, with 'no idea where I was going, but it was a joy to be on the move'. Paul Theroux has lost that joy and without it his writing loses much of its magic. The Last Train to Zona Verde is nevertheless a tale worth heeding. But no longer does one relish the company of an observant, knowledgeable guide; instead one travels with an embittered and introspective old cynic who cannot wait to get home.

Daniel Metcalfe: Blue Dahlia, Black Gold
A Journey into Angola
The Literary Review, September 2013

Pity the Angolans: rich in oil but mired in poverty, led by scoundrels, victims of as grim a history as any country in Africa. A Portuguese colony for over three hundred years, scarred by the slave trade, Angola was finally liberated from Lisbon in 1975, only to be traumatised by a 27-year civil war. Ever since independence the country has been the milk cow for a ruling elite dependent on the patronage of President José Eduardo dos Santos. In office since 1979, he has drawn on a slush fund of billions of dollars from oil exports, now running at nearly two million barrels a day, which he has dispensed to his cronies and family, including his daughter Isabel, Africa's wealthiest woman. For most travel writers, a destination with such a cornucopia of distress and excess—one Angolan fat cat is said to boast a statue that pees champagne—would have an overwhelming allure. Provided, that is, they have the resilience required. Paul Theroux found the sheer misery he encountered in Angola too much and abandoned a journey that he had intended to end much further north.

Daniel Metcalfe, a 34-year-old who won praise for his first book, *Out of Steppe: The Lost Peoples of Central Asia*, is made of sterner stuff—or perhaps he enjoys the resilience of youth. To prepare for a three-month stay in Angola he takes the trouble to learn Portuguese, reads widely and mixes with Angolan exiles in London. They share their memories of a homeland of warm welcomes and generous hospitality—a stark contrast to the travel guides full of horror stories that label Angola an 'anti-tourist' country to avoid. But far from putting off the author, these tales only whet his appetite: 'What kind of society', asks Metcalfe, 'sells hamburgers for £30 and awful hotel rooms for £300 a night? It is such an extreme situation it's almost laughable. It was also an irresistible challenge ... I wanted to prove the cynics wrong.'

This, surely, is the authentic voice of a travel writer driven by curiosity, fascinated by the chosen country, determined to share his journey with the reader. No further justification is needed. But it is not enough for Metcalfe, who lapses into academic speak, seeing Angola as a symbol for 'a broader turning point between the continents, the repositioning of the rich world versus Africa'. Fortunately, his heart isn't in it. He makes a passing reference to the irony of Angolans snapping up Portuguese companies, tosses in a meaningless statistic ('the new oil-fuelled boom ... averaging a staggering 15 per cent a year'—15 per cent of what?), and then gets down to what he is so good at: first-class reporting, descriptions of remarkable characters and easy-to-digest history lessons.

Arriving in Luanda via a stopover in São Tomé and Príncipe, a tiny archipelago once part of the Portuguese empire, Metcalfe gets to grips with the squalid *musseques* (slums) and soaring new skyscrapers of Angola's booming capital, before making his first excursion, appropriately enough to Benguela, today a railhead but once an embarkation point for the slave trade. He meets a specialist in Angolan colonial history who recounts how for more than three centuries Angola served the labour needs of Brazil. By 1700 the South American colony was demanding 10,000 slaves a year, decimating Angola's population. The route to the sea, writes one traveller from the time, 'was strewn with dead men's bones ... skeletons of slaves ... unable to keep up with the march'. By the late 18th century, notes Metcalfe, women outnumbered men by as much as 60 per cent, thanks to a trade aided and abetted by Angola's fat cats of their day—the local chiefs who collaborated with the slave masters. 'How many Angolans know ... the history of the slavery of their own people?' asks Metcalfe. The answer is one of the saddest lines in the book: 'Few know anything these days. Don't think they care much either.'

If the horrors of the slave trade have been buried in the national psyche, the town of Huambo and the backwater of Cuito Cuanavale provide an enduring reminder of the violent, recent past. Anything between six and twenty million landmines still litter the landscape, a legacy of the civil war in which troops from apartheid South Africa and communist Cuba clashed on Angolan soil. No wonder so much is *confusão*, says Metcalfe, using a word with a meaning unique to Angola, embracing the long queues at government buildings, the hazards of

Luanda traffic, a crippling despair and a soul-sapping lethargy. Just about wherever his travels take him, he finds a land that reeks of neglect —a land where there is one doctor to every 10,000 Angolans, where AIDS is on the increase, malaria kills thousands, tuberculosis is prevalent and polio still a risk; where 29 per cent of the budget is spent on one of Africa's biggest armies and 6 per cent on health services. All the more puzzling, then, is the optimistic note on which *Blue Dahlia, Black Gold* ends. As he sits in Luanda airport awaiting the flight home, Metcalfe recalls an exchange in London with an exiled Angolan who wondered what had happened to the country he had left behind, a land of 'humanity, family-run bars, of *kizomba* dancing, of joy'.

Metcalfe writes, 'I wanted to tell him that it was all still there, that there might be injustice and greed, but behind a kind of tortoise shell of armour you see it everywhere: in the hail of rumba music that christens every bus journey, in the longed-for rain that batters the roofs of the houses, in the polyphonic singing in Luanda cathedral and in the passion of the newspaper sellers.'

Given all that has gone before, this upbeat note is hard to justify. Indeed, it comes close to parody—the good-humoured native, proud and plucky, singing and dancing in the face of adversity. All that is missing is a reference to Angolans' wonderful sense of rhythm. A baffling conclusion to what nevertheless is still a very good book.

Nelson Mandela
Mandela's magic captivated all ranks
Financial Times, 6 December 2013

It was early morning at Buckingham Palace, an hour before breakfast on a glorious July day in 1996, that Nelson Mandela worked his magic on the *Financial Times*.

Outside, the gravel was still being raked and sightseers had yet to gather at the palace gates. But the Queen's distinguished house guest had long been up and about and was raring to go, ready for his first meeting—an interview with the FT.

Mandela, then a sprightly septuagenarian, entered the drawing room through a door held open by a palace official, who was looking firmly and fixedly ahead, his face set in an expression of robotic deference.

The first president of a democratic South Africa paused on the threshold. To the doorman's delight, Mandela exchanged a few words and then warmly shook his hand.

Thirty minutes later, another palace official, hovering in the background, was silently jabbing his finger at his wristwatch. Our time was up.

But before we got to our feet, there was a chance to put a final question. It had been entrusted to me, I explained to the president, by Alice, aged 12, daughter of an old friend.

'Would you ask Mr. Mandela if he has any pets—and if so, what are their names?'

The clock-watching official mouthed his irritation.

President Nelson Mandela sat back in his chair. Until this point, he had batted away our earnest questions about the health of the rand, and the pace of privatisation, with reassuring noises.

At last, said his body language, here was a real question, one that warranted thought, reflection and a considered and convincing response.

For the best part of five minutes, with the official gesticulating in the background, Mandela answered Alice's question, allowing insights into the pressures of life at the top for the world's most popular politician.

'No, I don't have any pets,' he began, 'but tell your friend Alice that while I would like to keep pets, my life does not allow it.'

He had gone through a painful, acrimonious divorce from his second wife, Winnie, a couple of years earlier and had yet to marry Graça Machel, who survives him.

The lonely man who sat before us continued: 'When I get back to my grandchildren the first thing they ask is: "Grandpa, when will you be going away again?" It is a painful question. Like my grandchildren, pets need love and company. How can I provide that if I am always away?'

It was in Pretoria, however, the South African capital, that I finally succumbed to the Mandela magic. By now I had met the man several times but I had never been able to bring myself to ask for a photo of us together. It seemed somehow unprofessional.

This time, however, I had prepared my excuse. 'It's for my mother,' I said.

The veteran FT photographer, the late Ashley Ashwood, took the pictures that now have pride of place on my study wall. We were done. Or so I thought.

'Doesn't Ashley have a mother?' Mandela asked. He pointed to an aide. 'Give him your camera, Ashley. Now come and stand by me.'

The hard-bitten photographer handed over his camera and stood alongside the president. Ashley beamed, Mandela smiled and the camera clicked.

They say no man can be a hero to his valet. By the same token, it would seem unlikely that a politician can ever be a hero to a journalist.

We protect ourselves with notebook and ingrained scepticism, which together serve as shield against the possibility that one could end up admiring the men or the women we write about. It worked for me— at least, until I met Nelson Mandela.

Nelson Mandela: Obituary

Sunday Telegraph, 7 December 2013

Once reviled as a 'terrorist' by adversaries who jailed him, acclaimed as a liberator by his people who venerated him, Nelson Mandela, South Africa's first democratically elected president, who became the world's favourite statesman, has died.

It is far too soon for a detached evaluation of the overall impact of this 20th-century colossus.

His record in office was not without blemish: though personally untainted by financial scandal, his fierce loyalty to comrades from the anti-apartheid struggle meant he often turned a blind eye to the corruption that spread in the new South Africa. Foreign-policy decisions suggested that Pretoria's support could be influenced by financial considerations rather than principles; diplomatic intervention in African conflicts proved ineffectual; trade reforms in South Africa were often at the cost of its African neighbours, leading to a resentment of the continent's superpower that persists to this day.

But few can dispute the claim that Madiba—the clan name by which nearly every South African knew him—changed the course of his country's history.

His extraordinary compassion and shrewd understanding of his enemies, sustained throughout and beyond his 27 years in detention, and his determined pursuit of racial reconciliation, were exemplary. Mandela rescued his country from the brink of disaster, doing so in a way that transcended South Africa's crisis, serving as an inspiration around the globe and giving generations of Africans a hero they shared with an admiring world.

In a life rich in drama, triumph and tragedy, four momentous events proved milestones. His conduct during South Africa's infamous Treason Trial (conducted over four years from 1957 to 1961) and at the trial in 1962 that led to his incarceration, where he made his defiant, electrifying statement from the dock—'democracy [is] an ideal for which I am prepared to die'—first alerted the outside world to the presence of a remarkable man. Sentenced to life imprisonment, he was taken to Cape Town's notorious Robben Island prison. No photographs were allowed and until his eventual release, his image was frozen in time.

On 11 February 1990, more than a quarter of a century later, having endured privations and hardships, and after nearly two years of secret negotiations, Mandela walked to freedom through the gates of Cape Town's Victor Verster prison, watched by cameras broadcasting live around the world.

Four years later, Mandela was again in the international spotlight when, at the age of 75, he celebrated the outcome of South Africa's first democratic elections, leading the African National Congress to an overwhelming victory with 62 per cent of the vote.

But perhaps the most enduring image of all is of a beaming Mandela, wearing the green-and-gold Springbok rugby shirt, shaking hands with team captain Francois Pienaar, just before kick-off in the 1995 Rugby World Cup final against New Zealand. It was a gesture rich in significance, given the sport's strong associations with the Afrikaners of South Africa, whose leaders did so much to entrench apartheid.

Nelson Rolihlahla Mandela (his middle name means 'troublemaker') was born on 18 July 1918 at Mvezo, a village on the banks of the Mbashe River in a poor but picturesque province between the rugged Drakensberg mountains and the blue waters of the Indian Ocean that is home to the Thembu people.

Although close to the royal household, he was not of the royal family. Instead he was groomed to be a court adviser, an upbringing that helps to account for the dignity and assurance that marked his conduct throughout his life, and that made him feel at home with commoners and queens alike—a quality shown during a state visit to Britain in 1996.

The visit cemented a friendship with the Royal family, the Queen in particular, whom he phoned regularly, addressing her as 'Elizabeth', inquiring after 'Philip', and offering a break in South Africa to the young princes William and Harry after their mother Diana, Princess of Wales, had been killed in a car crash.

Mandela's formal education was dominated by church-run institutions, whose schools prepared him for entry to the University of Fort Hare, founded in 1916 by Scottish missionaries and home to some of the leading African intellectuals of the time.

'We were exhorted to obey God, respect the political authorities, be grateful for educational opportunities and for the opportunities afforded us by the church and government,' he recalled in his autobiography, Long Walk to Freedom. He soon lived up to his middle name. Mandela resigned from Fort Hare's student representative council in a dispute over its role, and was suspended.

The episode led to Mandela setting off for Johannesburg, where he first became an articled clerk, and in 1943 began a law degree at the city's Wits University. By the time he went into partnership with Oliver Tambo, the man who was to lead the ANC in exile, he was deeply involved in politics, spurred on by a watershed event: the 1948 parliamentary election, won by Dr Hendrik Verwoerd and the National Party.

Under Verwoerd, racial segregation was formally entrenched as apartheid, turning into law the assumption that Africans were innately inferior to Europeans. The stage was set for confrontation.

Mandela played a leading role in the creation of the ANC Youth League and helped to launch the so-called 'defiance campaign', a series of non-violent protests against racial segregation including the pass laws, the hated permit system that required Blacks to carry identification that limited their movements to specific areas.

Although his life was now dominated by politics, he found time to box in a township gym. With the build of an athlete—tall, broad shoulders, tapering to narrow hips, light on his feet—he seemed a natural. Mandela, however, played down his ability: 'I was never an outstanding boxer ...' he wrote, 'but it was a way of losing myself in something that was not about the struggle.'

The 'struggle' took its toll on his first marriage to Evelyn Mase, a nurse, which ended in 1955. But he never lost his eye for an attractive woman. His relationship with his first wife was coming to an end when he was smitten: 'As I passed a nearby bus stop, I noticed out of the corner of my eye a lovely young woman waiting for a bus. Her name was Nomzamo Winifred Madikizela ... and I knew that I wanted to have her as my wife.'

Winnie won his heart, and later broke it, getting caught up in events leading to the death of a young boy during Mandela's long years in prison, and suspected of being unfaithful to her marriage vows. They separated in 1992.

For years he had been on the front line, instrumental in drawing up the ANC's Freedom Charter, with its memorable opening line: 'We, the people of South Africa, declare ... that South Africa belongs to all who live in it ... .'

'I cannot pinpoint a moment when I became politicised, when I knew that I would spend my life in the liberation struggle,' he wrote in his autobiography. 'To be an African in South Africa means that one is politicised from the moment of one's birth ... I had no epiphany, no singular revelation, no moment of truth, but a steady accumulation of a thousand slights, a thousand indignities ... [which] produced in me an anger, a rebelliousness, a desire to fight the system that imprisoned my people.'

In December 1956, Mandela and 150 others—black, white, Indian and coloured—were arrested and charged with treason. The marathon trial ended in 1961, with all defendants acquitted.

Mandela, however, feared re-arrest and went underground, where he concluded that the ANC policy of non-violence would never dislodge a regime so intransigent. 'In my heart I knew non-violence was not the answer.' In June 1961, the ANC leadership took a fateful decision: Mandela was authorised to create a military wing and sent on a mission abroad to secure support.

'I, who had never been a soldier, who had never fought a battle, who had never fired a gun at an enemy, had been given the task of starting an army—uMkhonto we Sizwe, the spear of the nation' (also known as MK). After a journey that took him through much of newly independent Africa and ended in London, he returned to resume his underground life.

It was only a matter of time before the dawn knock on the door. On 5 August 1962, after Mandela had been on the run for 17 months, the security police swooped.

The case of the State versus Nelson Mandela and others, better known as the Rivonia Trial, after the farm where he had been captured, opened in October 1963. He and the other defendants were charged with complicity in more than 200 acts of sabotage, hitting power pylons and electricity stations, aimed at 'facilitating violent revolution', according to the prosecution.

In a remarkable statement from the dock, Mandela admitted he had helped to form MK, defended his actions and ended on a note of defiance that rang around the world: 'I have cherished the ideal of a democratic and free society ... it is an ideal which I hope to live for and to achieve. But if needs be, it is an ideal for which I am prepared to die.'

Sentenced to life imprisonment, Mandela and colleagues were taken to Robben Island, a narrow, windswept rocky outcrop, 18 miles off the coast, where a group of white warders greeted them with the words: 'Dis die eiland! Heir gaan julle vrek.' (This is the island! Here you will die!) Conditions were harsh and unhealthy. Mandela's cell was damp, the winter bitterly cold, the work in a lime quarry arduous, the warders brutal. He was 46 years old.

From the mid-1980s, however, his status began to change. Apartheid was under increasing challenge. The government realised that Mandela's role was vital if centuries of white domination that began soon after Jan van Riebeeck landed at the Cape in 1652, and which culminated in 40 years of apartheid, were to end through negotiation and not violent confrontation.

After 18 years, he and other ANC officials were moved to Pollsmoor prison, near Cape Town, making it easier for contact between the two sides. The first formal round of secret talks got under way at Pollsmoor in May 1988.

Later that year he met P.W. Botha, the hard-line president, an occasion combining the historic, comic and bizarre. Shortly before the two men got together, South Africa's intelligence chief, Niel Barnard, noticed that Mandela's shoelaces were loose, and knelt to tie them.

Mandela, true to form, has kind words to say about Botha. 'He had his hand out and was smiling broadly and in fact from that very first moment, he completely disarmed me. He was unfailingly courteous, deferential and friendly.' Similar gentle appraisals mark just about every comment he makes about international figures.

Queen Elizabeth is 'a great lady, very sharp'; Pope John Paul was 'humble, very humble'; even Margaret Thatcher, who had called the ANC a terrorist organisation (a view shared by the US State Department well into the 1990s), was 'warm, caring … I was tremendously impressed by her'.

On 11 February 1990, nearly 30 years to the day after the British prime minister Harold Macmillan had warned South Africa's all-white parliament that the 'wind of change' gusting through Africa would inevitably reach the Cape, Mandela walked through the gates of Victor Verster prison, wife Winnie by his side, confronted by a battery of television cameras.

Mandela faced seemingly overwhelming problems. Black townships across the land were ungovernable. A conflict close to civil war raged in the province of Natal, where 20,000 had died. State security forces were given free rein to suppress dissent within South Africa's borders, using torture and hit squads. And the generals supported insurgencies in Mozambique and Angola.

Mandela arrived late for his appearance at Cape Town's city hall. A restless crowd had earlier clashed with nervous security forces, encounters marked by the sound of breaking glass, accompanied by the acrid smell of tear gas.

It was an occasion that called for a sensitive speech but what he delivered seemed hard, didactic and inflexible, and had, it turned out, been written by an ad hoc committee of the ANC.

'We are still suffering under the policy of the Nationalist government,' Mandela declared, ending his first address as a free man with a call to 'the international community to continue the campaign to isolate the apartheid regime'.

But the following day, at a press conference on the lawn of the Anglican Archbishop of Cape Town, Desmond Tutu, Mandela took charge. The good humour, civility, tolerance and compassion that guided his conduct were displayed at their best. Above all, he delivered a message that the minority race, about to surrender power, craved: 'The Whites are our fellow South Africans. We want them to feel safe.'

Reconciliation became the watchword as he met Percy Yutar, his treason trial prosecutor who had sought the death penalty, and took tea with Betsy Verwoerd, wife of the architect of apartheid.

Fortunately for South Africa, a heart attack had forced Botha to step down, for notwithstanding his courteous reception of Mandela, he was an irascible, finger-wagging conservative. The pragmatic F.W. de Klerk —with whom Mandela was to share the Nobel Peace Prize—succeeded him, and talks on a new constitution got under way.

The ANC, the National Party, Chief Buthelezi's Inkatha, and a host of smaller parties set about negotiating a new constitution, with few observers holding out much hope of success.

Mandela's relations with de Klerk were sometimes fraught, and on one memorable occasion Mandela displayed the steely side to his character. It was at the first session of the constitutional conference, the Convention for a Democratic South Africa (Codesa), in December 1991.

With the accumulated anger of centuries of humiliation and brutality borne by fellow black South Africans, Mandela laid into de Klerk, calling him 'the head of an illegitimate, discredited, minority regime' who was guilty of duplicity, trickery and lying.

In April 1993 the peace process was brought close to collapse when

Chris Hani, a charismatic ANC leader who was a hero to the radical youth, was assassinated by two white right-wingers. Mandela went on television to appeal for calm. An event that could have destabilised South Africa brought out the best in him, presidential in his quiet authority.

The election of 1994 turned out a triumph. At a celebration in Johannesburg that night, Mandela, surely then the world's sprightliest septuagenarian, strutted his stuff across the stage and into history, leading a joyous high-stepping celebration of South Africa's emancipation from apartheid.

After his term, Mandela gracefully handed over to Thabo Mbeki, his *de facto* prime minister, and gradually retired from public life, making his last appearance at the 2010 football World Cup accompanied by his third wife Graça Machel, widow of the Mozambican leader, whom he married in 1998.

Of the many images of Mandela—young boxer, treason trial defendant, walking to freedom, celebrating election victory—one surely stands out.

Mandela had chosen the anniversary of the 1976 student revolt, one of the country's most sensitive, to deliver a message to black youth, just days before the Rugby World Cup final. Right arm aloft, fist clenched, sporting a peaked cap in the green-and-gold Springbok colours, Mandela called on them to rally behind a rugby team that was overwhelmingly white: 'The cap I am wearing is to honour our boys ... I ask each and every one of you to stand behind them, because they are our pride, they are my pride, they are your pride. They are our kind.'

After the Springbok victory that Saturday, a small boy on a Johannes-burg street corner joined in the celebrations. With his hands cupped aside his head, forefingers jutting like budding horns, neck arched, back curved and rump high, a youthful black springbok pranced with delight at South Africa's success. A passing white motorist hooted in response. Driver and boy exchanged grins as wide as Nelson Mandela's on his team's victory.

The scene encapsulated the reconciliation Mandela tirelessly sought, personally demonstrated, and ceaselessly urged on a country that for centuries had been divided by race—a principle that will surely be uppermost in the thoughts of South Africans as they grieve the loss of this moral giant who wrested power from the hands of moral incompetents.

Nelson Mandela: Funeral circus
Unpublished, 16 December 2013

Nelson Mandela would surely have winced. After ten days of adulation, glorification and veneration came beatification in the guise of a funeral.

In his home village of Qunu, in accordance with the Mandela family wish for privacy, the final rites in the four-hour ceremony were attended by 400 'close friends and family'. Presumably this included Richard Branson and Oprah Winfrey, whose contribution to the anti-apartheid cause needs no elaboration.

But there was no way of knowing for sure who was on the guest list of the elite. The final act of interment was closed to cameras and commentators, part of a 2,500-strong media army, including 150 from the BBC. Many had paid up to 10,000 rands a night for a room in a mud-hut-turned-hotel by Qunu's entrepreneurial residents.

After more than a week of saying much the same thing, the broadcasters were confronted with a challenge even greater than coping with the palatal click in the word *Xhosa*—variously pronounced 'kaw-suh', 'co-sir' and 'cusser'. The burial site had been screened off—much to their evident surprise. And the commentators had no pictures. There was nothing to see or much to say. The anchor of Al-Jazeera was reduced to asking their hapless correspondent which crops grow in the Eastern Cape.

The anchors battled on, managing to make something out of nothing. Perhaps this was the first of the three miracles required by the Catholic Church as part of the beatification process.

Earlier, proceedings had got under way with an address delivered by a bishop with all the flair and passion of a man who reads aloud from a telephone directory.

The elephant in the room looked on, rumours and allegations of corruption circulating like ravens above President Jacob Zuma's head. Flanked by Mandela's widow Graça Machel and ex-wife Winnie Mandela, the two women seemed reconciled in life by the great man's death. Evidence, surely, of miracle number two.

The succession of speakers extolled the virtues of the man now called 'Tata' (grandfather).

Meanwhile, a glum-looking Desmond Tutu was recovering from a hissy-fit. The previous night, he had complained that he had not been invited and was not prepared to gatecrash. He would not, he announced, turn up. So there. The alternative explanation of his threatened absence is that he had had enough of the Zuma Government record of sleaze and incompetence. For a moment he cracked. Whatever the truth, he did turn up but took no part in the proceedings.

Looking back on these extraordinary days, it seems that Nelson Mandela, icon and inspiration, is both a beneficiary and victim of massive advances in information technology. We are now used to instant information provided twenty-four hours a day. The disadvantage is that we seem to have lost our capacity to sustain interest in any event for very long—even one as momentous as today's funeral.

As for the third miracle? Perhaps the very occasion of today's event can be seen as the culmination of a process which began twenty years ago when the man in the coffin walked to freedom and office.

Investors in corrupt 'new Africa' repeat old errors

Financial Times, 9 April 2014

Either memories are short or our ethical compass is faulty. Or do we simply no longer give a damn? When Barclays refused to end its ties with apartheid South Africa, protesting students in Britain took their business elsewhere. In 1986 the bank changed its mind and its policy. Three decades later Nigeria, despite being notorious for corruption, had no difficulty raising $1 billion by issuing sovereign debt. The bond was over-subscribed.

Of course, there is no moral equivalence between the evil of apartheid and the consequences of endemic graft in Nigeria and elsewhere in Africa. Apartheid ruined the lives of generations and its poison spread beyond South Africa. But corruption also ruins lives. Across Africa billions of dollars have been misspent and diverted into overseas bank accounts. Clinics have been left without medicines, schools without books, villages lack electricity, roads are potholed. Be it apartheid or corruption, potential is squandered and hopes are dashed.

So when investors buy bonds sold by sleaze-ridden governments, it is surely as dubious as giving a bottle of whisky to a known alcoholic. It is not against the law. But at best it is unethical and immoral, and the giver is complicit in the consequences.

What makes the act especially questionable is that it has happened before. Investors helped make Africa a debt junkie in a process that began 50 years ago. It is easy to forget that independence from colonial rule was accompanied by an optimism and a wave of lending reminiscent of the current enthusiasm about the so-called new Africa.

Africa's leaders proved deeply disappointing. Foreign lenders nevertheless indulged big men and their vanity projects. Grandiose power schemes, dams that silted up and irrigation projects that failed—few if any were viable or profitable. All were dependent on foreign loans.

The bubble had to burst. By the early 1970s the continent was unable to service its external debt. Arrears mounted, defaults became common. As the crisis deepened the search for a solution became desperate. Africa's finance ministers spent much of their time pleading for restructuring at meetings convened by creditors. By the 1990s, Africa was in effect bankrupt. Even then, western governments continued to indulge some of the most extravagant borrowers, such as President Mobutu Sese Seko of Zaire, whom they saw as allies in a Cold War in which Africa was a theatre of conflict.

But it became clear that the debt burden was unsustainable. By the turn of the millennium, the case for writing off the debt of some of the poorest states was overwhelming. Nigeria, one of the beneficiaries, decided to borrow afresh and became one of the first African countries to issue a sovereign bond, followed by a score of other states.

Foreign investors have piled in, pursuing profit but avoiding responsibility. They do not demand transparency in the award of contracts to the projects they fund, nor do they monitor implementation. 'We are competing with China' is an oft-heard excuse from the investors, suggesting an approach that excludes ethics but fails to explain their conduct when they had the continent to themselves. 'Anyway,' they add, 'why should Africa be singled out? Why subject it to scrutiny not applied to other corrupt borrowers?' The answer is that sub-Saharan Africa has long been treated as a special case. Closer checks are a small price for a debt write-off worth $190 billion.

Can Kenya, for example, which is planning a $2 billion bond issue, be trusted? Two massive scams that cost the country billions, based on bogus export claims and false invoices, have gone unpunished. Questions are being asked about construction of a $2 billion Kenyan railway, with contracts that lack transparency. Will Nigeria's bond be spent wholly on rebuilding the decrepit power system as promised? Or will a slice go the way of the $20 billion the state-owned petroleum company cannot account for?

We have been here before, but no lessons have been learnt. Three things are certain: the bond buyers will make their money on their loans, irrespective of how they are spent, the continent's elite will take their cut—and Africa's long-suffering people will pay the price.

A young continent that celebrates its elders

Financial Times, 23 December 2014

Suspend for a moment your concerns about religious extremists in Nigeria. Set aside your fears for Somalia. Take a break from the conflict in the Democratic Republic of Congo and the horrors of Ebola. There are glad tidings from Africa—you just need to know where to look.

This good news comes in different forms and can appear in unexpected places. It can be found in the continent's cultural renaissance, now well under way. It includes the bustling generation of internet entrepreneurs and the emergence of business leaders with global impact. And, finally, it can even be seen in the reception accorded my elderly mother on a holiday trip to Mombasa, in an assertion of values that seem eroded in the West.

From a conventional vantage point, democracy is struggling. Measuring good governance is a tricky task but the closest one comes to an authoritative annual yardstick is produced by the Mo Ibrahim Foundation, created and funded by the Sudanese-born mobile phone billionaire. Its latest report makes disquieting reading.

While overall 'performance has registered a slight improvement' in the five years to 2013, the pace of that improvement has slowed. 'Every African country has shown a decline,' according to the report, in one area or another.

Equally unsettling is the widespread failure in leadership. In 2006 the foundation set up a $5 million prize to honour leaders exemplifying a commitment to democracy and good governance. Last year, for the fourth time in five years, the prize was not awarded.

Despite these setbacks in governance, however, Africa is steadily recovering the self-confidence that had been shattered by successive traumas: the transatlantic slave trade, the arbitrary carve-up of the continent by European powers, the era of colonial rule, the convulsions of the Cold War played out in proxy by East and West, the horrors of apartheid and the harsh economic medicine imposed by the International Monetary Fund in the 1980s. All of this has been compounded by bad post-independence political and economic management.

Today there is a boom in Africa's culture. Its novelists thrive, its artists flourish, its music is pervasive. It exports style and fashion. Skills and talents are being liberated by the internet and the mobile phone, driven by an entrepreneurial 'born free' generation catering to a growing middle class. And part of this renaissance is an assertion of traditional values that have survived the continent's many upheavals.

Perhaps mine is a partisan perspective, for it is shaped by my upbringing in a small town in Rhodesia, today Zimbabwe. A white boy learnt to respect the elderly, the importance of family, loyalty to kin, hospitality to strangers—values that were all bound together by resilience under hardship, patience under pressure and the laughter that liberated.

I must have been six when I decided to run away from kindergarten. I had not gone very far when I was spotted by a delivery 'boy'—in fact a man employed by the local store to deliver the orders of their white customers, which were carried in an enormous wicker basket attached to the handlebars of the bike. He scooped me up and placed me in the basket, atop the various parcels, and delivered me to a grateful mother.

Decades later, my heart is warmed by the reactions of Kenyans to my mother when we pass through Mombasa airport, on the way to a beach-house holiday.

From airport staff to taxi drivers, from street vendors to house stewards, the response is the same. Faces light up, and the revelation that Mama is 93 is greeted by intakes of breath, polite whistles of incredulity, smiles and handshakes. How fortunate, they declare, how richly blessed, to have a parent who has reached such a venerable age.

Back in London, the reaction of almost all my British friends to the same news could not be more different. No congratulations. Their faces cloud over. They commiserate and murmur their sympathy and concern. Talk turns to retirement homes, to the failure of the state adequately to provide, and to the cost of private care.

Africa is youthful. Britain is ageing. Compassion comes at a price, demographics count. But in the meantime the continent would appear to be more caring and enlightened than its former coloniser, saluting and celebrating its oldsters, not commiserating with their youngsters.

The World Bank fails to credit the intelligence of the world's poor

Financial Times, 27 January 2015

When a report by the world's most influential development agency provides evidence that many of its staff are 'biased' in their perceptions of the poor and their needs, one might expect eyebrows to be raised. When the president of that institution—the World Bank, no less—acknowledges the flaw and goes on to call for 'measures to mitigate these biases, such as more rigorously diagnosing the mindsets of the people we are trying to help', jaws should be dropping.

One example of the bias uncovered by the report team is particularly striking. The authors conducted a random survey to examine 'judgment and decision making' among World Bank staff. Nearly 5,000 were invited to take part in the exercise, of whom 1,850 actually did—about half each from headquarters and country offices. Participants were asked to estimate how many of Nairobi's poorest residents would agree with the statement that vaccinations caused sterilisation. The same statement was put to the residents themselves. The result was remarkable. Forty-two per cent of the bank's staff estimated that the poor would agree with the statement. But when the statement was put to the residents, only 12 per cent agreed.

A similar gap between the bank's assumptions and actual responses was found in Jakarta and Lima. In this case, staff predicted that many more poor residents would express feelings of helplessness and lack of control over their future than actually did.

'This finding suggests that development professionals may assume that poor individuals may be less autonomous, less responsible, less hopeful, and less knowledgeable than they in fact are,' the report notes.

Yet beliefs like these shape policy choices. And development professionals, the report makes clear, 'are not always good at predicting how poverty shapes mindsets'.

Not since the economist Peter Bauer delivered his critique of foreign aid 50 years ago, famously arguing that the process amounted to a transfer of funds from taxpayers in well-off countries to enrich an elite in poor ones, has the concept of foreign aid come under such scrutiny —and from such an authoritative source.[38]

Yet reaction so far seems to have been a yawn of indifference and a shrug of the shoulders on the part of the rest of the multibillion-dollar aid industry.

The comments and conclusions not only raise questions about the World Bank's past performance and the extent to which its projects have been flawed as a result of the bias of its staff, it also raises concerns about the approach of other donor organisations and those thousands of non-government organisations that attempt to alleviate poverty in the world's poorest countries.

This 240-page study is not merely a theoretical treatise. It shows how insights into how people make decisions can have a wide-ranging impact, from helping households to save more, to reducing the prevalence of disease or increasing the efficiency of companies.

'Development professionals and policy makers are, like all human beings, subject to psychological biases,' reads a key paragraph. 'Government and international institutions, including the World Bank Group, can implement measures to mitigate these biases.' For one thing, it suggests that staff should work harder to understand the beliefs and preferences of the people they are trying to help. For another, it recommends introducing processes to ensure that, where biases remain, they do not filter through into the bank's decisions.

The consequences of bias are profound. The poorest in the world may be doubly burdened. Not only do they fight a daily battle against poverty, they may well have to cope with policies of well-meaning aid donors that owe more to the bias of those who frame them, than to the knowledge of those who are supposed to benefit from them.

---

[38] Peter Bauer (1915–2002) was a Hungarian-born British development economist.

David Beresford
The Guardian, April 2016

The journalist David Beresford, who has died aged 68 after a long ill-ness, was renowned for his reporting for *The Guardian* and *Observer* on conflict in two regions a world apart: Northern Ireland and his native South Africa. Equally distinguished was his account of the impact of his Parkinson's disease, diagnosed in 1991.

Posted to Northern Ireland in 1978, when The Troubles were at their peak, he turned his experience into a fine book, *Ten Men Dead* (1987), a harrowing investigation of the IRA hunger strike of 1981. *The Observer* newspaper, not then allied to *The Guardian*, described it as 'possibly the best book to emerge from the past 20 years of conflict in Northern Ireland'.

He took the same qualities of courage, empathy and perceptiveness to South Africa in 1984, where his coverage of the death throes of apartheid soon brought him an International Reporter of the Year award. David was in his element. Black townships were becoming ungovernable, black trade unions were flexing their muscles and the country's rulers were defending white rule by fighting its neighbours.

In 1990, Nelson Mandela was released, and David was in Cape Town for 'the biggest story journalism had ever known, the biggest human-interest story the world had ever seen'. However, as he reflected ruefully 25 years later, the media stampede when Mandela was sighted at the prison gates and pandemonium that erupted for his speech from the balcony of City Hall made it not quite the first-hand report he would have wished for.

For the local press it was a tumultuous time. In the 1990s there was a combative new weekly, the *Mail & Guardian*, in which the London

Guardian had a financial stake. David gave it his enthusiastic support, from editing copy to leading several of the paper's investigations into the abuse of state power. It was a passion for David, who played a pivotal role, unpaid and often unacknowledged, in making it so influential.

On one occasion he wrote an editorial saying that Mandela should stand down at the end of his term as president, from 1994 to 1999. He noted later that when asked why he had done just that, Mandela replied with a mischievous grin: 'Because the *Mail & Guardian* told me to.'

Particularly admired was David's magisterial obituary in 2013 of Mandela for *The Guardian*, well written, judicious and authoritative, drawing on a perspective that stretched back a lifetime.

David's reaction to Parkinson's disease provoked some of his best work. Variously comparing himself to a soldier trapped behind enemy lines, to a foreign correspondent sending despatches from a far-off land, or to a prisoner held for an unspecified offence, he used his writing skills to share with readers his experience of this debilitating condition.

His account of an operation to ease the symptoms—though not cure the condition—performed in Grenoble, south-east France, in 2002 is compelling. He had to be fully conscious throughout, his head bolted into a steel contraption while surgeons inserted an electrode into his brain.

David frankly admitted his terror, gripped by claustrophobia, yet provided an entertaining and moving commentary on the 13-hour procedure: 'The helmet was rather like being pinned down to the table like an ant by a massive thumb ... . When it was all over and I was unbolted by Brad [the surgeon] and wheeled away, I found myself weeping. Brad, bless his soul, could not figure that one out.

'"But it is all over," he kept repeating. "You've done it!"

'I couldn't find the words to explain to Brad that the operation was nothing ... . I was weeping at what had driven me to them: 10 years of living in another country known as Parkinson's disease.'

David was born in Johannesburg, the youngest of three sons of St John, a banker, and his wife, Faith (*née* Ashby). When he was seven, the family moved to Salisbury, in Rhodesia (now Harare, in Zimbabwe). He went to a boarding school, Falcon College, in Matabeleland. When he was 14, his brother Norman, the middle son and a hero to him, died.

After dropping out of his English and Law degree course at the University of Cape Town, he was a reluctant office worker, but then turned to journalism, with the Salisbury Herald and Cape Town Herald. Like many of his friends, in the mid-1970s he moved to Britain. His first job in the UK was with the South Wales Echo, and he also worked for the Argus group in Brighton and Hove, East Sussex, before joining The Guardian.

Although a sociable man, generous to colleagues who sought his advice, he avoided being part of the 'hack pack'. Contrarian by nature, scornful of authority, impatient with bureaucracy, he was a man who worked best alone. He was also a very striking figure: while most people run a comb through their hair when preparing to face the world, David gave the impression that he must have begun his day by deliberately dishevelling himself, with tousled hair, heavy-lidded eyes, wearing a crumpled shirt and stained trousers, for all the world like a South African farmer after a long night at the country club.

He had told me of his Parkinson's while we were at a funeral in Soweto surrounded by mourners dancing the toyi-toyi. The illness we shared created a lasting bond. We parted. I rejoined colleagues, but David, unkempt as ever, his battered canvas bag slung over his shoulder, notebook in hand, went on alone, and was soon swallowed by the crowd.

His last years were gruelling for him, but made easier by two remark-able friends: Alois Rwiyegura, his Rwandan researcher, and his full-time carer, Pasca Selepe.

In 1968 he married Marianne Morrell. She survives him, along with their children, Belinda and Norman; his partner, Ellen Elmendorp, and their son, Joris; and his eldest brother, Garth.

IT IS SAID that grief is the price we pay for love. We all loved David in different ways—as husband, partner, brother, father; as cousin, as friend, as colleague, companion and mentor.

We also enjoyed his huge talent as a writer and author, journalist, humourist and satirist.

David is in my heart for a further reason: Parkinson's. It gave us membership of an exclusive club we formed, which for some reason David called 'The Tremblers'.

I looked at the minutes of the club's last meetings before coming here and would like to read out some extracts:

'Word has spread about the Tremblers and about the privileges that membership offers. Unfortunately some colleagues are going to great lengths to gain entry to the club, affecting a shuffling gait, stooping, slurring their speech, and of course trembling. This does not deceive the trained eye. A doctor's certificate is essential.

'Three would-be Tremblers failed their medical when Dr. Andrew Lees—the club's neurologist—determined they were healthy and sent them packing.'

I read on from another set of minutes:

'Tips for travelling Tremblers: Tell the cabin crew that one has "trouble with waterworks" and the adjoining seat will stay vacant.'

And this popular tip for Tremblers: 'A number of members have expressed irritation that our slurred pronunciation and unsteady gait leads outsiders to assume that we have had one too many. Most tiresome is the tendency of airline cabin crew to ration the on-board drinks, on the grounds that we were the worse for wear well before we boarded the plane.' Lively discussion led to this useful tip: 'Wear a black armband and cabin staff assume you are in mourning and need the solace of a drink.'

Finally, I came across this message: 'Wheelchair members are asked once again not to abuse this privilege—it only excites the envy of non-members and puts the Tremblers and our Sebokeng helpers at risk. Unfortunately, there is only room for two wheelchairs at rallies and funerals.

'We've apologised to the Sebokeng ANC youth league chairman for the unseemly race that took place for the best position at the recent rally. Fortunately, the chairman agreed that "hotheads and radicals" who had infiltrated the list of volunteer wheelchair pushers were partially to blame.

'Four of the comrades responsible have been suspended from the pushers' rota and three have been reprimanded. The two Trembler members concerned have had their wheelchair passes withdrawn.

'The matter is now closed. It nevertheless provided a salutary illustration of the tension that lies below the surface on these occasions and could easily have gone wrong. Many members of the crowd had bet on the outcome of the race and resented the marshals' intervention.'

The last set of minutes reminded me that the next meeting is due to take place in the Mount Nelson Hotel: 'Given that most of its guests are themselves trembling, our presence would go unremarked.'

As I said, grief is the price you pay for love; but laughter and sorrow are also related, and so while I grieve for the loss of a much-loved comrade who was in the frontline of our battle, I take comfort from the laughter we shared as we mocked our tormentor.

What's next for Zimbabwe?

Financial Times, 6 October 2016

In September 2016, George Charamba, then Mugabe's powerful press secretary, authorised a visa that let me visit the country for the first time in 15 years. What follows is my account of my return to Zimbabwe. It appeared in the FT Magazine.

'Zimbabwe is dead.' It was the matter-of-fact tone of the local business-man, the note of exhaustion, of resignation and, above all, of defeat, that was more revealing than the bleak pronouncement itself. Had I left my return to the country that nurtured me too late? I wondered.

It had been 15 years since my last visit. This was my first day back. Would I be conducting yet another journalist's post-mortem, a political autopsy on a nation that had surrendered, beaten into submission by three decades of Robert Mugabe's despotic rule? Or would I find grounds for hope amid the forecasts of doom?

For years, Africa's political Houdini has rigged elections and got away with it. Now Mugabe is discovering that a rigged economy is ultimately bound to collapse. The state is running out of US dollars, creditors are running out of patience. On top of all this, the country is gripped by a severe drought, which has left a third of its 15 million people reliant on food aid. The frail 92-year-old autocrat is trapped, caught between reality and mortality.

I had been given a rare 10-day media visa for Zimbabwe, with no conditions or travel restrictions. It was a chance to explore, to refresh memories that stretched back to my arrival as a five-year-old child in a small town called Gwelo, since renamed Gweru, and to recall the events that helped shape the country's violent transition from minority-ruled Rhodesia to an independent Zimbabwe.

By my mid-teens, in the early 1960s, the reverberations of the African nationalist revolution sweeping the continent were being felt even in sleepy Gweru. A diary that I kept as a boy scout records the absence of the scout master, called up for police reservist duty; and the flight of Belgian refugees from the tumultuous birth of an independent Congo. In Rhodesia, tensions between the two main African nationalist parties erupted into violence, and clashes in Gweru's black townships became frequent, the start of the country's painful transition to independence in 1980.

Within a day of being cleared to visit, in late August, I was on a flight to Harare. The first 24 hours in the city reminded me of the opening sentence of a dispatch by a veteran foreign correspondent, based in Afghanistan. It had been a slow news day, indeed, a no-news day, but he rallied to the task of providing a daily story: 'A nightmarish air of normality hung over Kabul last night.'

So it was in Harare. But the appearance of normality was short-lived. The day after my arrival, the sounds and scents of violence drifted through the open window of my city-centre hotel room: the pop of tear-gas canisters, the distant cry of an angry anti-government crowd, smoke from a burning car forming a grey plume, stark against the blue spring sky. In the hotel lobby, security staff lowered a steel shutter over one door and stood ready to wind down the other. Hours later, all was quiet. A 'nightmarish air of normality' once again prevailed.

'Zimbabwe is dead,' repeated my companion, in the same flat, dispassionate manner. We were driving through Harare, once known as Africa's 'garden city'. Today it is a sprawling mix of security-walled homes and gated compounds, bleak slums, pavement markets and well-stocked malls. Jobless youths hang around street corners, emaciated children beg at traffic lights. There was no future, no jobs, said my companion. Corruption flourishes, he went on, so-called tender-preneurs thrived, a breed who use inside knowledge to make a mockery of the tender process, inflating costs while lowering standards. But where could he and his family go? Follow the example of as many as a million of his fellow citizens in the past decade or so and cross into South Africa?

But the neighbouring nation has difficulties of its own. Foreigners are not always welcome. My companion was one of the lucky ones. A teacher-turned-trader, part-time entrepreneur and occasional taxi-driver, he owns a plot on which he grows maize—although not for his family: the crop is sent to relatives in the countryside. Reversing the traditional direction of trade, workers in the city are now feeding the farmers. The drought, the worst for three decades and embracing much of southern Africa, is taking its toll.

Like most Zimbabweans—at least half the population is under 30—he had no direct experience of the era of white rule. He had no experience of the guerrilla campaign that brought nearly 90 years of white domination to an end in a war that intensified in the 1970s and cost more than 20,000 lives. He was too young to have known the relief of peace. And he had not heard Mugabe deliver a remarkable speech of reconciliation when he took office in 1980.

Then the FT's Africa correspondent, I had looked on from my seat in a packed, pulsating stand. The Union Jack was lowered; the black, red, green and gold of the new national flag took its place. The man reviled by many white Rhodesians as a 'Communist terrorist' turned forgiving pragmatist. The reggae thump of Bob Marley boomed out. It was a night when Harare became a giant street party. Since then Mugabe has become synonymous with despotism, a man who brutally suppressed opposition in the province of Matabeleland in the 1980s and presided over the often-violent seizure of the 4,500 white-owned farms, launched at the end of the 1990s. His black opponents fared no better. He abused the civil rights of his critics and rigged elections, flouting the law and emasculating the judiciary, gradually becoming the caricature of a liberation hero who stays too long in power.

Early in my stay I did see Mugabe, but briefly, and at a distance, at the annual Harare agricultural show. A convoy of police cars and armoured personnel carriers had escorted the presidential limo to the entrance of the VIP stand. I caught sight of a shuffling, unsteady old man in a dark suit and a wide-brimmed hat, propped up by solicitous aides. The ever-present ambulance that trails him in public was at hand, a reminder of his mortality. Show-goers looked on, their faces expressionless.

The next day I set off for Gweru, a 180-mile drive along the spine of Zimbabwe, following the so-called high veld into the heart of the country. What had happened to the landmarks of my youth: had the town's clock tower, erected by Jean Boggie, the wife of an early settler, become a casualty of the new reality? Or did it still stand in the shadow of the Midlands Hotel, whose upper-floor rooms with their high ceilings open out onto broad verandas, where my family had stayed during our first weeks in Gweru, in the early 1950s?

We were typical immigrants—my mother South African, my father a

Cornish-born teacher who had been based in South Africa during the Second World War. And what of the schools I went to, the stores frequented, the cinema attended? How had the town library fared? It had been a haven for me during a demanding year.

Arrested at dawn in August 1967, in my room on the university campus in Harare, I had been served with a government notice declaring me a 'threat to the maintenance of law and order', and restricting me, then a 19-year-old student 'troublemaker' and renegade, to the 'European' area of Gweru. After a night in the cells of Harare central police station, I was driven to my home in what was then a little town of some 15,000 Whites and 35,000 Africans. And there I stayed for the stipulated year, reading voraciously.

Warnings that I might be held up on this trip at predatory road-blocks were unfounded. There were fewer than half a dozen, manned by bored policemen, no doubt supplementing their salaries with arbitrary fines levied for trivial or non-existent traffic offences. But as I travelled south, I realised something was missing. Where were the bicycles, those ubiquitous workhorses of Africa, their ownership as much a measure of wealth as cattle or a new corrugated iron roof on a peasant farmer's hut? I started keeping count, excluding the bikes that appeared in the towns: the number barely reached double figures.

And where were the vegetable vendors, the curio sellers, the side-of-the-road pedestrians, striding to unknown destinations? There were only a handful in a landscape of parched golden veld and flat-topped msasa trees under a blazing clear sky—and hardly a white face to be seen.

At their peak, 'Rhodies', or white Rhodesians, the group to which I and my parents belonged, numbered no more than 250,000. A majority were immigrants, mainly from South Africa and Britain, attracted by the fine climate, the open-air life, cheap domestic servants, and believing the myths propagated by state-controlled media. They were portrayed as successors to the pioneers of the 1890s, forming a bulwark against the approaching Communist menace, united in their determination to overcome international trade sanctions imposed by the United Nations in response to the unilateral declaration of independence from Britain by prime minister Ian Smith in 1965.

They developed a remarkable maintenance culture, keeping Morris Minors on the road, steam locomotives on the rail tracks, ageing Viscounts and Dakotas in the air. Import substitution flourished: local manufacturers produced everything from marmalade to wine. But there was a brutal, repressive side to white Rhodesia. They voted overwhelmingly and regularly in support of the Rhodesian Front, a party that endorsed segregation. Their government tortured suspects, bombed refugee camps and forced 200,000 rural dwellers into fenced 'protected villages' that soon became little more than rural slums. In the scathing words of Donal Lamont, the Roman Catholic bishop of Mutare, the perpetrators were 'moral pygmies'.

Now only about 5,000 Whites remain, many of them trapped in poverty, dependent on charity to survive. As for the white farmers, all but a handful have now left, many driven off their land by violent mobs. Mugabe claimed he was redressing a historical injustice but there was no orderly redistribution of the farms. They were given to cronies, generals and party officials, reward for past favours or for services to come: injustice heaped on injustice.

One of my earliest memories of Gweru is being rescued by one of the men who delivered groceries ordered by white householders and carried in huge wicker containers strapped to the front of their bicycles. I was five, and had run away from kindergarten. As I set off on the long, hot journey and was spotted by an errand boy on his rounds. He scooped me up, deposited me in his basket and delivered me to my grateful parents.

Decades later I return to find that Boggie's clock still stands. It has been painted a sickly shade of green and is strung with coloured lights, baubles on a fading dowager. But there it is, a squat survivor of a bygone age, a monument to tolerance, or a defiant survivor of the colonial era. I have a cup of tea at the Midlands Hotel and a visit to a balcony room, under the elegant curving arches. Then I set off along the main street, once dominated by Meikles department store, until I reach the post office and the town council offices. I look in vain for Le Marché, the café where I met friends on Saturday mornings for a cool drink; Pelidis store, once a cavern of army surplus uniforms, is no more; the Royal cinema, strictly off-limits to Africans but where Indians and 'Coloureds' (mixed race) were allowed entry provided they sat in the back row, has long been closed.

I turn off the main street and stop outside a red-brick building. It is the memorial library, unchanged but for a protective steel gate at the entrance. It is as busy as ever. The books are grubby and well thumbed, the reading room full. A little further on I stop in front of an imposing entry gate and a grand assembly hall. It is Chaplin High School, the alma mater I share with Ian Smith. The hall is named after its benefactor, Sir Alfred Beit, who made his fortune at the turn of the last century.

Another surprise awaits me. The name of the primary school I attended so many years ago is also unchanged: 'Cecil John Rhodes Primary School' reads the sign outside. Sir Alfred Beit, Sir Drummond Chaplin, Cecil John Rhodes: enthusiastic colonialists all.

I look into my old classroom, sit in the shady garden and reflect. Poor Zimbabwe! It has suffered much at the hands of its rulers, white and black, since its inception in the late 1890s. It was built on fraud and deceit, the early settlers misleading local chiefs about the treaties they were persuaded to sign and the concessions they granted. An insurrection followed in 1894, known as the first *chimurenga*. By the 1940s Rhodesia had been formally divided, roughly half and half. The better half, including the best farmland, became the 'European' area; the African majority got the other half. Which leader, Mugabe or Smith, has done more damage, I wondered? Which system—white rule or Mugabe's rule—has caused more pain?

In style of leadership, the two could hardly be more different: Smith lived modestly; Mugabe milked state resources and built himself a vast mansion. Both men ran a *de facto* one-party state; both rode roughshod over their critics. Smith triggered a race war; Mugabe subjugated Matabeleland. Smith may have bequeathed a healthy economy but he also passed on a poisoned chalice, brimful with a toxic mix of past injustice.

Back in Harare, I meet a senior government official and ask about the statue that I briefly spotted outside the building. 'Rhodes?' 'Livingstone,' he replies. 'Another colonialist,' he adds, smiling. The day before I leave for London an envelope is slipped under the door of my hotel room. It contains photocopied pages of the prologue to a book by Timothy Holmes called *Journey to Livingstone: Exploration of an Imperial Myth*. Several passages are underlined, but one stands out. It's an extract of a letter from the Victorian explorer to a friend.

'My objectives are not merely exploratory,' he writes. '[The] ostensible object [is] the development of Africa and the promotion of civilisation but what I tell to none but such as you in whom I have confidence is thus I hope it may result in an English colony in the healthy highland of central Africa.'

Zimbabwe, it seems, is more tolerant of past colonisers than South Africa, where the wounds of apartheid remain sensitive. Rhodes lies undisturbed in his grave in the Matopos hills; Livingstone stands within sight of the president's offices.

But Mugabe's party, the ruling ZANU-PF, has its own problems.

Senior officials have been purged, or have resigned. Who will take over when Mugabe goes? The tough vice-president, Emmerson Mnangagwa, a guerrilla veteran, close to the army and in charge of food security, leads the field. Much may depend on the manner of Mugabe's going.

And what about Grace Mugabe? Does the president's wife really think she can take over? The official shrugs and suggests that much of the talk is the product of the Harare bubble, Zimbabwe's 'Westminster village'.

'Never forget that ZANU-PF is a party of the rural areas,' he says. I suggest that a transition to the post-Mugabe era is already under way and that the ruling party may be better prepared for the negotiations that surely lie ahead than they are given credit for. He neither demurs nor denies.

One of my last meetings is with Eddie Cross, a brave and outspoken opposition MP for the Movement for Democratic Change party. The economic pressures, he says, are remorseless.

'Our national debt is now approaching three times our GDP; interest on the debt alone is equal to one-third of all spending. The budget deficit has spiralled out of control. The civil service is being paid with virtual money by electronic means but they cannot draw their salaries out of the banks ... This state of affairs simply cannot go on.'

Since the US dollar is the national currency, there is little room for manoeuvre. Terms for fresh lending from the IMF and the World Bank, however, include a demand for transparency that would expose the patronage on which the ruling party depends. And the strains are starting to tell. There have been delays in paying the army and teachers; social media is increasingly critical, demonstrations and stay-aways (protests made by staying away from work) are becoming more frequent.

Zimbabwe is far from 'dead'. The country is free of religious divisions—although cursed by ethnic and clan tensions—and still has supportive neighbours, a battered but surviving infrastructure, a broad English-speaking skills base and a talented diaspora longing to return home. And above all, the military are still, for now, in the barracks.

It's the eve of my departure. I pack my bags. One of my novels, set aside as a farewell gift, has a passage from Camus's *The Plague*. The doctor in the rat-infested, cholera-struck town of Oran in Algeria prepares for bed and turns on the wireless:

And from the ends of the earth, across thousands of miles of land and sea kindly, well-meaning speakers tried to voice their fellow-feeling.

'Oran, we're with you!' they called emotionally. But not, the doctor told himself, to love or to die together and that's the only way. They are too remote.

At the airport I watch passengers embracing loved ones and imagine I can hear the traditional southern African words of farewell, part blessing, part exhortation. It signals the start of a journey to a new and challenging destination—but a journey that is made alone.

'Hamba gahle, Zimbabwe, hamba gahle'—go well.

David Coltart: The Struggle Continues

50 years of tyranny in Zimbabwe

Financial Times, 13 January 2017

What is it about southern Africa that creates so many moral heavyweights? It seems that adversity and repression in that part of the world stimulate rather than inhibit, and bring out the best in its citizens in response to the worst in its rulers. Hence the region's Nobel Prize-winners and feisty clerics, outspoken parliamentarians and courageous activists.

Whatever the reason for the disproportionate number of these men and women, all prepared to confront power with truth, David Coltart, a 59-year-old Zimbabwe-born civil rights lawyer, deserves to join their ranks.

The Struggle Continues is not only a comprehensive indictment of Robert Mugabe's brutal regime and the white minority governments that preceded it; it is a magnificent, monumental, two-fingered act of defiance by an extraordinarily brave man, made all the more remarkable by the fact that nearly all the main culprits from Mugabe's era are still alive—and that the author and his family still live in the southern Zimbabwean city of Bulawayo.

If a single theme emerges, it is Coltart's belief that the rule of law and the principles of democracy will one day triumph, ending decades of tyranny imposed by Zimbabwe's rulers, past and present, white as well as black. After digesting his book, it seems clear, alas, that it will be a very long wait.

What Coltart calls 'an autobiographical political history of Zimbabwe's last six decades' begins with a lyrical description of a 'blissful' childhood, albeit one that—as he readily acknowledges—was 'oblivious to the reality of life for most black Rhodesians'. He was still in his teens when political reality intruded in the form of the deepening confrontation between African nationalism and white resistance. A nightmare began.

Coltart, born in 1957, was just 17 when he chose to enrol in the police force rather than wait until the army would conscript him. Within two years he was on the front line of Rhodesia's guerrilla war, the consequence of prime minister Ian Smith's unilateral declaration of independence from Britain in 1965.

Initially sympathetic to Smith, Coltart's experience in the bush was life changing. Above all, he learnt that 'various interrogation methods, such as the use of water-boarding and electric shock treatment, were used to extract information from guerrillas. Bar talk in the mess,' he writes, 'was full of gory detail of how guerrillas had "sung" after being tortured ... War had exposed wholesale depravity on all sides, and I was being sucked into it, relentlessly ... Although I was aged just nineteen at the time, I am ashamed that I did not do more then to prevent its use or speak out against it.'

Granted permission to leave the police and take up a place at the University of Cape Town, he had his first encounter with Robert Mugabe, leader of ZANU-PF, victor in the 1980 independence elections and the new prime minister of Zimbabwe. In a telegram responding to a letter from Coltart, by then a supporter of the new government, we meet Mugabe the magnanimous, committing to 'a policy of reconciliation whereby our people must put aside the hatreds and animosities of the past'. Inspired by this promise, Coltart returned to Zimbabwe to set up as a human rights lawyer.

He soon discovered that the country was beginning to 'unravel'. Apartheid-era South Africa was determined to make life difficult for its neighbour, launching a sabotage campaign and supporting dissident former guerrillas. Mugabe the magnanimous soon became Mugabe the despot, planning the subjugation of the southern province, stronghold then as now of opposition.

To his horror, Coltart discovered that torture in the new Zimbabwe remained systemic. This time, however, he did not remain silent. Some readers may find that his exhaustive account of how he went on to enter Zimbabwe's brutal political arena tests their interest in a far-off land. They should read on. His account of his journey into parliament as an opposition MP, becoming a respected minister of education in a government of national unity, is more than an insider's account of the machinations of power: it is a blow-by-blow analysis of Zimbabwe's decline towards a failing state, with endemic corruption and a ruling party determined to retain power at all costs.

There is, however, a puzzling omission: there is not a reference to the destructive and bitter rivalry between the country's Shona majority and the Ndebele of the south.

As for Mugabe, he emerges as an enigma. Coltart records the president's solicitous inquiry after the health of his daughter Bethany after she had been mauled by a caged lion. At the end of a cabinet meeting Mugabe took him aside to ask after her welfare: 'He appeared genuinely concerned about her.'

It was 'ironic,' notes Coltart, 'given that operatives under his jurisdiction had done their best to kill me in Bethany's presence seven years earlier.'

Politics in Zimbabwe is a strange as well as a nasty business.

Can a crocodile change its spots?

Unpublished, November 2017

For 72 hours in November 2017, Zimbabwe was once more the focus of international attention as tanks moved into Harare's city centre and crowds numbering tens of thousands took to the streets. The army generals had had enough and Robert Mugabe was forced to resign. I could not keep away. A few days later I presented myself at the immigration desk at Harare's international airport.

The immigration official at Harare's Robert Mugabe international airport looked up from examining my passport, his face expressionless.

'Why have you come to Zimbabwe?'

'To celebrate,' I replied.

'What will you be celebrating?'

'Zimbabwe's liberation,' I said, and I held my breath. Journalists without visas have not been welcome in Zimbabwe for most of Robert Mugabe's autocratic reign.

I need not have worried. Joined by his colleagues, he burst into laughter, stamped my passport, and waved me through.

At one level at least, Zimbabwe has changed for the better. Despair has been replaced by hope. Views are expressed freely and openly. Optimism hangs in the air, albeit tempered by caution, but nonetheless tangible—almost as tangible as the musty smell of the parched earth as it soaks up the first of the country's summer rains.

But less than a month since the country's generals orchestrated the removal of the ageing dictator without the bloodshed and looting associated with coups the world over, concerns and doubts are creeping in.

Will the wave of goodwill be squandered by the new regime, will the optimism turn to cynicism, and plans for a fresh start become no more than an illusion? Are we seeing not the emergence of democracy but the modernisation of a one-party state, the overdue infusion of life into a sclerotic regime led by a despotic old man, increasingly under the influence of an ambitious wife? Or is the change in mood in itself an assurance that the process of reform will get under way, of a sufficient intensity to prevent back-sliding? On previous return visits to Zimbabwe, the land that nurtured me until I was twenty and on which I have reported for nearly 40 years, my time had been soured by tension and fear, generated by authoritarian regimes, whether white or black.

Would the mood of post-Mugabe Zimbabwe be sustained, would it be radically different?

TOGETHER WITH A filmmaker colleague, Peter Chappell, we spent the next week travelling across the country, talking to anyone who was prepared to talk to us: mission priests and teachers, roadside vendors and taxi drivers, civil rights lawyers and political activists, hotel stewards and opposition leaders, students and university—acutely aware that our journey barely touched on a land as vast as it is beautiful.

The journey would take us to the eastern border town of Mutare, picturesque but run-down, nestling in the green hills of the Nyanga mountain range, and on to Catholic mission stations a three-hour drive north of the city, on the border with Mozambique.

I had first visited these missions in 1975, at the peak of Rhodesia's guerrilla war. Four years later Rhodesia became independent Zimbabwe, as the conflict ended at the Lancaster House conference in London, but not before hundreds of children from the mission schools had sacrificed their careers and crossed the border to join Robert Mugabe's guerrilla army.

Back to Harare, and on to the town of Chinoyi, north of the capital, driving through countryside that had been home to many of the 4,500 white farmers forcibly evicted from their land by government-backed mobs.

Finally a 40-minute flight to the southern city of Bulawayo, stronghold of the opposition ZAPU party and capital of the province of Matabeleland, scene of one of the darkest events in the country's history—a massacre of some 20,000 civilians.

In different ways the journeys touched on many of the issues confronting the new president, Emmerson Mnangagwa.

Will the government agree to a commission of enquiry into the massacre? How would it handle compensation for the white farmers? Would the composition of the new cabinet reflect the new Zimbabwe?

And would the 75-year-old president, nicknamed 'the Crocodile', who had loyally served Robert Mugabe for the last 40 years, repent of his past and turn over a new leaf?

In his inauguration address no one was surprised when Mr. Mnangagwa ruled out a return of their land to the farmers: 'Dispossession of our ancestral land was the fundamental reason for waging the liberation struggle. It would be a betrayal of the brave men and women who sacrificed their lives ... if we reverse the gains we have made in reclaiming our land.'

He failed, however, to address the central concern of commentators who sympathised with the principle of land reform but were critical of its implementation. Not only was it conducted violently, many of the farms were allocated to cronies of Robert Mugabe, including the army generals who would later remove him.

Mr. Mnangagwa did make one concession: 'My government is committed to compensating the farmers from whom the land was taken.' But the farmers will not be holding their breath. The government has not the funds to cover even modest compensation.

Of far greater concern is the tragedy of Matabeleland.

We spoke to David Coltart, a Bulawayo-based human-rights lawyer and a former senator widely admired for his work as education minster in the government of national unity.

He has no doubt about Mr. Mnangagwa's complicity in the slaughter of civilians in the early 1980s. At the time he was head of the country's Central Intelligence Organisation and had access to the membership records of ZAPU. The impact of the information was devastating. Party officials were singled out, interrogated and summarily executed, effectively destroying ZAPU, says Coltart, who has detailed this infamous campaign in his book, *The Struggle Continues: 50 Years of Tyranny in Zimbabwe*.[39]

The only way this boil can be lanced, say survivors, is for Mr. M to admit his role, to apologise, agree to a public enquiry and provide compensation in the form of schools, clinics, boreholes and other community services. A senior ZAPU official was doubtful that such steps would ever be taken. The alternative, he warned, was an embittered, resentful people who account for one in five of Zimbabwe's population.

---

[39] Reviewed in this book, p. 225.

One obstacle to an enquiry is the loyalty of the new regime to the former president, who after all bears overall responsibility for the slaughter, just as he does for the state of the country today.

Far from condemning the man, his successor has gone out of his way to praise him: 'He remains a father, mentor, comrade in arms and my leader ... history will grant him his proper place and accord him his deserved stature as one of the founders and leaders of our nation.'

Mnangagwa continued: 'I have no doubt that over time we will appreciate the solid foundation laid by my predecessor.'

Needless to say, this view is not shared by most Zimbabweans.

We were in Bulawayo when the names of the new cabinet were announced, seen as the first sign of the president's intentions.

Hopes that it would include new blood and fresh talent were dashed. With an average age in the mid-fifties, only one woman, and four ministers with army backgrounds, it was seen as business as usual.

It should have come as no surprise. An editorial in the state-controlled daily newspaper, the *Herald*, had early given advocates of a cabinet of talent short shrift.

'ZANU-PF has a clear mandate,' read the headline.

'Why have a government of national unity ... when ZANU-PF has a clear mandate?' the paper asked. 'The challenge is to reconcile the interests of the revolution with those of the people who went into the streets ... those who have struggled for years to put ZANU-PF in the dustbin of history.'

The message was unmistakeable. The ruling party has no intention of surrendering its grip on power.

Neither the government of Zimbabwe nor the international and bilateral donors are comfortable in the relationship now being forged. The former will resent the conditions attached to urgently-needed financial support; the latter will surely feel uncomfortable at having to deal with such an unsalubrious group of ministers.

Only China will have no qualms, well ahead of the field as it provided substantial emergency funding.

The outcome is uncertain.

Is a process of genuine reform under way or are we witnessing the salvaging of ZANU-PF, rescued by Western donors from a crisis of its own making yet unrepentant and arrogant, intolerant of dissent, the opposition in disarray, keeping the press and the social media on a tight rein?

In the meantime Zimbabweans and donors alike are waiting for a concrete gesture from the president that allows them to believe that the crocodile can change his spots.

Many Zimbabweans express pride at the bloodless nature of the coup. Only in Zimbabwe, they say, could there have been such a peaceful transformation from dictatorship to a celebration that brought hundreds of thousands of joyful dancing citizens onto the streets, embracing soldiers as they celebrated.

But there are two sides to this coin. Zimbabwe appears to have a culture of deference to authority, and a veneration of age.

What else explains the full-page advertisements in the country's newspapers, extoling the virtues of their new leader, whose brutal past is well known and who must surely share the responsibility for the sorry state of Zimbabwe today?

'We pledge our unwavering support and absolute dedication ... your wise counsel and visionary leadership ... your astute quality,' read one especially obsequious endorsement. Not since the days of Ian Smith, the former prime minister hero-worshipped by white Rhodesians, has there been such a fawning welcome to the man in office.

MEANWHILE IMAGES AND scenes from the journey recur like flashbacks.

Workers painting road signs in the farming town of Rusape, on a Sunday; grass growing in Mutare's main street; the colonnaded, wood-panelled, century-old Bulawayo Club; women selling mushrooms by the roadside in the Nyanga national park; the polite treatment at a roadblock north of Mutare; *guti* (mist) clearing as the sun rose over the resort of Troutbeck ...

But most vivid, most memorable, are the students at the mission where we spent a night. Confident youngsters, smartly turned out, free from the horror of war that had destroyed the lives of an earlier generation, expressing a determination to succeed in their chosen professions.

Today a cabal of old men run Zimbabwe. If they have the good sense not to cling to power, the country's future is in safe hands.

Robert Mugabe: creature of colonialism

Michael Holman, Victor Mallet, David White and Andrew England
Reserve obituary, unpublished, last updated November 2017

First drafted in the 1990s, this obituary of Robert Mugabe was updated several times over the course of his life. It has since been overtaken by events. In November 2017, Zimbabwe's army generals forced Mugabe into retirement in what was in effect a bloodless coup. Even then, we underestimated his capacity for ruthless resilience.

When Robert Mugabe celebrated his overwhelming victory in Zimbabwe's 1980 independence elections with a speech as magnanimous as it was pragmatic, the country's fearful white minority and an anxious British government heaved a sigh of relief.

The man reviled as a 'Communist terrorist' during the Rhodesian guerrilla war not only brought Whites into his first cabinet, awarding them the portfolios of finance, agriculture and health. He also sought the advice of the late Lord Soames, the departing British governor, treated with courtesy Ian Smith, the former white Rhodesian leader who was once his gaoler, and retained Smith's intelligence chief. He even made a point of seeing Margaret Thatcher, then UK prime minister, on his visits to London.

After years of conflict, peace and reconciliation seemed within reach.

It was not to be. Seldom have such high hopes been so comprehensively dashed, near-universal goodwill lost and resources so needlessly squandered.

Robert Gabriel Mugabe, recently forced into retirement, leaves behind a country in crisis. Its economy remains damaged by a brutal and often chaotic take-over of white-owned farms; corruption is rampant; the infrastructure, once among the best in Africa, is failing; millions of the 14-million population are hit by severe drought and depend on external food aid; the loyalty of the army is uncertain, and a venal political elite is squabbling over the succession. The leading contender happens to be his wife, Grace.

Mugabe's successor faces a daunting task. Aside from the need to restore an ailing economy, they will have to reconcile the country's Ndebele people, target of one of Mugabe's most shameful abuses, reform the hated Central Intelligence Organisation, bring to justice the perpetrators of the torture that became routine, and secure of the country's army.

MUGABE'S REPUTATION AT home and abroad has been determined by three landmark events: the brutal suppression of civilians in the Ndebele-dominated province of Matabeleland in the 1980s; the take-over of nearly all the 4,500 white-owned farms; and the election of 2008, when Mugabe dropped any pretence at democracy and used party thugs to kill and intimidate opponents.

The fault line in Zimbabwe's politics was reflected in the 1980 election result.

ZANU, led by Mugabe, dominated the north, home of the Shona people, winning 57 of the 80 seats: 20 were reserved for Whites for a limited period. ZAPU triumphed in their southern stronghold of Matabelelend with 20 seats, while all the 20 seats reserved for Whites for a decade went to Ian Smith's party.

It soon became clear that Nkomo's guerrillas were being largely excluded from the new national army dominated by Mugabe supporters.

Resentful ZAPU guerrillas took to the bush in Matabeleland. With the covert backing of apartheid South Africa, they attempted to undermine Mugabe's authority. Nearly 70 farmers and their relatives died, and six foreign tourists were ambushed and killed on the road from the provincial capital of Bulawayo to the Victoria Falls. Much of rural Matabeleland had returned to war.

Mugabe's response was massively disproportionate to the modest threat posed by a force of about 300 dissident guerrillas. In 1982 he deployed the North-Korean-trained 5 Brigade, which soon became a byword for brutality. Over the next four years at least 10,000 civilians— some estimates put the loss at 30,000—including women and children, were slaughtered or starved to death. Western governments made no public protest; the local media failed to report. Only when eye-witness accounts were gathered and published by the Catholic Church did the scale and savagery of the campaign become clear.

The next defining event for Mugabe was his assault on the country's white farmers, a violent, chaotic exercise which, unlike the horrors of Matabeleland, was followed and recorded by media from around the world.

The history of land occupation in Zimbabwe, formerly Rhodesia, begins in 1890 when Cecil John Rhodes offered 15 gold claims and 1,200 hectares of land to settlers prepare to enlist in an expedition to Salisbury, today Harare. Some 200 responded, and between 1908 and 1915, Rhodes's British South Africa Company put 1.5 million acres of the country's best land into settler hands.

Ian Smith's unilateral declaration of independence in 1965 was intended to entrench a system that apportioned half the country, including most of the best farmland, to 250,000 Whites, who were outnumbered by the black majority 15 to 1.

One subject in particular topped the agenda in the many attempts to end the war that followed: land.

Concerned to avoid the exodus of white skills that marked the chaotic transition to independence in Congo, Angola and Mozambique, Western governments launched a series of settlement initiatives which shared a vital component: an assurance of compensation abroad should property rights be abused.

At the end of 1976, the US and other governments were contemplating the creation of a trust fund of as much as $2 billion (substantially higher in today's prices), to which Britain formally invited 25 countries to contribute. By the time the independence negotiations in 1979 got under way at London's Lancaster House the plan had been shelved, say British diplomats.

African nationalists maintain that the proposal was still alive, and helped break a deadlock over land that threatened to derail the negotiations. But a meeting called by Sonny Ramphal, then Commonwealth Secretary General, and attended by Mugabe and Nkomo and senior conference officials, appeared to make a crucial difference.

The two men issued a statement the next day, saying they accepted assurances that Britain, the US and other countries would 'assist in land, agricultural, and economic programmes ... which go a long way in allaying the great concern we have over the whole land question'.

In the event, Britain provided £30 million in the early post-independence years—far short, Mugabe maintained, of what the Lancaster House negotiations had led him to expect and far less than the amount provided to Kenya in the early 1960s.

The spirit, if not the letter, of the Lancaster House agreement, had been broken, he argued.

Mugabe was in Kuwait when the land issue flared. What began as a mob invasion of a handful of white farms had risen to more than 300 by the time he returned.

From the turn of the millennium, the land grab spread across most of the country. Many of the Whites who had been at the heart of Zimbabwe's commercial agriculture were forced to abandon their farms and their workers, who bore the brunt of attacks by so-called veterans of the country's guerrilla war. By 2003 the 4,500 white-owned farms had been reduced to 600. Today barely 300 are under white ownership.

It is a measure of Mugabe's folly and Zimbabwe's decline that a once self-sufficient country came to depend on donors to avert food shortages affecting up to half its population. But later he warned of retribution against Whites if Britain and other countries maintained their pressure against his government.

'The more they work against us, the more negative we shall be to their kith and kin here,' he said. The country's white population, once more than 250,000, has shrunk to perhaps 30,000.

Zimbabwe has yet to recover from the economic and social consequences of the dislocation caused. A spiral of political repression and economic disintegration gathered speed after a stinging defeat in a constitutional referendum in 2000.

Two years later he secured a fifth presidential term in an election that incurred international condemnation for violence and cheating and caused Zimbabwe's suspension and subsequent withdrawal from the Commonwealth. In 2008, Mugabe faced the greatest threat to his power when he and ZANU-PF lost elections to Morgan Tsvangirai, the former trade unionist and leader of the opposition Movement for Democratic Change.

With Mugabe facing the prospect of a run-off in the presidential vote, thugs and militia loyal to ZANU-PF unleashed a wave of violence against MDC supporters. Scores of people were killed and the bloodshed caused Mr. Tsvangirai to pull out of the poll.

A measure of stability returned when regional mediators convinced the MDC to join ZANU-PF in a unity government, which took office in 2009. The administration was largely dysfunctional, with Mugabe retaining the presidency and the loyalty of security forces, while Mr. Tsvangirai took up the post of Prime Minister, with the MDC as a weak junior partner.

Perhaps the unity government's most significant decision was to introduce the US dollar as the main currency in 2009, a move that helped counter hyperinflation and provided an initial boost to the collapsed economy. (Zimbabwe dollars, 35 quadrillion of which were by then required to buy one US greenback, were finally withdrawn in 2015.)

After much political manoeuvring, fresh elections were held in 2013.

Mugabe once again displayed ruthless political skills as he and ZANU-PF defied critics by sweeping to crushing victories. The MDC, Western diplomats and activists all alleged there had been widespread vote rigging and denounced the results as a sham. But voting passed peacefully, and regional and African Union observers in effect endorsed Mugabe's victory. Much-needed investment was stymied by a liquidity crunch, not helped by ZANU-PF's record and its calls for the indigenisation of foreign-owned companies.

Mugabe had every reason to feel bitter.

His time in detention began in 1964. His only son by his first marriage died of malaria in Tanzania in 1966 and Mugabe was refused permission to attend the funeral. Born in Kutama in north-west Mashonaland on February 21 1924, the son of a labourer, Robert Gabriel Mugabe completed his secondary education at the local Roman Catholic mission school. After teaching for eight years, during which time he did his first year of university by correspondence, he went on to graduate in English and history at Fort Hare, South Africa.

When back in what was then Southern Rhodesia, he taught again at secondary schools while continuing his private studies by correspondence, eventually obtaining an education diploma and a BSc in economics from the University of London. In 1956 he went to teach in Accra, Ghana.

His return to Rhodesia in 1960 marked his formal entry into the political arena as publicity secretary for Joshua Nkomo's National Democratic party. Mugabe broke with Nkomo in 1963 to join Ndabaningi Sithole in forming ZANU and was arrested the following year. He put his decade in detention to good use, taking university degrees in law and administration by correspondence.

Although he made concessions to market-driven reforms, he never really believed in them, nor abandoned the idea of building a socialist state. He clung to power, riding waves of public protest at home and ostracism abroad. His defiance of measures imposed against members of his regime by the US and the EU, and of criticism by Tony Blair's UK government, was typified by his declaration at the 2002 Earth Summit in Johannesburg:

> We do not mind having and bearing sanctions banning us from Europe; we are not Europeans; we have not asked for any square inch of that territory. So, Blair, keep your England, and let me keep my Zimbabwe.

Although he sometimes appeared cold and aloof in public, the more so after his Ghanaian-born wife Sally died in 1992, his private persona could be charming. This enabled him to forge a close working relationship with Lord Soames, the British governor who ran Rhodesia during the weeks of transition to independence. Mugabe also enjoyed his private talks with Margaret Thatcher, who as UK prime minister oversaw the independence process.

But relations with the Whites were irretrievably soured in 1984, when in the country's first post-independence election—long before farmers lost their land and before the horrors of Matabeleland were widely known—the white electorate once again backed Ian Smith. Mugabe's olive branch had been rejected, and he never forgave or forgot.

In 1996 he married Grace Marufu, with whom he has three children. Grace became infamous in her own right, accused of lavish spending at home and while accompanying her husband on his frequent trips abroad.

By the end he had become a parody of a vain dictator, dying his hair to keep the signs of ageing at bay and meticulously trimming a tiny moustache.

He commandeered the national airline for his frequent trips abroad, and moved into a palatial residence that cost millions of pounds.

Sometimes a finger-wagging pedant, prone to homophobic rants, sometimes a benign father figure who enjoyed watching cricket at the ground that adjoined his official residence, he was an enigma—a man of great talent who terrorised his people and abused his office.

Although loathed in the West, however, he retained a remarkable popularity across the continent. Partly this was because many of the continent's leaders themselves retained office by irregular means, partly because they enjoyed the spectacle of an African leader tweaking the tail of the former colonial master and partly because Mugabe was seen as supporting the interests of the landless—a particularly sensitive issue in neighbouring South Africa.

A man besotted by his lust for power, shaped by the colonialism he spent a lifetime opposing, Robert Mugabe bequeaths a divided nation and a devastated economy. Zimbabwe will take many years to recover from his poisonous legacy.

Zimbabwe's broken dreams: book review

Kingdom, Power, Glory by Stuart Doran, Weaver Press (Zimbabwe)
Garfield Todd: The End of the Liberal Dream in Rhodesia by Susan Woodhouse,
Weaver Press (Zimbabwe)
Financial Times, 13 July 2018

Pity Zimbabwe. For over 30 years its people have endured deepening poverty, rampant corruption and systematic abuse of their human rights.

But nothing has matched, for scale or wanton brutality, the slaughter in the early 1980s of some 15,000 men, women and children in the southern province of Matabeleland by soldiers of the North Korean-trained Fifth Brigade. And no single act has done more to widen the divide between the Ndebele-speaking people of the region, long an opposition stronghold, and the Shona-speaking majority in the rest of the country—a divide all but certain to be reflected in the election due at the end of this month (July).

Stuart Doran, an independent Australian historian, is by no means the first person to investigate the Fifth Brigade killings. But he has surely produced the most authoritative account of the atrocity, drawing as he does on hitherto classified files from the archives of the British, Australian and Canadian governments, as well as material and informants from Zimbabwe's Central Intelligence Organisation.

The result, *Kingdom, Power, Glory*, is a chilling account of the evolution of a *de facto* one-party state and of Robert Mugabe's ruthless rise to power, driven by ambition as well as motivated by his loathing for fellow nationalist leader, Joshua Nkomo.

Victory in the 1980 independence elections was not enough to satisfy Mugabe's lust for power, Doran maintains. The 'real enemy' was not white Rhodesia but Nkomo and his supporters. Mugabe seized every opportunity to humiliate or intimidate his rival.

This included the planting of an illegal arms cache on property owned by ZAPU, Nkomo's party, sustained harassment, and an attempt on Nkomo's life, leaving relations between the two men irredeemably poisoned.

Early in 1983 Mugabe ordered the deployment of the Fifth Brigade in Matabeleland, then as now a ZAPU stronghold. Their campaign of indiscriminate killings, torture and random executions left the people of the province mentally scarred, seeking in vain a public acknowledgement, an official apology and reparation.

For the British government the book raises some awkward questions. Judging by the frequency with which UK diplomats are cited in the book and the details they disclose, it seems clear that they were well informed about the massacres. Yet they did little to alert the outside world about the unfolding horror. Ten years later it seemed that all had been forgotten or forgiven. Mugabe was invited on a state visit to Britain and awarded an honorary knighthood (rescinded in 2008).

His despotic reign finally ended last November, when army generals deposed him in a bloodless coup. But the link with the past was not broken. The man they endorsed as Zimbabwe's new leader was none other than Mugabe's counsellor and confidante for more than 30 years, an ex-guerrilla called Emmerson Mnangagwa—and the first Western diplomat to congratulate the president leader was a British minister.

Describing him as Mugabe's 'point man', Doran describes how Mnangagwa 'had from the beginning [of the Matabeleland slaughter] played a key role in the campaign against ZAPU and ZIPRA (ZAPU's guerrilla army), from his chairmanship of the Joint High Command through to the provocation of the Entumbane conflagration [when the rival guerrilla armies clashed], the fabrication of the arms caches and the intelligence on which operations such as the attempt on Nkomo's life depended. ... With others he provided the day-to-day bridge between the political leadership and the killers in the security services.'

Zimbabwe has paid a high price for this violent past, prompting two questions: was there any stage in the country's history when hopes for a non-racial society might have become a reality? And was there a white politician who could convince their constituents of the need for radical change?

Susan Woodhouse suggests there was a window of oppottunity in the 1950s, and the man she believes would have been able to lead the way is the subject of her monumental biography, 25 years in the making, indispensable to anyone who seeks to know white Rhodesia.

Garfield Todd, a New Zealand-born missionary, arrived in Rhodesia in 1934, having been appointed to the post of superintendent at the Christian mission of Dadaya, in the south east of the country. An eloquent and persuasive speaker, he rose in the ranks of the ruling United Rhodesia Party, winning respect for his work as minister of education, before becoming premier in 1953.

Ms Woodhouse portrays him as the standard-bearer of the multi-racial cause, who looked for a middle way, creating what she calls 'a multi-racial buffer zone' between two powerful forces: African nationalism, backed by 'Marxist rhetoric', sweeping down the continent from the North, and apartheid, triumphant in the south.

She draws on an exceptional range of material as well as a personal knowledge of her subject, having worked as a secretary in Todd's private office when he was premier, later joining Todd and wife Grace at Hokonui Ranch, near Dadaya.

Despite these resources, her book is not so much a biography as a compendium of information about Todd: an essential source but short on analysis. Yet the information she has unearthed raises concerns that will disconcert Todd's admirers and provide ammunition for his critics. There is scant evidence of his commitment in office to radical reform.

He lost his job in 1958, as much because he alienated cabinet colleagues as because of the policies he advocated

On the contrary, the legislative pillar of white rule, the country's 1948 Land Apportionment Act which consolidated the division of Rhodesia into white and black areas—with the white minority allocated the best land—was left untouched during his premiership, minor amendments apart. Indeed, the Act was supported by Todd. As late as 1957 he wrote: 'It had seemed a completely sensible and natural proposal when it was introduced, and it continues to have a most important part to play in the life of the country.'

Some of his early views on the franchise seem to echo those of Cecil John Rhodes. 'To say that most black people are uncivilised and, therefore, unworthy of the vote is, I am afraid, quite correct.' For a Todd supporter like myself, who grew up in Rhodesia in the 1950s and 60s, such comments make disconcerting reading.

But if Todd the politician was unable to square the circle between African nationalist aspirations and white unease, Todd the champion of human rights was inspirational, spending a total of seven years confined to his home, condemning the abuses of both Ian Smith and Robert Mugabe, in this way at least the personification of the liberal dream.

Robert Mugabe: Obituary

Financial Times, 6 September 2019

When Zimbabwe celebrated its independence from Britain on April 18, 1980, the newly elected Robert Mugabe received a succinct message from a staunch supporter.

'You have inherited a jewel,' declared Julius Nyerere, then the Tanzanian president. 'Keep it that way.'

Zimbabwe's founding president, who has died aged 95, ignored the advice. Throughout his 38 years in power he rigged elections and sanctioned torture, crushed opposition and embezzled billions of dollars, treating the state as a milk cow that served him, his family and the ruling ZANU-PF party.

The consequences were disastrous.

Life expectancy fell from 60 years at independence to a low of 44— from one of the highest in Africa to one of the lowest in the world. At least 1 million Zimbabweans fled to neighbouring South Africa in search of jobs and sanctuary. Hyperinflation wiped out savings and made pensions worthless. And a country that at independence could boast of food self-sufficiency now regularly needs foreign aid to feed its people.

The fall in production was the result of Mugabe's often-violent seizure of most of the country's 5,000 white-owned farms. Ostensibly it was done to redress a historic injustice that had left the country's best land in the hands of Whites, outnumbered 15 to one by the black majority. The reality was that most of the seized properties were gifted to Mugabe's cronies.

But this was no ordinary despot, no run-of-the-mill dictator. Inside the political thug he undoubtedly became, there was a very different persona. For all his homophobic diatribes and the rants against Britain, he was a closet Anglophile, a man who loved to watch cricket at the ground that adjoined his official residence in the capital, Harare.

He admired the British royal family and loathed the Labour party. He spoke fondly of Conservative prime minister Margaret Thatcher and regarded Christopher Soames, the last British governor, who oversaw the independence election in 1980, as a friend. He spoke excellent English, had no less than seven university degrees and diplomas—most of them taken by correspondence, some during the nearly 11 years he spent in detention.

To meet him was to come face to face with an icon, a man in possession of the aura that surrounds those who wield absolute power —and who are unfettered in its use.

That was enhanced by the fact that he was a living link with pre-independence colonial Zimbabwe, the last survivor of a small group of African politicians who endured detention without trial and went on to lead their countries to independence.

In this context Mugabe's age became an asset and not a liability, a reason for veneration rather than grounds for revolt. His ministers were not only indebted to him, for all were beneficiaries of his patronage: they were in awe of him and afraid of him. Far from acting as a constraint on his power, they became complicit in a web of corruption. Above all, he was a canny politician, skilfully manipulating the ethnic and clan rivalries that bedevil Zimbabwe's politics, ruthless and brutal in his treatment of opponents, and shrewd in his use of patronage.

The bleak state of Zimbabwe today is in stark contrast to the cautious optimism that marked the birth of the new country. The guerrilla war triggered by white Rhodesia's unilateral declaration of independence in November 1965 was over. Economic sanctions had been lifted and hope was in the air.

'If yesterday I fought you as an enemy,' Mugabe asserted in his eve-of-independence speech, universally acclaimed for its theme of reconciliation and forgiveness, 'today you have become a friend and ally ... If yesterday you hated me, you cannot avoid the love that binds you to me, and me to you. ... The wrongs of the past must now stand forgiven and forgotten.'

Robert Gabriel Mugabe had come a long way from his humble beginnings.

Born in Kutama in north-west Mashonaland in 1924 and educated at the local mission school, he was soon singled out by his Jesuit teachers as a pupil of rare talent. But he was also a loner who made no close friends, and missed the presence of his father, who walked out on the family when he was a boy.

For the next 15 years he taught at schools around the country. It was not until 1960 that he entered politics, inspired by a visit to newly independent Ghana, where he met and later married Sally Hayfron, a fellow teacher, who died in 1992. Now in his thirties, he became publicity secretary for the party headed by the man he would later do his best to destroy—Joshua Nkomo, soon to be leader of the Zimbabwe African People's Union (ZAPU).

He broke with Nkomo in 1963 to co-found the rival Zimbabwe African National Union (ZANU). Both men were detained the following year. It was while in detention that Mugabe was given the devastating news that his only son, Nhamodzenyika, had died of malaria. His request for parole in order to attend the boy's funeral in Accra was turned down.

Mugabe was released from prison in 1974 along with other detained leaders, as part of an international effort to end an intensifying guerrilla war that threatened white rule. Early the following year he slipped across the border into neighbouring Mozambique, the rear base for ZANU's military wing; ZAPU's fighters operated from Zambia, the two parties nominally united as the Patriotic Front.

Successful negotiations at London's Lancaster House in 1979 paved the way to independence elections the next year. Mugabe triumphed. But his victory reflected the faultline that runs through the country's politics. Mugabe was Shona while Nkomo was Ndebele. ZANU won 57 of the 80 seats at stake (20 seats were reserved for Whites); in Ndebele-dominated south, ZAPU secured 20 seats.

Within months of his conciliatory eve-of-independence address, the dream of a new era was turning into a nightmare. Mugabe began preparing for the elimination of ZAPU and the subjugation of the province of Matabeleland, the party's stronghold.

In 1982 he sent in the North Korean-trained 5 Brigade, equipped with a list of ZAPU officials obtained by Zimbabwe's Central Intelligence Organisation. In the hands of the brigade, it was the equivalent of a death list. Over the next two years, more than 10,000 men, women and children were slaughtered in what was called *gukurahundi*, a Shona word that means 'spring rains that wash away the chaff'. Although British diplomats were well aware of what was happening, they made no public protest about this atrocity.

But memories can be short. Ten years later, Mugabe was a guest of

Queen Elizabeth and given an honorary knighthood, which was rescinded in 2008 on the advice of the government.

His ruthless and callous side was displayed again when he launched a campaign to purge the urban areas of the increasing number of jobless flooding the cities in search of work. In what was called Operation Murambatsvina—'clear out the rubbish'—700,000 people were left without even rudimentary shelter as police razed shanties and bulldozed vendors' stalls.

By then it had become apparent that only force would dislodge Mugabe. In the run-up to the 2008 election Morgan Tsvangirai, a former trade unionist who led the opposition coalition Movement for Democratic Change (MDC), was publicly assaulted by police, one of whom wielded an iron bar. Pictures of the MDC leader's bruised and battered face and head went around the world.

As the 2008 elections drew closer, the violence and intimidation got worse. A hundred MDC election agents had disappeared, and supporters were being beaten up in their thousands. Tsvangirai felt he had no option but to withdraw from the presidential poll.

An extraordinary assertion by Mugabe confirmed that the MDC leader was right to withdraw: 'The MDC will never be allowed to rule this country—never ever ... only God will remove me.'

Mugabe's lust for wealth went beyond the boundaries of Zimbabwe. In 1998 he sent 11,000 troops from the Zimbabwe national army to fight on the side of the Kinshasa government in the Congo war. But this was no act of solidarity. Rather it was part of a lucrative deal in which Mugabe and his generals were rewarded for their efforts with mining and timber leases in a mineral-rich country with extensive forests.

As age took its toll, Mugabe's second wife Grace, whom he married in 1996, emerged as a contender for the presidency. Forty years his junior, mother of his three children, unpopular but ambitious, she could have been a formidable candidate. The intervention of the army in November 2017 may well have killed two birds with one stone.

Meanwhile the new president, Emmerson Mnangagwa, 74, the former guerrilla and long-time Mugabe confidante, is saddled with a problem that will not go away: his role as Mugabe's 'point man' in the gukurahundi massacre.

He has inherited not an African jewel but a country that is getting dangerously close to becoming an African basket case, its economy shattered, its foreign debt unpayable, its assets squandered by Robert Mugabe and a corrupt elite.

Counting the geckos

Review: *Factfulness* by Hans Rosling
Unpublished, May 2020

Sitting on the balcony of an Indian Ocean beach-house on the Kenyan coast, looking out for geckos while watching the sun go down, may seem an incongruous place from which to take issue with a best-selling writer.

A writer, moreover, whose book—*Factfulness: Why Things Are Better Than You Think*, first published in 2018—quickly reached fifth place in the *New York Times* best-sellers list, and was endorsed by no less than Bill Gates ('indispensable') and Barack Obama ('a hopeful book about the potential for human progress when we work off facts rather than our inherent biases').

If author Hans Rosling, a disease specialist by profession and a statistician by choice, who died in 2017, has it right, Africa is in far better shape than the rest of the world realises. Whether through ignorance or malice, prejudice or misconception, the continent has been given an undeserved rough ride by its critics—including people like me.

Drawing on UN and World Bank statistics to make his case, Dr Rosling argues that we have failed to acknowledge the substantial progress made in post-independence Africa—progress at a rate that in several respects compares favourably with that of his home country, Sweden.

He admits that he has an agenda—and an ambitious one at that. He refers to his 'lifelong mission to fight devastating global ignorance' and 'to calm ... irrational fears' using 'data as therapy'.

'I want the audience to realise how wrong their intuitions can be,' he declares. Without having evidence to back up his own claims—odd for a statistician—he somehow knows that we all us have an 'overdramatic worldview'.

Ten years before his book came out, a young academic from Denmark was producing very different findings. In 2007 Morten Jerven visited the Zambian department of statistics and visited it again in 2010. What he found both times appalled him. The office was in 'disarray'.

Thirty years earlier, I was based in Lusaka as a correspondent for the *Financial Times*. I remember the office being shabby, the staff under-resourced, and the data unreliable, based on assumptions rather than fieldwork.

Little changed in the intervening years. 'GDP numbers and other statistics would be often treated as facts,' commented Jenver, 'but they are products, and they are produced under difficult conditions. This is the knowledge problem.'

'Our knowledge problem in economic development is doubly biased,' added Dr Jerven, now a professor. 'We know less about income and growth in low-income countries, and we know less of the economic condition of those who are the poorest in those countries.

'The paucity of accurate statistics is not merely a technical problem; it has a massive impact on the welfare of citizens in developing countries.'

In *Poor Numbers: How We Are Misled by African Development Statistics and What to Do about It*, the book that was the outcome of his research, Dr Jerven showed how the statistical capacities of sub-Saharan African economies had fallen into disarray. The numbers substantially misrepresented the actual state of affairs, he argued.

'As a result, scarce resources are misapplied. Development policy does not deliver the benefits expected. Policymakers' attempts to improve the lot of the citizenry are frustrated. Donors have no accurate sense of the impact of the aid they supply.'

The consequences are profound. Rich countries and international financial institutions such as the World Bank allocate their development resources on the basis of such data.

False or unreliable statistics produced across Africa in neglected offices like the one in Lusaka may not have an immediate bearing on the lives of villagers. But the location of a hospital or a school may well have been the result of government or donor policies, all determined by flawed data.

Meanwhile in the village of Msambweni, near my beach house, the warnings are clear.

The geckos that used to patrol the ceiling of my balcony bedroom have all but disappeared, as indeed have the lizards that used to sunbathe during the day on the red-polished veranda. There are fewer butterflies weaving across the lawn that lies between my room and the sea.

And where are the shiny black *shongololos* (millipedes) with their hundreds of tiny legs moving in miraculous coordination?

Biodiversity is in crisis. During walks along the beach, dotted with plastic debris, I discover why the fishermen of the village, who used to stay within sight of the shore, now go further and further beyond the reef to maintain the size of their catch.

The reason, they tell me, is that the fish are becoming less plentiful, while the reef itself is dying. The money they earn from selling fish also barely meets their daily needs. Much of it goes towards school fees for their children, who play with their home-made footballs on the dusty lanes of their village.

Each year there seem to be more and more children. The hospital, built in the 1960s, is run down and lacks essential drugs. The schools are short of books and desks.

At independence from Britain in 1963, there were five million Kenyans. Today there are more than 40 million. And every year, the government has to find social services for the million newcomers, as well as jobs.

In the past, those Kenyans who were unable to find work in the formal sector would return to the *shamba* (farm) that had been in their family for generations. No longer. Today those plots have been subdivided to the point where many are economically unviable. Instead, there is a steady drift to the cities—notably the capital, Nairobi, where street children hang about at every corner.

In the village, clues give away the state of the local economy. The size of bars of soap, or packets of washing powder, or piles of salt, all vary according to the cost of living.

THERE ARE NO local statistics on the number of butterflies, nor is there a count of geckos, but their growing scarcity is evidence as powerful as any data of fundamental change affecting the village environment.

Dr Rosling, nonetheless, is determinately upbeat. And he is not alone in wanting to challenge the pessimistic view of Africa.

'Lions on the Move', a report by the consultancy firm McKinsey, published in 2000, and updated in 2016 as 'Lions on the Move II', portrayed a continent bursting with potential. Africa's one billion population, nearly two-thirds under 30, was seen as an asset, not a liability.

What makes Dr Rosling different, however, is not simply his evangelistic fervour but the extraordinary response he gets from readers. His message—'things are far better than it appears'—has appealed to an audience throughout the world.

'The idea that Africa is destined to remain poor is very common,' he writes, 'but often seems to be based on no more than a feeling. If you like your opinions to be based on facts, this is what you need to know.

'Yes,' he concedes, 'Africa is lagging behind other continents, on average. [But] the average lifespan of a newborn baby in Africa today is 65 years ... and five large African countries—Tunisia, Algeria, Morocco, Libya and Egypt—have life spans above the world average of 72. They are where Sweden was in 1970.'

I doubt these figures. Life expectancy at birth in sub-Saharan Africa was 47 in 2005, in Zimbabwe it was 37, and in Sweden it was 81, according to the World Bank's development indicators.

Further, is it hard to reconcile this figure of 65 with the UN claim that one in five African children dies before reaching age five.

In the last 60 years, African countries south of the Sahara almost all went from being colonies to being independent states. 'Over that time,' according to Dr Rosling, 'these countries expanded their education, electricity, water and sanitation infrastructures at the same steady speed as that achieved by the countries of Europe when they went through their own miracles.'

Would that this were true.

Had they concentrated their resources on education and social services, the continent would be in better shape today. Instead, prestige projects and 'cathedrals in the desert' took priority. Rosling goes on to claim that 'each of the 50 countries south of the Sahara reduced its child mortality faster than Sweden [his yardstick for comparison] ever did.'

This is simply implausible. One only has to take into account the legacy of wars in southern Africa, including the ongoing war in the Congo, to put the claim into perspective. The infant mortality rate per thousand live births in Sweden in 2005 was three, in sub-Saharan Africa, it was 96.

Rosling acknowledges that 'though things are much better, they are still bad. If you look for poor people in Africa, of course you will find them.' He adds: 'When I was young, China, India and South Korea were all way behind where sub-Saharan Africa is today in most ways, and

Asia's destiny was supposed to be exactly what Africa's destiny is supposed to be now.'

He fails to explain how countries like South Korea, which once lagged behind Ghana, have today left the African nations trailing in its economic wake.

Twenty-five years ago, he says, 'India was where Mozambique is today. It is fully possible that within 30 years Mozambique will transform itself, as India has done. Mozambique has a long beautiful coast on the Indian Ocean, the future centre of global trade. Why should it not prosper?'

The answer is that Mozambique, which endured a struggle for independence and a civil war, has squandered its income from mineral resources and lost billions of dollars through corruption. Dr Rosling does not see fit to mention this.

I am no statistician, nor am I an economist. I am a journalist and I rely on my own experience and observation. And what I see all around me, not only in Kenya, is evidence of a region under severe strain.

The causes are many. Sub-Saharan Africa had numerous obstacles to overcome when nationalism created independent Africa in the 1950s and 1960s. The trauma of the slave trade and the death toll of 20 million on the passage from Africa to destinations abroad is still felt in the region to this day.

The carve-up of Africa at the Berlin conference of 1884 left African nations divided and then shattered by colonialism. In the twentieth century Washington and Moscow conducted proxy wars across the continent. The intervention of the World Bank and the IMF and their insistence on austerity did more harm than good.

Ill-prepared for independence, African leaders became venal and corrupt, and replaced civil servants with party loyalists and toadies.

The list of problems does not end there. UN agencies have also largely failed Africa. Too many appointments have been made not on merit but as a result of political patronage. Land ownership cries out for reform, with the communal system of ownership tying up capital and inhibiting investment. NGOs have become increasingly intrusive, sapping initiative and pursuing their own agendas.

So when Dr Rosling tells me that journalists like me have given Africa a bad press, and that the continent is young and starting to thrive, I beg to differ. I don't trust the statistics he cites, and I dispute his findings.

I believe I am supported in this view by Prof. Jacqueline Rose of

Birkbeck, University of London, who has written recently that while statistical figures are 'always approximate and imperfect, ... knowing this appears to make no difference to their quasi-sacral status. It is as if intoning numbers according to the same recognisable formula ... allows us somehow to feel on top of a situation which everyone knows—and not just because of governmental incompetence—is out of our control.'

Prof. Rose is writing here in the context of coronavirus data but her conclusions apply equally well to Africa. 'At the very moment when we appear to be taking ... reality on board, we might also be deluding ourselves,' she writes. 'Counting is at once a scientific endeavour and a form of magical thinking.'

So, as a journalist, I feel justified in being perturbed by the declining number of geckos on the ceiling of the beach house near Msambweni, and regretting the dwindling number of butterflies swooping over the lawn, and missing the *shongololos*. And I will continue to note the size of the soap bars and the packets of washing powder in the village market.

I wish the late Dr Rosling had done the same. His data might have been more robust.

APPENDIX 1

Rhodesian Government: Cabinet minutes Z535
Extract, August 1967

... In further discussion the Minister of Law and Order asked Cabinet to consider the policy to be adopted towards students sent down as a result of disciplinary action. It was expected that these students would seek admission to universities overseas. The question had been raised whether, in this event, they should be deprived of their travel documents and prevented from leaving the country. It was pointed out that the Government stood to gain little by withholding travel document; on the contrary it could be brought into disrepute, particularly if it was represented abroad that the Government were preventing Africans from being educated at outside universities. In fact, the Government's interests might be better served if these agitators did leave the country. The point was made, however, that one of the Europeans—**Holman**—should be treated in isolation and made an example of. The attitude of the others could be understood but Holman was more of a renegade. Outside the country Holman had the makings of a very militant opponent and therefore it might be in the Government's interest to restrict him within Rhodesia and so prevent his leaving the country. Here again it was pointed out that such action would only turn him into a hero and martyr and build up his cause. It would make him more important than he was at present and give him the entré overseas to numerous subversive organisations. Furthermore, the Government was pursuing in Rhodesia a policy of freedom of thought and it would be inconsistent with this policy to prevent a man leaving the country if he wished to settle in another country. ...

APPENDIX 2

Exemption Board hearing
Salisbury, Rhodesia, 13 January 1977

When military call-up papers were served on me in 1976, Anthony Eastwood, my lawyer, warned me that there was no way out other than to leave the country, but he devised a strategy that could buy me time.

The exemption board's word was final and they would certainly not release me from the obligation to do military service. Nor did the regulations allow an appeal against their decision.

But Anthony devised a loophole. The board was bound by the principles of natural justice, which required that anyone appearing before them received a fair hearing. If, when I put my case for exemption, my expression of support for the nationalist cause prompted such fury on the part of the panel that they were unable to resist interrupting and cutting me short, Anthony reckoned he could petition the high court and seek an order that the board's ruling be set aside. In this way he reckoned he could keep me in the courts, and out of the army, for about a year.

He would, however, need a transcript of the exemption board proceedings. And so, with a tape recorder concealed in my bag, and relishing the prospect of an exchange in which my insincere deference was likely to infuriate the panel as much as my support for the guerrillas they were expecting me to fight, I appeared before a retired district commissioner, an army officer and a prominent businessman.

I got what I wanted, but I was to have a narrow shave a few months later.

I had lost in the high court, as Anthony expected, and we had taken the case to the appellate division. I thought I was safe until they pronounced. But the rules were changed. A government gazette altered the law overnight: anyone appealing against a decision by the exemption board would serve in the army while his case was being heard.

The military police came to arrest me on the Friday the gazette was published. Fortunately they went first to an office where I did freelance work. A phonecall alerted me that they were on their way to the Salisbury office of the Johannes-burg Financial Mail, for which I worked as the Rhodesia correspondent. I went down the stairs as the police travelled up in the lift.

After three weeks in hiding, I turned up in London, soon to be despatched to Lusaka by J.D.F. Jones, the Financial Times's managing editor, as the paper's Zambia stringer.

First Session

Present: Chairman of the board, two members, secretary, stenographer.

Chairman: (inaudible) ... for military service, Mr. Holman?

Holman: That is correct, Mr. Chairman.

Chairman: One point I wish to make and bring to your attention is that although this board is called an exemption board, we have no powers regarding exemption; we can merely grant deferments.

Holman: Yes, I looked at the Act and it seemed there was that power precluded, that you could not grant exemptions.

Chairman: You have made various statements here, Mr. Holman. You are regarded by the government as an undesirable inhabitant of Rhodesia for security reasons. This has nothing to do with this particular board. You happen to be a resident of Rhodesia and in terms of the Defence Act, you are liable to call-up for service by mere virtue of the fact that you are resident in Rhodesia. You say that you have been declared, well, you don't say, but it is common knowledge that you are—have been declared—a prohibited immigrant. You won an action in the High Court to have this set aside, therefore you obviously intend to carry on residing in Rhodesia, and as such you are therefore liable to service. It that understood?

Holman: Well, I'm making note of your points, Mr. Chairman.

Chairman: The second statement I find rather alarming. You say the military forces are the main instrument of preserving the institutional violence of minority rule. This being the case, I wonder that you have the temerity to stay on in this country, if you feel that. You believe that the military forces are guilty of systematic oppression. I treat that statement with the contempt it deserves; and you agree that the nationalist cause is legitimate. This I am afraid I can't accept at all from my point of view. You've asked if you can be permitted to call a number of witnesses. To start off with, Mr. Holman, this is not a court. Perhaps you are unaware of that fact.

This is a deferment board. Any witnesses that need be called are called by the board and not by you. You merely state your case and we weigh up your case, the pros and cons of your case, and decide whether or not we are prepared to defer you. Is that understood?

Holman: I take your point, Mr. Chairman, but that does not mean that I accept it.

Chairman: (*inaudible*) ... you are an applicant for defence exemption, we have already established that.

Holman: Well, I would like to make two points, Mr. Chairman. I wonder if I could begin. I would appreciate it if I could have the names of the board. I don't know any of them.

Chairman: I don't think this is really necessary.

Board member: It is not normal practice that names are disclosed to persons appearing before the board.

Holman: Is your ruling, Mr. Chairman, that you are not prepared to give the names?

Chairman: That is correct.

Holman: I see. Mr. Chairman. The first point I wish to raise is that I would seek a postponement of this hearing. The grounds are that in terms of the Act—if you will give me time to refer to the appropriate regulations—it says that the chairman of an exemption board shall give reasonable notice to an applicant of the place and time at which the exemption board will sit for the purpose of considering his application. That is Section 4, Subsection 3, of the Exemption Board Regulations, Government Notice No: 786. Mr. Chairman, I was informed at 3.30 yesterday afternoon that an appointment had been made for 11:10 today. With respect, Mr. Chairman, I do not believe that this gives me sufficient time to prepare my case, and certainly not reasonable time in terms of the Act. I pointed this out at the time, when discussing the matter with the person who informed me, that this did not give me either time to prepare my case, or to prepare my witnesses. I was told...

Chairman: To that I make two statements ...

Holman: I haven't finished, Mr. Chairman ...

Chairman: I am not prepared to listen to you to that extent, Mr. Holman. First of all, the thing is, what is reasonable time? In our estimation, reasonable time is a matter of twelve hours or so. Quite often before this board we have senior executives, chairmen of companies, appearing at half-an-hour's notice. The second point is that you received your call-up papers at least a week to ten days ago.

You therefore had ample time in which to prepare your case as soon as you received your call-up papers ...

Holman: With respect, Mr. Chairman, that is not the case.

Chairman: I am not prepared to argue on that, Mr. Holman

Holman: I want to state that I have been unprepared in the time available to present my case before this board. Secondly, Mr. Chairman, I want to bring it to your attention that I am of a mind to take the validity of the call-up to court because I think there are grounds for challenging the validity on two issues ...

Chairman: That has nothing to do with this board, Mr. Holman, in fact you can take yourself to the devil if you like, but we are not to go into that matter, we are merely prepared to see whether we can grant you a deferment or not.

Holman: One of the points that I wish to raise, Mr. Chairman, both in the courts and before this board, I think does fall within your functions and within your authority. You will note that the terms of the Emergency National Service Act, Section 18, Subsection 2, Clause (a) says that when the minister, with the approval of the Minister of Defence and the Minister of Law and Order, deems it necessary or desirable in the interests of defence, public safety or public order, he may authorise the call-up of residents in any class of residents who are liable to emergency National Service. Now, Mr. Chairman, I think that any reasonable interpretation of this would suggest that the minister was not in possession of the facts when he decided to call me up. I don't think that any reasonable man, given that I have been declared a security risk and an undesirable resident of this country, would at the same time have thought it either necessary or desirable in the interests of defence, public safety or public order to call me up, and I wish to put that point for your consideration, Mr. Chairman.

Chairman: You can take that to the High Court, or any other court ...
(*Inaudible comments from board*)

Holman: Mr. Chairman, I wish to move on to a further issue, and that is the matter of calling witnesses to bear out the four main points that I have made in the document that is before you.

Board member: Mr. Holman, the Chairman has already stated that those do not constitute having good reasons for this board to consider a deferment, so it is quite pointless your endeavouring to call witnesses to discuss the points which are not relevant as far as we are concerned.

Holman: Well, I wonder if I could outline the names of the witnesses and the evidence I think they could provide, before the Chairman and makes a final ruling on this.

Board member: This is purely procrastination, is it not, Mr. Holman?

Holman: No, I believe it is entirely relevant to my case.

Chairman: What you believe doesn't really concern this board. We are purely here to see whether we can grant you a deferment or not.

Holman: I ...

Chairman: We have finished that case, Mr. Holman. Will you carry on please.

Holman: I want your ...

Chairman: You have finished with that point.

Holman: No, I haven't, Mr. Chairman ...

Chairman: I have, the board has. (To board members) I take it you are in agreement with that?

Holman: I wish to say who I wish to call, so you can assess the validity of my claim. If your ruling is that I might not continue, then of course I will not continue, but do so under protest.

Board member: (inaudible) ... ruled out of order Mr. Holman, and it is quite pointless your bringing them forward.

Holman: I simply ...

Board member: May I be permitted to explain to you the workings of this board. We consider cases that are brought by employers. In this case yours is not a matter that has been brought forward by employers. It is one that you have brought forward personally. We therefore consider personal reasons why you should not attend at a given date and we examine reasons why you want a short-term deferment: nothing else. Now these can be compassionate reasons, it can be reasons of health and matters of that sort, or in the case of an individual who is self-employed they could relate to the nature of his business or his employment. None of the points you have raised bear in any shape or form on the normal workings of this deferment board.

Holman: I think that in terms of the Act, your functions exceed beyond which you've described. If I present reasonable grounds for deferment you can consider them ...

Chairman: Mr. Holman, it has already been brought to your attention that your interpretation of the Act and Regulations are not the interpretation this board places upon them.

Holman: I simply have ...

Chairman: Your next point, please.

Holman: Well, could I be clear in my own mind, Mr. Chairman, that you are not allowing me even to bring up the names of the witnesses whom I wish to call and whom I believe I have a right to call.

Chairman: That is correct.

Holman: That is your ruling?

Chairman: That is my ruling.

Holman: Well, Mr. Chairman, I must accept your ruling but I continue wanting to make it perfectly clear that I continue with the utmost reluctance.

Chairman: We quite understand that, Mr. Holman. Would you carry on? ... (*inaudible*)

Board member: Mr. Holman, is it correct that you have received your call-up papers?

Holman: They have been received.

Board member: On what date were they received?

Holman: They were received, it was a Monday morning. Monday of last week. That would be about the 3rd of January.

Board member: Have you got them with you?

Holman: Yes ... I'm afraid I've left one of my folders in the reception, but I've got the papers there. I don't know if you want to refer to them because ...

Board member: No, I think we'll take your word that you received them on the 3rd of January.

Holman: Mr. Chairman, I want to go into the point relating to my circumstances as a security risk and an undesirable resident of Rhodesia ...

Chairman: We have already told you, Mr. Holman, both myself and the honourable member on my right, that this has no relevance to your application whatsoever. You are a resident of Rhodesia, a self-confessed resident of Rhodesia in that you have contested an action in the High Court as to why you think you should not be declared a prohibited immigrant, and you appeared to, well, I withdraw that word, you were granted residence in this country. As a resident you are therefore liable to military call-up ... (*inaudible*)

Holman: I think nevertheless, Mr. Chairman, it is important that in your interests and mine, the grounds on which I think I am regarded as a security risk and as an undesirable resident of this country should be put to you when you consider my application for what you say in terms of the statutes is a deferment. May I proceed, Mr. Chairman?

Board member: I would suggest, Mr. Chairman, that the background of this case is known to the military authorities when they made the call-up. It is for them and not this board to evaluate such matters. I don't see its relevance to our particular meeting this morning.

Holman: I don't know on what grounds you say the defence authorities (*inaudible comment from the board*) would be aware of this. Secondly, I don't see how the defence authorities could have been aware of all the issues which I personally wish to raise *vis-à-vis* my attitudes to the state ...

Chairman: And Mr. Holman, I am getting tired of your continual interruptions ...

Holman: I have not interrupted, Mr. Chairman ...

Chairman: ... and your 'with respects' and all the rest of it. I am telling you right now that this board does not call up personnel. This board is merely to see whether we can accommodate employers in respect of their employees, or persons wishing to ask for deferment for compassionate or personal grounds. These are the only terms of reference which this board has. Will you kindly confine yourself to these particular matters now.

Holman: Mr. Chairman, I take exception to your personal references. I have conducted myself respectfully, and when I say 'with respect' I mean exactly that. If you choose to interpret it in a derogatory fashion, then I am sorry about that but, I repeat, I am putting forward my position with respect and I will continue to do so. I wish to state that I do think that it is of considerable validity and it also falls within the board's authority to consider the issue that I am a security risk to the state. Mr. Chairman, if your ruling is that I cannot present this evidence, then I will accept it but, Mr. Chairman, as each point is taken I would request a definitive ruling, and my request now is that you are going to rule one way or the other as to whether I am allowed to present evidence (*inaudible interjection*) relating to the issue as to whether I am a security risk.

Chairman: You have been told already, Mr. Holman, that it is not a matter for this board to consider, it is a matter for the defence authorities to consider. Can we take it that this point is fully covered now?

Holman: Are you refusing me the opportunity to put forward the evidence that I have?

Chairman: That is so.

Holman: Mr. Chairman, I will then move on to point two, in which I say that I believe that the military forces are the main instruments of preserving the institutional violence of majority rule. Mr. Chairman, I would seek the opportunity to give an elaboration of this point, backed by documents, and think that it is pertinent to my beliefs to go into my personal background and the fact that I have been brought up in this country for most of my life ...

Board member: Are you a Rhodesian citizen, Mr. Holman?

Holman: Mr. Chairman, in terms of the legislation, the minister would have been able to deport me, were I not a domiciled citizen. I am a citizen of this country and I have lived here longer than the Minister of Immigration himself. I have been here since 1951 ... and I believe that my background is relevant in my points that I wish to put forward on point two. I would like to proceed, Mr. Chairman.

Chairman: Proceed.

Holman: Mr. Chairman, I was brought up in the small Rhodesian town of Gwelo. I went to kindergarten there, I went to junior school there, and I went to secondary school there. From secondary school I went to the University of Rhodesia. In 1967 I was served with a restriction order, but in the light of your earlier ruling I feel that I cannot elaborate on the security grounds for that restriction order. Am I correct Mr. Chairman?

Chairman: That is correct.

Holman: After serving one year in restriction in the town of Gwelo from 1967 to 1968 the order was renewed for a further year. The minister gave me the opportunity to study in Britain, which I took, and I returned to this country in 1973. Mr. Chairman, for I think I can say for as long as I can remember, I have found the policies of this country thoroughly distasteful, I have found them racist and demeaning. Demeaning, Mr. Chairman, not only to the African majority of this country, but to myself, because it has circumscribed my relations with them and I have felt that, simply as a white man, my relations with black Rhodesians can never be on an equal footing. I have intimate knowledge, I think, of the characteristics of white rule. I think I have an intimate knowledge of the legislation on which white rule is based. This legislation I regard as designed to perpetuate the control by a white minority through a number of devices. These devices, Mr. Chairman, include basically the Land Tenure Act, which decides what part of the country a man can live ...

Board member: Just a moment, may I butt in for a moment please. Mr.

Chairman, do we have to listen to this? I don't think it's got anything to do with his case. (*Inaudible comments between members of the board*) It's pure procrastination, Mr. Chairman; we have said this before. It in no way turns on whether Mr. Holman as an applicant to this board has in the board's opinion adequate grounds, compassionate or otherwise, for a deferment from call-up which is scheduled for the 15th. (*Inaudible comments*) Are you asking for a short deferment, Mr. Holman? If so, what are your reasons?

Holman: I am sorry I can't refer to you by name. The position is that I have applied for exemption. You have said that the board's powers are limited to deferment. I think that under these circumstances you can exercise your powers of deferment to meet my request for exemption. My request for exemption is based on a number of issues. I must stress, members of the board, that my case is unique. Nobody has appeared before you, on these grounds, with the evidence that I could present if permitted.

Board member: How long are you asking for exemption, or deferment rather, and what are your reasons, Mr. Holman?

Holman: First of all I would like to say that I wasn't given the opportunity of completing my elaboration on the point ...

Chairman: Mr. Holman, we are asking you a question now: can you answer or can't you answer it? How long are you requesting a deferment for call-up? You have now stated after some prevarication you wish deferment for an indefinite period which this board is not allowed to grant.

Holman: Well, Mr. Chairman, you are empowered to grant a deferment and I could appear before you on subsequent occasions, and I stress that my case is unique. There is not another man like ...

Chairman: We have heard a considerable amount of this already, Mr. Holman. We are not prepared to listen anymore. Can you tell us now the reasons why you need a deferment from 15 January, that is until next Friday, 15 January is a Saturday ... (*inaudible*)

Holman: The reasons are as I have outlined, Mr. Chairman, but I haven't had an opportunity to fully present my case.

Chairman: We have listened to a lot of words and we haven't heard one reasonable reason yet, or one glimpse of a reason yet, why we should continue to listen any longer. I don't know ...

Board member: Can I, on behalf of the board, put it that the points you have raised in your written submission do not in the opinion of the board constitute valid reasons for us to consider granting a deferment. Any matters that you have verbally expressed to us relate to those, or in the same category. They are not relevant in respect of an application for deferment. Could you therefore give us any other reasons, other than those that you have touched on and listed here, why we should grant you a deferment?

Holman: Well, I believe that were I to have an opportunity to elaborate on these points, you would then be able to come to your conclusion, but it seems to me you have reached your conclusion simply on the basis of those points, and say that they are not relevant to your authority.

Chairman: That is correct.

Holman: Well then, I have simply not had the opportunity of presenting my case. For two reasons: partly because of the short period of notice that I received for this meeting; partly ...

Board member: You could have started preparing your case as and when you received, on your own admission, notice of your call-up on the 3rd January.

Holman: Mr. Chairman, I am an extremely busy man, I have got an extremely demanding job, I have got many responsibilities. The law is an unfamiliar subject to me. I have to find out how exemption boards work. I am in sufficient doubt, as I say, to intend to proceed to the courts about the validity of that call-up. There are a number of issues, Mr. Chairman, which occupied my mind, and further ...

Chairman: We have now got one reason for your applying for a deferment, Mr. Holman, and that is you wish to present your case to the High Court or to some court in order to question the validity of your call-up documents. Is this in fact a reason or don't you wish to consider this?

Holman: I am simply notifying you, Mr. Chairman, that having looked at these statutes, I am of a mind to seek a challenge to the order in terms of its validity, in the High Court. Now because one of the grounds is the security issue, I feel that I should also have had the opportunity to present to you, because I think it does fall within your jurisdiction, to decide whether the minister was well advised in calling me up, given that the legislation is specifically in terms of the security of the country.

Chairman: Thank you very much Mr. Holman, I have heard enough ... (*inaudible conversation between members of the board*) Quite frankly not one reason that has been produced before this board today has any validity towards any application for a deferment.

Holman: I haven't had the opportunity to deal with points three and four, Mr. Chairman ...

Chairman: We are now (*inaudible*) ... you have had ample opportunity, which you have not used to very good advantage if I may say so. Will you now please withdraw, Mr. Holman, while we discuss your case.

Holman: Mr. Chairman, I do not feel that I have had the opportunity to present my case. I withdraw if that is your ruling, under protest, making it clear, as I say, that I have not had the opportunity to present my case.

Chairman: Will you now withdraw.

Holman: Will you reconsider your attitude towards giving me your names, Mr. Chairman?

Chairman: Negative.

Board member: There are sound reasons, Mr. Holman, why names of members of the Defence Exemption Board should not be known. They are published in the *Government Gazette* and you can see them *en bloc* but it would be quite wrong that members of the board should be pestered by persons wishing to have exemption who would approach individuals in their private capacity and seek to get exemption on those grounds.

Holman: Mr. Chairman, I repeat that I withdraw, not having had the opportunity to present my case. Do I wait for your decision?

Chairman: (*response inaudible*)

Second Session

Chairman: Mr. Holman, the board has considered the matter. While we are not prepared to hear anything further on the first grounds of your application as we consider this beyond our powers, we would welcome a little bit of elaboration on points two, three and four.

Board member: That is where I interrupted you, Mr. Holman.

Holman: Which were the points on which I can produce further evidence?

Chairman: 'The military forces are the main instruments of preserving the institutional violence of minority rule'. You haven't got on to point three, I don't think, where you believe the military forces are guilty of systematic oppression; and you were talking about point two.

Holman: Mr. Chairman, I was giving an account of my background in this country, because I think it important that you know that my views stem from long experience and intimate involvement. If the shorthand writer would just indicate when I go too fast, I will slow down—'intimate involvement in the country and careful study' ...

Chairman: Just a point I would like to ask. Do you speak either of the main languages of the country, perhaps?

Holman: Mr. Chairman, I don't, and I attribute that to one of the characteristics of the racist nature of this country, and that is, when I was at school, Mr. Chairman, instead of being given the opportunity to learn one of the languages of the majority of the inhabitants of the people, I was given the opportunity to learn French or Afrikaans. This was really puzzling but, as I say, I think it can be explained in the light of the policies of the administration.

Chairman: You're not going to carry on beyond one o'clock? You've already said you are a busy man. I happen to be an extremely busy man and I can't waste too much time on these things. You have until one o'clock, Mr. Holman.

Holman: I see it's eight minutes to twelve: is that right?

Board member: Yes.

Holman: I think that should provide enough time, Mr. Chairman, but perhaps if it doesn't we could adjourn the hearing and meet on another occasion.

Chairman (*inaudible comment*)

Holman: Mr. Chairman, I was saying that my attitudes are based on intimate involvement with the government of this country, with the people and with race relations in this country. I was saying I had been brought up here, had gone to university here ...

Board member: And that you are in fact a citizen of Rhodesia.

Holman: I am a domiciled citizen of Rhodesia. The experience that I had left me convinced that the policies of the administration were to perpetuate white minority rule. I was saying that I regarded this as demeaning, not only to the African majority, but as demeaning personally. It circumscribed the terms of my relations with them; it was not possible to co-exist with fellow students and friends without risking the opprobrium of the society or indeed the punishment by law when one contravened the law, such as the Land Apportionment Act, or the Land Tenure Act as it now is. It is therefore quite incongruous, I think, that somebody with my long and deeply held persuasions—to which you should have received testimony, were you to have agreed to listen to witnesses—should now be prepared to fight for the system which is perpetuating minority rule, to fight for segregated schools, Mr. Chairman, to fight for segregated land, to fight for the right of a café owner to refuse service to a black man, to fight for the right to segregated toilets, or to fight for the right for segregated hotels, or a civil service in which advancement is predominantly on race rather than merit, and within a military structure which itself bears the racist characteristics of the system itself. I have followed, for example, with great interest the educational policy of this country in which education is compulsory for one race; that race receives ten times as much public funding for the education of their own kind, compared to the black Rhodesians. Education is not compulsory for them, Mr. Chairman: no doubt other members of the board are well aware of this. As a result, there is a substantial drop-out of young African children for whom education is not compulsory. This I regard, Mr. Chairman, as one example of the institutional violence that I referred to, which the military forces are protecting. Another example, Mr. Chairman ...

Chairman: Are you on point three now?

Holman: No, I am still on point two, Mr. Chairman. Another example is the segregated system of land tenure, as a result of which I believe that half the country is not only gravely deteriorating, but has led to hunger and malnutrition amongst the African people. This, Mr. Chairman, I regard as another form of institutional violence. I think institutional violence is also incorporated in the financial structure of the country inasmuch as the bulk of subsidies, loans, assistance, access to capital, access to expertise is denied Blacks. This is also a form of institutional violence, in my opinion, Mr. Chairman. I also believe that the laws of this country in other respects, often nominally non-racial, are in fact racial. Their intent is to suppress the black majority. For example, the Industrial Consolidation Act is nominally non-racial but in fact ensures that control of unions and thus influence on the wage structure remains in white hands. The vast majority of black wage earners in this country, Mr. Chairman, earn much less than a subsistence wage. This is maintained by the manipulation that is carried out by both those skilled members of the union who are in the majority white, and government legislation. I also refer, for example, to the fact that half the Blacks in employment in this country have their working conditions determined by the Masters and Servants Act, which allows them neither the opportunity of wage bargaining nor the formation of a legally recognised union. I think there is evidence of gross malnutrition on farms, including farms in the European areas, and I think this is a situation which cannot be remedied because, in part, the Masters and Servants Act, an archaic and punitive piece of legislation, is maintained on the statute books. This, Mr. Chairman, I regard as another example of the institutional violence of minority rule. Mr. Chairman, I would want the opportunity to go further into these points because these are deeply held and sincere views, but in light of the fact that I had such short opportunity to present my case has been limited. I have not been able to collect evidence that I would require, to cite various papers, for example on the issues that I have mentioned.

Chairman: (inaudible interjection)

Holman: You take my point that I have not had the opportunity to prepare my case fully, Mr. Chairman?

Chairman: No, we take your point that you have already produced plenty of evidence of the so-called preservation of institutional ... preservation of minority rule by institutional violence. We've got that. (Inaudible comments) We are purely here, as has already been explained to you, to decide whether you are entitled to a deferment or not. Carry on.

Holman: Yes, I am simply making the point ...

Chairman: We heard that, thank you very much, please carry on.

Holman: ... that I have not had the opportunity of preparing my case.

Chairman: The point has been amply made.

Holman: I am looking for one of the documents which I wish to cite in raising my case, point three, Mr. Chairman, in which I say I believe the military forces are guilty of systematic oppression.

Chairman: You are quoting from a Justice and Peace report?

Holman: That is correct. I will identify the document and the page numbers. I might say, Mr. Chairman, that in the course of my work I have had to investigate some of the allegations that have been made and I am satisfied that, both out of my own experience and the material from the Justice and Peace Commission, that torture, brutality, oppression are officially sanctioned by the authorities of this country. If I might cite one case of which I have personal knowledge, since I was in part responsible for investigating it and bringing it to the attention of the authorities. It is from *The Man in the Middle*, subtitled *Torture, Resettlement and Eviction*, a report compiled by the Catholic Commission for Justice and Peace in Rhodesia, published in 1975. This case says that one Anthony

Dzvimarungu—I am sure, Mr. Chairman, you will be better capable than I of pronouncing that surname ...

Chairman: It should be D–Z–I ...

Holman: D–Z–I. I see. Perhaps it's misspelt in this document. This man alleges that, following an attack by insurgents on the chief's building in the Mudzi district of Mtoko, about 100 miles from Salisbury, soldiers came to his kraal by helicopter and questioned the people. In the course of the questioning, his sisters-in-law were assaulted by the soldiers. One was pregnant at the time and was whipped. Anthony immediately went to Salisbury to report the incident to the Catholic Commission for Justice and Peace. At the time he expected more trouble. He alleges that on his return he was picked up, before he got home, by the police. He was then held at Mtoko police station where, he reports, he was repeatedly beaten on the buttocks and feet with sticks. Hair was pulled out of his head and a pair of scissors was placed against his genitals, with a threat to cut them off. A firearm was pointed at this head and a threat to shoot was made. A few days later, after his release, he was examined in Salisbury, and found to have patches of hair missing, severe bruising on the soles of his feet, and marks of the assault on this buttocks. The government is defending his claim, but has not given details of its action. This, Mr. Chairman, is a case of which I have personal knowledge, and I am satisfied that the man is telling the truth and that he was indeed assaulted. There are other cases, Mr. Chairman ...

Chairman: Do you have personal knowledge of them, Mr. Holman?

Holman: Personal knowledge, Mr. Chairman, inasmuch that I have followed the activities of the Justice and Peace Commission closely and in particular cases kept in touch at each stage of the case, and will have had the opportunity to look at the evidence.

Chairman: I think that then you haven't really had personal knowledge involving the cases and I therefore think you should confine yourself to those cases.

Board member: (inaudible interjection) If you know the individuals concerned and saw the brutalities ...

Holman: But I had to follow these cases closely, as a journalist, Mr. Chairman and ...

Chairman: Do you know the actual people or don't you?

Holman: Not in subsequent cases. There is one case which I will find ...

Chairman: I think you've made your point, Mr. Holman. ... (inaudible)

We don't want to listen to any more. Have you personal knowledge of these wounds, bruises, injuries and other hurts? ... (inaudible)

Holman: As I have said, Mr. Chairman, the basis on which I have knowledge is close connection with the Justice and Peace Commission. I think it must be ...

Board member: I think Mr. Holman is prevaricating now ... (inaudible)

Second Board member: You have made reference to two publications and that is the information in those publications is known...

Board member: ... to the general public ...

Second board member: ... and that is adequate. He does not need, I believe, to highlight any of the matters in the two publications to which you have made reference.

Holman: I don't think it is public knowledge.

Board member: Unless he has personal knowledge ... (inaudible)

Holman: I think that ...

Chairman: The mere fact that you have heard people say these things is hearsay evidence and we can't accept it in a court of law.

Holman: They haven't gone to a court of law because apparently the government is afraid to challenge them.

Chairman: Point taken, Mr. Holman. Can you carry on to the next point, please?

Holman: May I simply say, Mr. Chairman, that these cases, as I say, involving the use of electric shock torture, make a profound impression on me and I think it is of considerable relevance that you should have knowledge of these cases when bearing in mind my attitude to serving ...

Chairman: As has been stated by other members of the board, these two publications have been made public and they are known, so there is no further need for any ...

Holman: Are you saying, Mr. Chairman, that I cannot continue taking these extracts and making the point that they have a profound effect on me?

Chairman: You are absolutely correct.

Board member: You have made your point, Mr. Holman.

Holman: I don't believe that I have had the opportunity to make my point, but if the chairman's ruling is such, then I will under protest pass on to other material. The material which I have here deals with the grounds on which the minister came to deport me.

Chairman: We have already stated that we are not prepared to listen to any further evidence on that point.

Holman: I again accept your ruling under protest, Mr. Chairman. The other documents are dealing with my restriction, when the minister said that he was satisfied that I had been actively associated with activities prejudicial to the maintenance of law and order. Again, I understand that your ruling has been that I cannot go into this. If this is correct, Mr. Chairman ...

Board member: There only remains point four that I think we wish you to elaborate on, that you believe nationalist guerrilla forces are legitimate.

Holman: Well, Mr. Chairman, as I said at the beginning, I haven't had the opportunity for marshalling my material and as I go through it, points that I might want to raise, and I want you to confirm that you have ruled that I cannot raise them. Can I refer, for example, to my affidavit in the recent High Court case involving my deportation and take an extract from that?

Chairman: What extract, Mr. Holman?

Holman: This touches on the issue, I should say to you, Mr. Chairman, of the minister acting unwisely, and presumably without the information available to him, in considering me a fit person to do call-up.

Chairman: I will come back to my original ruling that we are not here to judge whether the minister is acting *ultra vires* or not; this is beyond the jurisdiction of this board, so I now say you cannot continue ... (*inaudible*)

Holman: If that is your ruling, Mr. Chairman. I would also wish to refer to points in the Immigration Act under which I was deported, referring to my undesirability. Does your ruling affect that?

Chairman: (*inaudible*) ... that is beyond the jurisdiction of this board.

Holman: I would also wish to refer to Mr. Broomberg's comments in parliament about me, in which he described me as a security risk.

Chairman: We'll take your point on that ... (*inaudible*) ... elaborate suffici-ently on that one.

Holman: Well, I think it would be better, Mr. Chairman ...

Chairman: What you think doesn't matter. We have got your points that Mr. Broomberg has said that you are a security risk. That is sufficient.

Holman: Well, I would have thought you would have wanted the full text of what he said and the context in which it is about.

Chairman: Unfortunately Mr. Holman ... (*inaudible*)

Holman: Well, if that is your ruling, Mr. Chairman, I place the document to one side. I here have a document, Mr. Chairman, which I think is certainly based on my personal knowledge and ...

Chairman: Are we dealing with point four, Mr. Holman?

Holman: Well, can I refer to a case in which I investigated circumstances in a protected village, Mr. Chairman, and wrote a substantial article for the London *Observer* in which I ... (*comments among members of the board inaudible*)...

Chairman: We don't wish to hear this, Mr. Holman.

Board member: I don't think so. I don't think it's relevant ...

Holman: Well, you haven't given me an opportunity to tell you what the article deals with.

Chairman: It's completely irrelevant. Can you put it to one side and go on to the next point, please.

Holman: Well, Mr. Chairman, if you insist that this document is irrelevant, again I put it to one side, but I think it's got a personal connection not only with my experience but with the duties I am expected to perform. How far are we? I don't think I will need to keep you 'til one o'clock, Mr. Chairman. I am sure you and members of the board will be relieved. I see these are points dealing with the fact that I don't believe that I have had reasonable time. We have dealt with those, or rather in my opinion, we have not dealt with those. This, Mr. Chairman, is a list of the witnesses who I would have called, had you given me the opportunity to do so, but you ruled that I might not call the witnesses or indeed give an account of their names or their relevance. So I therefore, Mr. Chairman, turn to point four and say that I think that this represents a summation of my points, because if indeed I feel that the military forces are guilty of systematic oppression as I do, though I don't think I had the opportunity of expounding on this, and if I also believe that those forces are the main instrument of preserving the institutional violence of minority rule, and for these views presumably I have been declared a security risk and undesirable, I must therefore look at alternatives, Mr. Chairman, and I must look at the objectives of those who oppose the existing authorities. Now, Mr. Chairman, I think I should make it clear that at no stage have I ever advocated violence, or have I ever participated in violence, and that remains my commitment, Mr. Chairman. Notwithstanding this I think I can take the detached attitude that though I find violence repugnant I can decide whether violence under certain circumstances is legitimate. I feel that the nationalists have taken to arms only after 80 years of white rule, having exhausted peaceful opportunities to come to an accommodation with the ruling minority in this country.

Mr. Chairman, I deeply regret having exhausted ... the opportunities for peaceful change of the ruling minority system of this country. Mr. Chairman, I deeply regret what is happening, and it causes me profound distress. People I know have died or have been injured. I believe that I have friends on both sides of the conflict. The objectives of the military wing of black nationalism, as I understand it, are to establish a democratic system whereby each adult has a vote, and to do away with racial discrimination, and to do away with the forms of institutional violence which I was referring to. These, Mr. Chairman, I believe are the objectives of the military wing of the nationalist movement and ...

Chairman: By nationalist movement are you talking about ... (inaudible)

Holman: That is the broad term, Mr. Chairman, for the nationalist groups who function as political parties.

Chairman: So you are including the ZANU and ZAPU?

Holman: Muzorewa.

Chairman: Muzorewa, FROLIZI.[40]

Holman: Well, FROLIZI is no longer in existence, to my knowledge, but it will include nationalist groups, Mr. Chairman, and in all conscience I believe that efforts to establish a government on that basis is one which I support. Mr. Chairman, bearing in mind the reservations and reluctant acceptances of your rulings that I made in the time I have been here, and bearing in mind that I have not had the opportunity to prepare my case, bearing in mind that I was given short notice and was not able to call witnesses which I believe should be my right, I think at this stage there is no further point to raise.

Chairman: Thank you very much Mr. Holman. As far as I can see, the only good reason (inaudible) for a deferment, or a request for a deferment, is that you require time to bring your call-up papers before the High Court, to decide whether in fact they are ultra vires or not. Am I correct?

Holman: No, Mr. Chairman, you are not correct.

Chairman: If I am incorrect, I see no reason whatsoever to even consider an application for deferment.

Holman: I made it clear, Mr. Chairman, that I informed you of the grounds on which I had in mind going to court, because I would raise an issue, and I continue to believe it raises an issue which falls within your authority. Now, you dispute that, Mr. Chairman ...

---

40 Front for the Liberation of Zimbabwe.

Board member: Mr. Chairman, Mr. Holman is out of touch on the question of call-up. He has given us a lot of other information. I would like to suggest we ask him to leave us for a moment and we will then give him our decision, and we will answer one or two of the points that he has raised and he believes to be relevant.

Chairman: I take your point. The only thing that I would make is that you know, the only reasons we could grant a deferment in this case is because of time to bring the matter before the High Court, and I asked him this and he said no ... (*inaudible*)

Holman: Well that is a different point Mr. Chairman. If you feel that the other points I have raised are outside the ambit of your authority, that is a decision you bear in mind when considering my request for a deferment, but in addition I am simply informing you that I am in mind to go to court and I am setting out those grounds, because I think that these, in addition to the other points I have made, are worthy of your attention. You might, for example, feel that the minister should have the opportunity to be aware of my background before deciding to go ahead with this call-up, which is indeed essentially an issue which I am also going to raise in the courts. But I don't think this falls without your authority.

Board member: Can I ask one question to you, Mr. Chairman, and that is this: is this Mr. Holman stating that he is not asking this board to accept as a point in his favour that he proposes to move towards action in the High Court. You do not wish us to take that matter into account?

Holman: Yes, certainly, Mr. Chairman, take it into account ...

Board member: Are you asking us to take note as a point for ...

Holman: Yes I wish you to take note of it, I wish you take note of it and I wish you also to take note of the fact that I believe the points which I want to raise are also valid in your consideration. You see, I don't think it would have been legitimate for me to say I am going to take this issue to court, take legal advice and consult an advocate, but I am not going to refer to it, I am not going to deal with it any further. If I thought it was on a technicality then it would be different, but I think it is on grounds which are of importance to yourselves.

Board member: (*inaudible comments*) ... in view of the fact that he wishes to take it to the High Court ...

Chairman: Well this is the question. I put the question to him and he said, no, this wasn't the point. (*Inaudible discussion between members.*)

Holman: If I might make a point from the floor, as it were, I think that the board has to consider first of all, given my background and circumstances, whether I should be deferred, perhaps pending the close consideration by the minister of my circumstances. The board must also consider, I believe, the grounds on which I think I have a case to take to court ...

Chairman: Do you mind not telling the board what to do, Mr. Holman. We're aware of our duties Mr. Holman.

Holman: With respect, Mr. Chairman, and I mean that, I am not telling the board what to do ...

Chairman: And will you now withdraw please because we wish to discuss your case. Thank you.

Holman: Well, Mr. Chairman, I would have thought that my further contribution would have been helpful to just set out the precise grounds on which I think the board now is considering, but if the order is that I withdraw, I will do so Mr. Chairman. Mr. Chairman, I want to make sure that there is no misunderstanding. I have not given my solicitors instructions to take it up in the courts, I have studied the ... (inaudible)

Third session

Chairman: Mr. Holman, the board ... (inaudible) ... that you have given it ample evidence of the ... (inaudible) ... for your written submissions and also the historical background leading to the views you have expressed. The board has already stated, however, that in its opinion your submission does not constitute a valid reason for any deferment. The board does not consider that it is empowered to the defence authorities ... (audio missing) ... reasons for calling any resident for military service. Its duties lie solely in granting deferments to those that warrant it. The board notes that you are considering the possibility of referring this matter to the High Court. It submits that you can proceed with this action while undergoing service. For these reasons, your application is rejected and you will report for duty on 15 January, 1977. Thank you very much.

Holman: Do I get a copy of that Mr. Chairman?

Chairman: It's not normally done.

Holman: I see. If I needed to, perhaps I could get one through the shorthand writer.

Chairman: (inaudible) ... We have spent quite a lot of time on you already. Thank you very much for coming.